Southern Lies and Homicides

Tales of Betrayal and Murder

Susan Waller Lehmann

WHITE RHINO PRESS
ESTABLISHED 2016

The people, places, and events described in this book are real. However, the author has changed names and identifying characteristics for some of the people referenced in these stories to protect their privacy. The author has relied on the memories of those who shared their experiences to make these stories as accurate as possible. Events, conversations and timelines have been recreated from interviews, personal and work notes, newspaper and media accounts, legal testimony and police reports. Any errors are the sole responsibility of the author.

Copyright ©2025 Susan Waller Lehmann

All rights reserved. No part of this publication may be reproduced, stored, or transmitted in any form or by any means, including electronic, mechanical, photocopying, recording, scanning, or otherwise without written permission from the publisher, except for the use of brief quotations in a book review. It is illegal to copy this book, post it to a website, or distribute it by any other means without permission.

Susan Waller Lehmann asserts the moral right to be identified as the author of this work.

ISBN 978-0-9992300-6-0 (Soft cover)
ISBN 978-0-9992300-7-7 (Hard cover)
ISBN 978-0-9992300-8-4 (E-book)

Library of Congress Control Number: 2024903832

Susan Waller Lehmann has no responsibility for the persistence or accuracy of URLs for external or third-party Internet websites referred to in this publication and does not guarantee that any content on such websites is, or will remain, accurate or appropriate.

Author Photo Credit: Phil Rose Photography

For Peter, My North Star

Contents

Praise for Southern Lies and Homicides	xi
Southern Hospitality and Other Myths	1
On Becoming an Investigator	3
The Rottweiler	11
The Process Service	17
The Choices We Make	25
The Day Smoking Saved My Life	35
Garbage	41
Life in Wartime: The Custody Game	49
Chicken Feathers	105
The Hoover Affair	111
Fool Me Once	127
My Final Divorce Case, Part One	135
The Road to Nowhere	141
My Final Divorce Case, Part Two	151
Lies, Alibies, and Homicides	181
The Phoenix	183
The Redhead in the Blue Rambler	189
Lunch with Frankie	201
Lost Time	217
A Trail of Breadcrumbs	231
The Persecution	245

The Predator	261
The Armory	271
Murders in the Black Belt	279
The Tornado	293
The Murder House	299
The Execution of Robert Butts	**313**
Robert Butts, Jr.	315
A Note from the Author	349
Acknowledgements	351
About the Author	353
Also by Susan Lehmann	355
Notes	357

Praise for Southern Lies and Homicides

In Susan Lehmann's line of work, cheating spouses, custody combatants, and child castaways turned killers are among the subjects of her investigation. In her latest book *Southern Lies and Homicides*, she takes the reader along in her quest for evidence as she sets up cameras in risky stakeouts, sifts through garbage looking for telltale receipts, escapes the target of an investigation in a high-speed chase, and interviews the family of a young man sentence to death. Whatever you think you know about private investigators, forget it. Susan Lehmann tells you what it's really like to be one. It can be dangerous and heart breaking. The book's finale is the case of Robert Butts, a young man executed in Georgia after a prosecutor lied to a jury and Butts's shoddy legal defense team failed to reveal a childhood of unimaginable hardship, abandonment by family, and finally despair. Susan brings the injustice of our legal system to light as she deftly leads readers into realms unimaginable to most. *Southern Lies and Homicides* is comprised of finely told stories of deception, of unforgettable plots and characters, of a fractured legal system and its victims.

—Larry Schnell, Author, Reporter, Journalism Instructor

Susan Waller Lehmann is that rarest of private investigators, and storytellers—one driven by curiosity and dedication and a powerful, perhaps nameless compulsion to dig as deeply as necessary, peeling away layer after layer, through complication after complication, to get at something like the truth—no matter how painful in the end. From her start in the business as a Sue Grafton-reading PI wannabe, to her years-long work on complex cases as a death-penalty mitigation specialist, Lehmann has maintained not only her investigative tenacity, and the skills to match, but also her deep and abiding sense of humanity, all of which she explores in this must-read collection of true tales of her lifetime in the business. As compelling as it is, the title of Lehmann's book—*Southern Lies and Homicides: Tales of Betrayal and Murder*—barely scratches the surface of her deep dives into dark underworlds the rest of us are reluctant to openly acknowledge, but that we fear are there nonetheless, eroding the tenuous foundations of our lives. Lehmann's memoir reads at times like the best PI procedurals, and at times like a literary genre of her own making—a meditation on family, and caring, and fear, and loss, and what can be salvaged from all the lost souls among us—including, at times, our own.

> —Steve Watkins, Award-winning author of the nonfiction book, *The Black O: Racism and Redemption in an American Corporate Empire*, and winner of the Golden Kite Award for Young Adult Fiction for *Down Sand Mountain*.

This was an engaging trip into the world of a private investigator, not just any PI, but one very particular PI, the author Susan Lehmann. While Susan and I spent countless hours together in rural Alabama doing death penalty mitigation field work, much of her story was new to me. The stories in *Southern Lies and Homicides* shine a light on the work and the people, the tribulations and surprises and gifts. But in these stories also witnessed Susan's personal journey through events that made her swear and rant and laugh—and the things that battered her heart. Her very big heart.

> —Catherine L Boyer, Ph.D., Clinical and Forensic Psychologist

Author Susan Lehmann applies with dazzling results her keen observational skills and captivating journalistic voice in *Southern Lies and Homicides*, a collection of remarkable stories about her experiences over two decades as a private investigator and capital mitigation specialist in the South. Her accounts are often funny, sometimes tragic and always compelling as she serves legal papers, sifts through garbage for evidence and catches cheating spouses in the act. In detailing her

PRAISE FOR SOUTHERN LIES AND HOMICIDES

work with death row prisoners awaiting execution, she brings into sharp focus the heart-rending effects of poverty and injustice. Read *Southern Lies and Homicides* not only for entertainment, but also enlightenment.

—P.M. Castle, Award-winning Journalist and Novelist

From completing her first assignment to knowing what to do when a client lies, private investigator and author Susan Lehmann never disappoints in the riveting accounts she's collected for her new book *Southern Lies and Homicides*. Lehmann includes in this reader-friendly and personalized book the varied cases that made up a PI business that began with serving legal papers, meeting lawyers and their assistants and befriending the secretaries and gatekeepers who became essential to her success. Her background as a reporter on the crime beat in a Florida newsroom provided the foundation for her expert sleuthing. Every scenario includes Lehmann's personal dialogue exchanges and thoughts about these intense cases. She offers sound advice along the way. "Never, ever purchase a house that's down the street from your former spouse." And this to describe sorting through garbage to gather evidence. "One man's trash is the plaintiff's treasure." Lehmann handles all these cases with finesse and grace. What unfolds in this excellent volume is a non-stop read that will have readers turning pages faster than her ability to locate her clients and capture the culprits.

—Laurie Scheer, Writing Mentor and Media Goddess

At once a how-to and fearless *Bildungsroman* of a private investigator, with squirmy details of client indiscretion and rife with PI skullduggery, Lehmann's new book also has heart.

—Sean Feral, Writer

This book is a powerful and deeply personal journey through the world of criminal defense investigation and mitigation, as experienced firsthand by the author. Set against the backdrop of the South—primarily Alabama and Georgia—these stories delve into the lives of death row convicts and individuals caught in private crises. With unflinching honesty and compassion, the author brings to light the humanity behind these often-overlooked lives. It took tremendous courage not only to engage with these difficult realities but also to share them so openly. This work stands as a testament to the author's resolve to ensure these voices are heard.

—Krista Bentley, Creative Strategist at Paddles & Paragraphs

Susan Lehmann's collection of in-the-field case stories is an entertaining and candid peek behind the curtain at the real work of private investigations. With a former journalist's storytelling instincts and a detective's eye for the perfect, telling detail, Lehmann offers a fascinating highlights reel of her investigative life, describing the daily tediums, human dramas, case-breaking discoveries, and alarming confrontations that make up a PI career. Interspersed with thrilling action sequences are flashes of empathy and insight, as Lehmann illuminates the complicated human lives at the heart of her cases. *Southern Lies and Homicides* is part memoir and part field guide to process service, surveillance, and mitigation investigations. It's an essential read for rookie PIs, anyone considering this profession, or spy-curious civilians.

—Kim Green, Managing Editor, Pursuit Magazine

The lucid stories in Susan Lehmann's *Southern Lies and Homicides* are deceptively forthright. and move along at a steady pace holding one's interest and sparking imagination. Whether recounting tangled lives pursuing the coldly determined ruin of others or the convoluted journeys to tragically inevitable resolution, Lehmann's narratives are devoid of sentimentality, or the purple language invited by the often unseemly facts. Yet gradually, a humanity emerges built upon the salient details that fleetingly, but movingly expose deep sorrows and lifetimes of never having a chance. It's not always the guilty who stand convicted in the more poignant stories. Profound and longstanding

PRAISE FOR SOUTHERN LIES AND HOMICIDES

poverty, a justice system that layers itself over a community's life, compounding harm rather than relieving it, people living almost next door to redeeming possibilities that never materialize, like ships in the night, these are the elements in her more compelling stories. Each tale is a brush with some forlorn aspect of Americana. We can count ourselves lucky to be on the outside looking in.

—Paula Stahmer, Attorney

Read *Southern Lies and Homicides*. In the second part of the book, the author leads the reader through several of her investigations of death penalty appeals. Besides entertaining writing, you will find yourself questioning our justice system. A rare book that entertains and provokes thought.

—Kevin Wolf, Award-winning Author, including *The Homeplace*, 2015 Tony Hillerman Award for Mystery set in the Southwest, 2016 Strand Mystery Magazine Best Debut Mystery, *The Belthanger*, 2021 Western Writers of America Spur Award Best Short Fiction, *The BootHeel*, 2024 Finalist, Western Fictioneers Peacemaker Award for Best Traditional Western, and *Trailridge*, 2025 Finalist, Colorado Authors League Best Mystery (Amateur Sleuth)

I
Southern Hospitality and Other Myths
1996 to 2005

On Becoming an Investigator

By the early fall of 1996, a sense of routine was achieved after our move from Florida to Alabama, and it was time to find a job. I applied for a few professional positions, and went in for second interviews, but couldn't seem to close the deal. Taking stock of my skills, I pondered this question:

Who do I want to be?

My passion was journalism, but those jobs were hard to come by, especially in a new town where I had no connections. In 1978, I began my professional career in a newsroom in Tallahassee, Florida. I worked through college as a paid staff news reporter, toiling on dull stories until I landed on the crime beat, my dream assignment. The challenge of developing sources and encouraging people to publicly share their secrets were a few of my best skills. Bylining a front-page story, above the fold, was euphoric. I exited newsrooms shortly after becoming a mom. I missed the spontaneity of gathering and writing the daily stories. But with three kids and a new marriage I knew I couldn't meet daily deadline demands.

In the intervening years, I reinvented myself multiple times, but I always missed reporting. Alabama brought a fresh start, this time in a flea-bitten small town north of Montgomery. I thought working as a private investigator could be exciting, even glamorous. Casework seemed like journalism: I remembered the reporter's formula of:

$$5W + 1H$$

… the who, what, when, where, why, and how rules might apply to domestic problem-solving. A little research showed there were no state-issued professional investigator's licenses offered in Alabama. All I would need was a county business license.

But how to begin? I didn't want to work alone. I was concerned about sleuthing without training. The word "stalker" comes to mind. I envisioned a business environment where I could draw a paycheck without the aggravation of marketing, billing, banking, taxes, and management headaches, on top of performing work. I'd been self-employed before and wore all those hats.

In those days, the internet was rudimentary and incomplete, a new way to access information certainly, but I had to rely on familiar sources. Turning to the telephone directory, I saw there were eleven private investigative agencies listed in Montgomery. I studied their Yellow Page ads. Most had telephone numbers but no addresses, a clue the detectives worked from home, which quickly scuttled my plan to show up at their offices. I mustered my courage and began making phone calls. Half of the numbers were out of service or disconnected. I reached several answering machines, leaving messages with little confidence of a return call.

A man answered on my 8th or 9th attempt. I blundered through the conversation, and the PI, whom I'll call Aaron, was not impressed.

"We're not hiring now, and especially not anyone I have to train," he said.

"I don't need much training… I used to be a journalist, and I have a lot of skills," I said.

"Such as?"

My mind blanked. "I'm good at interviewing people, gathering records, writing reports, taking photos, things like that…"

"When was the last time you sat in a car, by yourself all night, working surveillance?"

Um, never.

"Call me when you get some training."

On Becoming an Investigator

"Listen, I've dined with a serial killer and found the hideaway of another one. That must count for something," I said.

But he'd already hung up.

Undaunted, research was next on my list. This was the time before Google or Amazon, so I visited the main library in Montgomery and thumbed through the card catalog, looking for a 'how-to' book; someone must have written one. While some dealt with law enforcement training, there was nothing on the non-fiction shelves that could teach me how to conduct skip traces or run a surveillance operation. The reference librarian sprang into action, and she dutifully checked the same catalog I'd already examined.

Eyebrows knit, she was puzzled and perplexed but intent on helping. She checked drawer after drawer of index listings. She closed the last one and leaned against the cabinet for a moment.

"I'll be right back," she disappeared. Eventually, she returned with a huge grin and an armload of books.

"I think these may be helpful," she said.

One by one, she displayed her finds. *One for the Money* and *Two for the Dough*, written by Janet Evanovich. And three books by Sue Grafton. At the bottom of the pile were two novels by Dashiell Hammett, one featuring hard-boiled detective Sam Spade, the other with sleuthing couple Nick and Nora Charles solving the whodunnit. I loved the Hammett books in college, and the movies made from his stories were among my favorites. I hadn't read the women authors, although my last literary agent wanted me to write like Grafton. I got a library card. The books came home. I devoured them, made notes, and worked through to the endings with the characters.

The Stephanie Plum books were educational if you were going to be a bond enforcement agent, particularly a hapless one. I had interned briefly with a bounty hunter in Gainesville, Florida, until he dropped dead from a massive heart attack outside a convenience store after buying a carton of cigarettes. He was 46 with too much stress in his life. Nope, not for me. The plots in these books were laugh-out loud funny and served as a what-not-to-do in the field of process serving, skip tracing, and fugitive apprehension.

But it was Kinsey Milhone, the female protagonist of Sue Grafton's alphabet books, who captured my heart. She was exactly the kind of investigator I longed to be—but with a husband, three kids, a reliable car, and hopefully, a bit more money.

I took notes on the techniques Kinsey used to solve cases. I then called Aaron again. He answered the phone.

"Look, I may not be trained, but I'm a fast learner," I said. "Please, do you have something I can help you with?"

Silence. A measurable pause. And then…

"Come in tomorrow morning."

Nine-thirty was the time set. The early morning found me exhausted from a lack of sleep; my brain afire all night, burning with a million questions; my most pressing concern was how to dress for this meeting. I was in turmoil over an outfit, because, I reasoned, this was a job interview.

Thankfully, the kids made the school bus, which allowed me to shower, style my hair, and put on a little makeup. I had decided on the Kinsey Milhone style of dress: blue jeans with a blouse and blazer. My sole departure was to wear leather flats rather than tennis shoes. My left arm and wrist had barely come out of the cast I'd worn for three months since a dumb canoeing accident on the Coosa River over the summer. I hadn't fully regained use of it because I didn't want to go to physical therapy. I was left-handed, and my ten-year-old daughter was my assistant: she wrote checks at the grocery store, paid bills, and signed school progress reports. Michelle was so adept at forging my signature it was hard to tell them apart. Later, this proved to be a useful skill for her, expressly for the benefit of her brothers.

But I digress.

On Becoming an Investigator

Thirty minutes had been allotted to drive into town and find the agency, and it was a good estimate. Aaron's office was located behind a strip mall in east Montgomery, next to a diner. At exactly 9:30, I knocked on the door, which was opened by a woman in her mid-twenties. She looked me up and down.

"Are you a new client?"

After I explained my appointment with Aaron, she raised a carefully tweezed eyebrow. "He won't give me a raise, but he's hiring someone new," she grumbled and shuffled back to a desk with a ringing phone. "He's not here."

Uh-oh.

The woman ignored me; she chatted away on the phone about an evening spent drinking at a local bar, trying to catch the eye of a guy. I wandered around the bare-boned office: two desks, a handful of mismatched chairs, a couple of battered filing cabinets, and blank walls. A dining table was pushed against a back wall. Film cameras, pagers, voice recorders, and a camcorder with tapes were strewn on the surface. A dead plant was the centerpiece. Half-filled soda bottles and an opened bag of pretzels lay amongst the equipment. There was an old Mr. Coffee with a couple of dirty mugs.

The floor of the one-room office was bare concrete. A door led to a storage closet, which held a set of golf clubs and a man's shoes and clothing inside. The office did not have a bathroom or a kitchen. At 10 a.m. I prepared to leave. The woman continued with the phone call. The door opened, and she slammed down the receiver.

"Go clean out my car," he said to the woman, whose name was Jennifer. "There are bottles in there. Get 'em out." She groaned and shuffled from her desk; the door slammed shut behind her. I soon learned Aaron urinated into empty soda bottles while working. He shared this "tip" with me while explaining why women were badly suited to PI work.

"You can't pee in a bottle. You'd have to leave your post to find a bathroom, so women fail at surveillance," he was fond of saying.

Aaron was a tall man. He was in his late forties, bearded and tattooed with a shaven head. He was a competitive triathlete and spent his off-hours training.

Over several months, Aaron taught me spy craft like the basics of surveillance and how to trail subjects without getting caught. He specialized in workers' compensation and cheating spouse investigations. I learned how to eavesdrop on unencrypted cordless and cellular phone conversations between lovers with a Bearcat analog scanner taped to a mini-cassette recorder. He'd let the air out of car tires in the cover of darkness, then return the next morning to videotape the "injured" person changing the flattened tire. Some weekends, he forwarded the business calls to my home phone and urged me to simply take messages, like I was his answering service. Callers often awakened me hours after midnight, wanting case updates or looking to hire a PI. Many of these people were lonely, seeking conversation. I couldn't say much other than I'd relay their information to the investigators.

After a month or so, I began to spot a pattern in his behavior. For two weeks, Aaron was fun to work with. He made jokes and our interactions were companionable. Soon, I had my own cases, but I was never allowed to speak with clients or meet them. I was a contractor and paid $10 an hour plus mileage, better pay than substitute teaching in Alabama. I was doing decent work, and the weekly checks were welcome.

But by the third week of the cycle, Aaron became moody, agitated, and quick to anger. He found fault with Jennifer, and with me, often making cutting remarks. Jennifer would cry at her desk. Aaron was cycling steroids, she confided in a rare moment of friendliness.

She never came into the office during those fourth weeks. I answered calls, took messages, and did little else. Legal secretaries called often, wanting to know the status of court documents they'd sent to Aaron for service. I found a bulging file folder stuffed with subpoenas and summons and complaints. The dates had lapsed on some. I offered to help him with these, to try to serve the papers, but Aaron said those were his bread and butter and he was worried I'd take the business away from him. But no one served those papers. The next time I was alone, I jotted down the names of the attorneys and their paralegals, *just in case*, I reasoned.

One day, Aaron demanded I empty the bottles from his car. I picked up my purse and keys and left for the day.

Curious and alone in the office, I investigated my employer. Aaron was a gambler. He was lousy at it and often over-drafted his bank account. When he contracted a cheating spouse or custody case, he would get a client's credit card number and expiration date to bill a retainer and subsequent charges, and this information was written inside a client's folder. I routinely worked on several cases each week, assigned my hours and mileage to a client, and submitted my billing reports every Thursday afternoon. Fridays were paydays.

One afternoon during a fourth week, Aaron was out of town following a philandering husband. Bored and looking for something to read, I pulled out case files. The folders contained my reports, photographs, and other evidence. I scanned the invoices Jennifer prepared for clients. I earned $10 an hour, but the clients were billed at rates of $40 or $50 per hour.

Aaron was the boss, it was his agency, he had to make a living, I understood the mark-up.

But attached to my billing were yellow sticky notes instructing Jennifer to inflate the number of billable hours. If I had logged ten hours for a case, he told her to double, or even triple, the number of hours on an invoice. A one-hundred-dollar fee could turn into a thousand-dollar charge.

Aaron didn't mail invoices to these clients. He would call them and request more money, or he'd run their credit cards without permission. Twice, I fielded calls from angry clients when thousands of dollars in charges appeared on their statements. Once, I overheard Aaron talking with an irate client about billing errors made by his investigator.

He blamed me for his fraudulent activities.

That Friday, at the end of yet another fourth week, I got my paycheck and walked out. I never returned to the office, and it would be a decade before I saw Aaron again.

I'd learned enough. It was time to go into business for myself.

The Rottweiler

Excitement blended with terror when the legal secretary handed me a set of service papers. Thrilled to get my first PI task, I was alternatively overwhelmed by a stark fear of failure.

"File these with the Clerk's office," Barbara said, rifling through a stack of papers. "There's a check attached for the filing fee; invoice us with the service return. We'll file the return with the court."

Unsure about what she'd said, I smiled and thanked her.

Legalese. A new language to learn.

Although working for Aaron's PI agency had taught me a few things, like catching people faking workers' compensation claims, or cloning cordless phones, I never served court documents. I had found a stack of these on Jennifer's desk, but neither she nor Aaron seemed obligated to serve them. Prior to walking out the door, I jotted the names of the attorneys from the papers.

One week after leaving his agency, I had my first client, a woman lawyer in downtown Wetumpka. Jacqueline Austin had a formidable reputation in this small town. We had yet to meet; all arrangements had been made through her secretary. Home to my computer, I got directions to the Dallas County courthouse.

I was going to Selma.

The drive was 68 miles from my house to the courthouse. The U.S. 80 route had recently been designated The Selma to Montgomery National Historic Trail, some thirty-plus years after the marches for Civil Rights. West of the Montgomery airport, the drive became scenic, with rolling hills, bucolic landscapes of farms, pastures, horses, and cows. There were small shotgun houses overgrown by kudzu and large, well-manicured and gated estates. It was 1996, but I was put in mind of the Harlan Ellison story, *From Alabamy, With Hate*, an essay detailing his experiences during the 1965 civil rights marches, marked by hostilities and violence, to bring voting rights to all Black U.S. citizens.

A century after the end of the Civil War, a decade since the historic Montgomery bus boycott, four years after the famous Freedom Rides through the South, there were three attempts by civil rights supporters to complete the 54-mile march. The first effort lasted six blocks when the Alabama National Guard, under orders by Governor George Wallace, attacked and brutally beat the 600 protesters, mostly college students, at the Edmund Pettis Bridge.

The day became known as Bloody Sunday, which spurred a second march, led by the Reverend Martin Luther King, from downtown Selma to the Pettis Bridge, where they were turned back by law enforcement officers.

The third march was successful. On March 21, 3,200 protesters, with some limited and reluctant federal protection, set out from Selma and walked twelve miles a day, sleeping in fields at night. Many were spit on and attacked by hostile residents, others were given water and food by sympathizers of the civil rights movement. By March 25, when the marchers reached the Alabama capital city, the number of protesters had swelled to 25,000.

Five months later, President Lyndon Johnson signed the historic Voting Rights Act providing all adult U.S. citizens the right to vote, regardless of color or ethnicity.

As I drove, I visualized people marching down Highway 80 East, toward Montgomery, demanding the recognition of all Americans as equal, set against the backdrop of the vitriol hostile southern Whites spewed toward Black people.

And outsiders. Even decades later.

The Rottweiler

Our journey to Alabama was a work move for my husband, so some kids on the school bus called us "Carpetbaggers," and "Dirty Jew Carpetbaggers." Although we weren't dirty or Jewish, we were all targeted by hatred, and this set the tone for our tenure.

I crossed over the bridge and entered Selma, vowing one day I would walk the bridge, in solidarity with all the people who tried to bring equality to this state. There had been some progress, although for many Alabama natives, the Civil War is still commonly referred to as "the War of Northern Aggression."

Over the years I would learn what the Civil Rights Legislation would cost Selma.

There is always a price to pay in Alabama.

Prior to picking up the papers, I studied the Alabama Rules for Civil Procedure. These were the guidelines for serving court papers; each state has them. For example, I didn't need to physically touch people with the documents. I could leave them with a suitable member of a household at my discretion and return a copy to the agent, meaning the lawyer who had issued the subpoena or summons.

The clerk at the Civil Court counter examined the papers, took the check and one set of documents, stamped the rest, and wished me good luck when I said I'd be executing the service.

"Have a blest day," the woman with the improbable beehive hair said to me.

Dumbly, I had forgotten to get directions to the address, so I asked if she had a map of Selma. She directed me to a counter on the first floor. I picked up a city map, stepped outside, near my car, and unfolded the map.

"Ma'am, you need some help?"

A Black man straddled a boy's banana seat bike on the sidewalk.

"Um, I don't think so."

"Who are you looking for?" He leaned the bike against a light post. I showed him the address.

"I don't have my glasses, I can't see too good to read," he said, squinting at the papers. Close up, I realized he was older than he initially looked, his face marked by too much sun and hardship. I read the address to him. He nodded his head.

"Git your car and follow me."

Mystified, I slowly trailed this old man on a boy's bicycle into a neighborhood of small homes built mostly of wood, with occasional red brick. He stopped and pointed to a house.

"There it is," he said. "I'll wait here."

The neighborhood, built in the 1930s for prosperous White families, had declined into low-wage, working-class rentals long ago. This house was a particularly sorry sight: paint faded to dirty gray, with a broken front window, cardboard taped over splintered glass. The frame of a storm door was twisted, torn screen hanging. Other yards had blooming bushes, azaleas, roses—but this yard was dead grass lost to weeds and broken glass.

A car rested on blocks in the driveway, the two back tires missing. I looked back at my escort, he smiled and waved, encouraging. A Rottweiler, drowsy in the sun, was chained to the back bumper.

The wood porch sagged with rot. I noticed the front door was partially open. Clutching the service papers and a pen, I knocked. The door inched open. I heard the noise of a too-loud television.

"Who's there?" A woman's voice.

"Um, ma'am, I have some papers for you."

A hand snaked through the door.

"Mrs. Harris?" I asked.

The Rottweiler

"Uh-huh."

Quickly jotting the date and time, with my signature on the front page, I put the papers in her hand, which quickly disappeared. The door slammed shut.

Walking back to the car, I saw the man stroking the dog's head.

"That go a'right?" he asked.

"I suppose it did."

He smiled, showing a mouth of beautiful white teeth.

"This is my dog, Fred," he said, climbing back on his bike.

"Hi Fred," I said, but couldn't make myself touch the huge animal. "Why's he chained to the car?"

"Well, Fred is a working dog. People fixing to get their cars repo'ed rent Fred from me, until they can pay up. No one's gonna hurt my dog."

"People pay you to chain Fred to their cars?"

"Yes, ma'am. They do. Well, glad to help you."

With a wave, he pedaled down the street. I wish I had asked his name or slipped him some cash to pay him for his time. I never saw him again, but occasionally, over the years, I would see Fred the Rottweiler chained to the bumper of a car in Selma.

The Process Service

I built my business by serving legal papers. It was the first work I got as a private investigator and it's the best way to meet lawyers and their assistants. Befriending secretaries—the gatekeepers—has been essential to my success. I rarely saw most of the attorneys I've worked for; they were merely names on the papers. But some of the secretaries became my friends.

Early one morning, I got a telephone call from one of those friends, Paula. She was the assistant to the first attorney to give me work.

"Jacqui wants to know if you can serve some papers either today or tomorrow," Paula said.

"I think I can, today probably. What am I serving?" I pulled out a notepad with my list of tasks.

"There's a woman here in Wetumpka who's been taking care of her great-niece. She needs to come to court next Tuesday and bring the child with her."

I knew there would be more to the story. Most attorneys filed papers through the court clerk's office and paid eight dollars to have off-duty sheriff's deputies serve them. I charged fifty dollars plus mileage, but I had an advantage—no one expected me to be serving court papers, so they were likely to open the door. In all my years of serving papers, only once was I unable to complete a service. I had some tricks.

"Okay. Go on," I said.

"The sheriff's office has tried. No luck."

"So, she's expecting the papers but doesn't want them, correct?"

"Correct. The great-aunt is quite attached to the little girl and doesn't want to turn her over to the mother. She's afraid of what might happen."

"Because of what happened before?"

"You could say that."

I sighed. "Okay, I'll be over after lunch."

"Jacqui wants you to get into the house."

Paula hung up the phone before I could say anything else. I knew what I had to do.

On the way to Jacqui's office, I stopped at the Winn Dixie grocery store and went straight to the floral section.

The clerk and I picked out some lovely white carnations, a small bunch of daisies, and one yellow rose. She added a spray of baby's breath then wrapped the flowers in lavender paper with a bow. I picked out a pink helium balloon. The flowers and balloon cost less than twelve dollars, a business expense.

I swung by the law office and got the papers. I drove to a neat little house off Alabama Highway 170 and parked my car in the driveway. The grass was mown; the bushes were trimmed and tidy. I inhaled deeply, exhaled slowly. I had one shot at successfully putting the papers into this woman's hands.

I gathered the documents, flowers, and balloon and carefully positioned myself right in front of the peephole, making sure the flowers were visible. I rang the bell and counted slowly to myself.

"Who is it?"

The Process Service

"Ma'am, my name is Susan, and I have a delivery for you," I said, smiling brightly.

The deadbolt clunked, and the door opened. A middle-aged Black woman stood before me. She was dressed in a neat cotton blouse and slacks.

"Come in." She smiled.

"Ms. Williams, I actually have some papers for you," I said as I walked into a spotless living room.

"What kind of papers? Do I need to sign something?" She eyed the flowers and balloon.

"No, ma'am. These are regarding your niece and your great-niece." The woman's hand trembled as she took the papers.

"What's this about?"

I explained that her niece, Alysha, had petitioned the court to have the little girl returned to her. She'd have to bring the girl to court. I pointed to the date and time on the document.

"She'll miss school; it's a school day." Her voice broke. Her eyes filled with tears. I patted her shoulder.

"What are you afraid of?"

"What am I not afraid of?" Ms. Williams said. "Her mama, my niece, she ain't nothing but a baby herself, got in with a bad bunch, a bad man, and they was getting high and stealing things, and baby wasn't in school."

She was crying now, but her voice was angry. "If my niece wants to go down that path, I suppose it's her business, but I will not let her take this baby with her."

She motioned for me to sit.

When I asked Ms. Williams the little girl's name, the whole story poured out.

Shantell was named after her grandmother, Ms. Williams' sister, who was murdered by a boyfriend ten years earlier. "Happened in the kitchen," she told me. "He didn't like the way she was cooking chicken. He was drinking and acting crazy and carrying on. She gave him some lip. He picked up his gun, and bang! Shot her in the head."

The room was silent. Through an open window, a distant lawn mower hummed.

In a quiet, measured tone, she said, "My niece, Alysha, was sitting at the kitchen table, doing her homework. She was a little bit of a thing, like her baby now."

Ms. Williams had raised Alysha while caring for her own dying mother and holding down two jobs. "My niece found the streets quick. She liked the men."

She'd been caring for her granddaughter for a year after collecting her from Family Services. And now, after a stint in rehab, Alysha wanted the little girl back.

"Oh, that baby was dirty," said Ms. Williams. Now she was angry, her back ramrod straight in the chair. "She had scabies, and it took me weeks to get her scalp clean and her skin healed, and her hair fixed. She was left in filth, and God knows what happened to her with those people. I'm afraid to think about it too much."

"Poor little thing, she was so afraid when she came here." She looked at the paperwork. "I don't have much, but I keep a nice home, and I take good care of this baby."

"Yes, you do, Ms. Williams. I see you care very much for Shantell."

"Come see her room."

I followed her down the hallway, peeked into a little girl's room swirled in pink. Her bed was decorated with a fluffy pink comforter, hand-knitted pink Afghan, and a tidy arrangement of pillows, dolls, and stuffed animals. A small white dresser stood in one corner, with a matching white desk and lamp in another. A neat row of pretty dresses hung in a closet. A picture of Jesus hung on the wall.

"She was quiet as a little mouse when she got here," said Ms. Williams, smiling again. "She's still quiet, but I hear her singing sometimes in the bath and in her room. Her little heart is calmer now. We go to church and she's beginning to sing aloud during the services. At night, when she says her prayers, she asks Jesus to take care of her mama—and me. She didn't even know about Jesus until she came to live here. Will you tell the judge that for me?"

"No, ma'am, I can't speak to the judge, but I will tell the attorney as soon as I leave here. You can speak to the judge yourself."

Everything I saw told me Shantell was thriving with her grandmother. Family Services had checked up on her and found no problems. Shantell initially had a tough time adjusting to school. After a rocky start in first grade, school officials placed her in kindergarten. She was catching up fast. Shantell was reading a little bit now, and she was slowly making friends.

"She's getting to be a happy little girl," said Ms. Williams. "Please don't let them take my baby from me."

I didn't know what to say. Most of the legal papers I served were routine court actions. Divorces, money owed, and requests for documentation were normal actions. But this was a different situation.

I stood up, a bit unnerved and ready to leave. I held out my hand to shake hers. She grasped it, pulled me close to her, and looked me straight in the eye.

"What would you do, if this was your mess?"

I sat back down and thought for a moment. How much should I insert myself into this legal battle? I decided to suggest a solution.

"You have a third bedroom here. Perhaps Alysha could come here to live, and the three of you could learn to be a family," I said.

"I don't trust her to live here, and I don't think I can allow myself to be heartbroken again." Conflicting emotions ran across her face.

I told her it seemed to me her heart would break more if the judge turned over Shantell to her mother.

"Oh, Lord! That will surely kill me." She wrung her hands. "Would the judge take her from me?"

"I don't know," I said. "But if Alysha moved in here with you, you could keep Shantell here in the house and see how Alysha is doing. You'll know if she's working, and how she's living, and if she's hanging around with the wrong people." Ms. Williams shook her head in disagreement, but I continued.

"You can help her learn how to take care of Shantell, too. And you'll be here for the little girl, always. I think the judge, and the social workers from Family Services, may like this idea very much."

"I don't know. I can't trust that girl to not take the baby and leave again."

"I understand. I know this is a difficult situation." I pulled out my business card. "Why don't you give it some thought and call me if you want to talk again?"

She sighed. "I appreciate your time, Miss Susan," placing the card on the table, next to the papers. "I'll be in court. I'll bring Shantell, but I don't know if I can do what you said. I need to pray on it."

"I hope this works out well for you, Ms. Williams. I really do." I picked up my paperwork, sunglasses, and car key from the coffee table. "It was so nice to meet you." I walked out the door.

"Miss Susan?" I turned to look at the woman.

"May I keep those flowers?" she asked. "No one's ever given me flowers before."

I smiled. "Yes, of course. I brought these flowers for you. The balloon is for Shantell."

The Process Service

Ms. Williams watched from the doorway as I got into my car. She cradled the flowers in her arms. Tears flowed down her cheeks.

I fought my own tears as I backed out of the driveway.

The Choices We Make

On the morning of April 20, 1999, I put my teenagers on the school bus, kissed my husband, and packed an overnight bag. I headed north to work on my first criminal defense case. I would be away at least one night, perhaps two, so I brought clothing for three workdays, just in case. I tucked the printed driving directions into the folder that contained very scanty information about the case. Pens, notepads, cash, credit cards, and a tape recorder with extra cassette tapes and batteries went into a leather shoulder bag. I was excited, nervous, and blissfully unaware that the effects of several recent choices would come into play on this day. I've since pondered the significance of randomness and chance in our daily lives.

The decisions we make.

The court-appointed attorney didn't brief me before my trip. Everything I knew about this case was typed on a single sheet of paper, handed to me by his secretary. A year prior, on the afternoon of May 1, 1998, two young Black men allegedly beat an elderly neighbor to death with a cinder block during a robbery in Prattville, Alabama. They had been told the old man cashed his Social Security check at a neighborhood store that morning.

This fatal robbery netted the suspects an older model car with a tank of gas and less than twenty dollars.

The two men decided to drive north, to evade arrest. They made it to Franklin, Tennessee, where the car ran out of gas. It's doubtful either were expert drivers or even had licenses. They split up and went off in different directions with little money, wearing bloodstained clothing, and no clear idea of what to do.

Southern Lies and Homicides

My client, 21-year-old Timothy Barnett, backtracked forty miles, either on foot or by hitchhiking, where he located a payphone near an interstate exit in Columbia, Tennessee. He called 911 at 4:11 a.m. on May 2. He surrendered to several law enforcement officers. He was described as hungry and cold.

The second suspect was apprehended in Brentwood, a wealthy Nashville bedroom community. Upon learning a murder suspect had been making phone calls from their garage, the Tennessee homeowners swore they'd never leave the door open again.

Both suspects were charged with capital murder. I was retained to locate and interview anyone who had encountered Barnett during his brief sojourn in Tennessee.

Unsure about what made a murder capital, but not wanting to expose my ignorance to the secretary, I asked an attorney friend for clarification. It's capital murder, she said, when there is at least one other crime committed, called an aggravator, which leads to murder. In this instance, the robbery led to murder.

My primary task was to determine Mr. Barnett's state of mind from the moment he surrendered to Tennessee authorities until Prattville officers arrived in Columbia to arrest him.

The secondary reason was to figure out why Barnett made the choices he did: to rob, to kill, to flee, to surrender.

Psychological studies find the average adult makes over 35,000 decisions every day.[1] Most of these are minor decisions: what to eat for breakfast, what to wear for work, how to style our hair, which shade of lipstick goes with an outfit, and so on. We make many of these easily without assigning them much thought or importance. There are times when we make big decisions, and while we may agonize over the options, we make our choices and act accordingly. With hindsight, we later realize the importance of some of these decisions: that these choices signified turning points, forks in the road, and what may have seemed like a random decision could have either caused, or averted, dire consequences.

The two murder defendants decided to rob the elderly gentleman because they heard he'd cashed his Social Security check. During the robbery, they believed the victim was withholding money. Enraged, they killed him.

When Barnett was taken into custody in Tennessee, he had $6 and a disposable lighter in his pocket.

Peter and I had spent Thanksgiving week of 1997 house hunting in metropolitan Denver, Colorado. Knowing our move to Alabama the previous year had been a difficult transition, especially for our teenage sons, his employers gave Peter the option of moving to the Denver office rather than remaining in Montgomery. It was a move we wanted to make, but it would be financially tough. His salary would remain the same, but the cost of living was higher in Colorado. I was barely a year into my agency work, just beginning to establish my reputation, build clientele, and make a little money. I would likely give up my business to find a real job if we made the move.

We spent two days with a realtor. The houses we could afford were not as lovely nor the neighborhoods as bucolic as our home in Alabama. On the second afternoon, we sat in a rental car across the street from the Littleton High School our boys would attend. We discussed our options, when, like flipping a switch, we decided to cancel the Realtor, forgo the move, and spend the rest of the week exploring Colorado and having fun.

Seventeen months later, on April 20, 1999, I was on my way to Columbia, Tennessee to work on a capital murder case. I never dreamed what this day would come to signify.

The printed directions took me to the outskirts of Columbia, a mid-sized town of 33,000 citizens, an hour south of Nashville. The day was overcast, drizzling, and chilly as I drove rolling hills, the air thick with foggy humidity. Trees were greening, the azaleas and dogwoods blooming, and spring was coming... but the weather screamed winter. I didn't know to look for the tall emergency broadcast towers atop law enforcement buildings, so I was effectively lost. I pulled into the parking lot of a convenience store, seeking a restroom and directions. I'd made the 250-mile trip in under four hours and needed a break before I began work.

Entering the store, I was hit by a frantic news broadcast and a cloud of cigarette smoke. Mid-stride, I asked the clerk for a restroom. She pointed toward the back of the store, never moving her eyes from the television.

Refreshed, I grabbed a bottle of water and a candy bar and headed to the counter. She tore her gaze from the screen, and I saw she was sobbing, tears streaming from her eyes.

"What's wrong?" I asked. She turned back to the news.

"Have you seen this?" She nodded at the TV mounted on a wall. She stubbed out a cigarette, drew another from a pack, and lit it. She slid the smokes and the lighter across the counter toward me. We were the only people in the store.

This was the horror of a mass school shooting.

At 11:19 a.m. mountain time, two students opened fire inside their high school and killed thirteen people, wounding twenty others. Few details had been confirmed when I watched the broadcast at approximately 3 p.m. eastern time. The scene was chaotic, frantic, and surreal. A war zone.

"Where in Colorado is this?" I asked the clerk.

"Outside of Denver, somewhere."

I read the chyron at the bottom of the screen. Goosebumps crawled my body. I pushed the candy bar aside and reached for a cigarette.

Columbine High School. Littleton, Colorado. Mass Casualties.

The Choices We Make

Peter and I parked across the street from the school and randomly chose to stay in Alabama.

My sons would have been there today.

The clerk gave me a strange look when I asked for directions.

"You can't miss it," she said. "It's across the road. Look for the antennas."

I bought the water but left the candy bar on the counter. I drove for a couple of minutes, then saw the Columbia Police Department. I pulled open the double glass doors and approached the desk officer, a young woman seated at a long counter behind a Plexiglas partition.

I pasted on a smile and introduced myself to the woman. A male officer sat near her and pretended to read something while I stated my business.

"Do you have an appointment?" she asked, clearly avoiding eye contact.

The answer was no. Ideally, I wanted copies of all the reports referencing Barnett and to speak with everyone who had encountered him. Quickly, she cut me short, picked up a telephone, and pressed a button with the eraser of a pencil, to protect her beautifully manicured nails. She spoke briefly, then hung up.

"The lieutenant will be with you shortly," she said. "You can wait over there," she pointed to a small reception area, dismissing me. She took the list of officers' names from me and left her desk, briefly, then returned to her seat.

I stood in the reception area and waited. I studied the woman, guessing her age to be about 24. Her face was beginning to harden into an expressionless mask as if to shield herself from the men around her. I'd seen this hardness before, on the faces of women drowning in male-centric careers.

Eventually, the female officer was replaced by a young rookie male who flashed a brief smile but subsequently ignored me. Eventually, a lieutenant came through a set of locked double doors. He was a tall, well-built man with graying temples and exemplary posture, polished in his uniform, accustomed to a daily workout. I was self-conscious that I smelled like an ashtray.

"Ms. Lehmann?" He introduced himself, and we shook hands. A professional greeting. He held several sheets of paper in his hand. On top was the list of officers I had given the female desk officer.

"You're here for the defense, right?" I nodded. "You do know we didn't arrest Mr. Barnett? He called for assistance, we took him into custody, to hold him for the Alabama police."

"Yes, I do understand, but I would like to see any paperwork you have and speak with the officers who dealt with him."

"We don't have any reports per se. Once we learned there was a murder warrant out of Alabama, we brought him here, processed him, and took him over to the court to have an extradition waiver signed, then transported Barnett to the county jail. That was the extent of our involvement.

"What about the officers? May I speak with them?"

"Sorry, shift change," he explained. "None of the men are here now. Are you staying in Columbia tonight?"

"Yes," I replied.

"If you come back here at 10:30 tonight, Officer Delk will meet with you then. Barnett surrendered to him. He'll find the others for you." He handed me the papers.

"If you're looking for a good supper, try Betty's."

The events at the school in Colorado had devastated me, and the cool reception at the police department depleted any remaining enthusiasm for work. I was weary, body and soul.

The Choices We Make

"I'll be back tonight," I told him.

It was well after 5 p.m. by the time I checked into the motel and called Peter. We discussed the Columbine shootings, the Littleton high school, and how we randomly chose to remain in Alabama.

"What if," I said, then burst into tears.

He assured me all three kids were okay, and he was taking them for Mexican food that evening. He groaned when I said I'd have to do interviews at the police department when the night shift reported for duty. I honestly didn't know how I would spend the evening, other than going to dinner. The motel room was shabby, and I was dubious about sleeping in the bed. The bathroom seemed clean, but the towels were threadbare, the toiletries basic. Needing to cleanse the odor from the convenience store, I took a quick shower and washed my hair.

I promised to call Peter later that night, to check in. I anticipated at least one phone call from Michelle, and one from Danny. The two younger children liked to tell me stories from their school days. They both had quite a flair for drama, and, on occasion, self-righteous indignation with a dollop of hysteria.

But it was Jacob who called. He had seen the news. "Was that where Danny and I would have gone to school?"

After I assured my eldest son we were lucky, we were okay, I sat down at the small breakfast table and wrote up the details of the day for billing, tallying travel hours and mileage, and focused on the upcoming interviews, to work out questions for the officers. I studied the papers the lieutenant had given me: he had written margin notes about each officer, noting one was on vacation, and another was away for training. This left three men for me to interview. He had given me a copy of the Alabama murder warrant, as well as the extradition waiver Barnett had signed.

People stared at me as I entered the family restaurant, a woman alone, a stranger in this small town. The hostess was puzzled when I asked for a table for one, asking again for clarification. She led me to a four-top in the middle of the dining room. I ordered a small steak with salad and a plain baked potato. While I wanted a glass of the house red wine, I settled for coffee.

The salad arrived with the coffee. Iceberg lettuce, carrot scrape, a slice of tomato. I pulled a paperback book from my bag and settled in to read while I ate, a rare treat. A friend had lent me a Greg Iles book a few days prior, and I looked forward to losing myself in a mystery for a little while.

"Excuse me," a man said.

I looked up from the book. A man stood by the table.

"Sorry, I don't mean to disturb you, but I saw you today at the police department."

I nodded. He was the quiet officer from the reception desk. "Yes, that's right."

"Well, I wondered if I could join you. I was on duty when he was arrested; I might be able to give you some information.

In confidence, the man told me what I needed to know, to ask the proper questions of the officers. He encouraged me to go to the county jail and speak with a particular guard, one who had spent the most time with Barnett. We spoke about the two men, Barnett, and his accomplice, and how, in perhaps a drug-induced, spurious frenzy, they killed a man they intended to rob. We compared this crime with the horrific school shooting in Colorado. Details had emerged about the meticulous planning conducted by two teenage boys, with diabolic exactitude, causing the horrific terrorist attack at the high school, in which they both perished.

If the two had not died at the school, likely they should have faced the death penalty.

The Choices We Make

The next week, Timothy Barnett was tried and convicted of capital murder for the death of the elderly gentleman. He was sentenced to life in prison without parole. I never met him, but I had learned about the decisions he had made in Tennessee: he was frightened, yet cooperative. He dialed for emergency help from a payphone, then surrendered to the police. He willingly gave them his name, even though he didn't have any identification. He asked if there was an arrest warrant for him in Alabama, tying himself into the homicide. He denied participating in the murder, although his clothing and shoes were splattered with blood.

When asked if Barnett was intoxicated, one officer said, "Not on alcohol." When asked to elaborate, the officer, off the record, told me the story of a high school friend who, high on crack cocaine, killed several family members. I caught the suggestion but knew it was useless to use inebriation as an excuse for murder.

The judge who had prepared the extradition waiver had died, so I couldn't get his opinion of Mr. Barnett's mental state.

Armed with some information, I returned to Alabama.

Sometimes our decisions can mean the difference between life and death, or a lifetime of trauma. Timothy Barnett received a sentence of life without parole. My children were spared the Columbine tragedy.

The Day Smoking Saved My Life

"It's a quick trip up to Auburn," I told my husband over coffee. "It shouldn't take more than two hours, over and back, to serve these papers, then let's go up to the boat."

"Want to invite the kids?" he asked.

"Nope."

It was a Sunday in mid-July 2001, blazing hot with an expected temperature of 98 degrees, with high humidity but zero chance of rain in the forecast. A set of papers had come in earlier in the week, and I'd put them aside. I'd been consumed by a custody case that kept me working in multiple locations. I reasoned this would be a quick service and best to catch the guy at home in the early morning. I rose with the sun, anxious to be done with the task. Peter offered to go with me, but I suggested he pull together a lunch, and we'd head to the marina on Lake Martin.

The drive was quiet; most people were either home or in church this early on a Sunday morning. A legal secretary at a New Jersey firm had called prior to sending the documents; she'd gotten my information through a Deponet referral. This was a petition to terminate parental rights. She suggested I approach the subject with caution. I always do, I said.

By this day, I'd been serving papers for over five years. The work had become plentiful but routine. While I typically read the court petitions, I'd merely glanced at these when the FedEx package arrived.

The address brought me into an affluent area of Auburn, reflective of lawyers and university professors, not student housing. Yards were expertly manicured; homes were brick with sweeping driveways, decorated with Mercedes or BMWs. The address was a two-story, white-washed brick home, with dark trim, and a tall, wooden privacy fence surrounded the back yard. A late-model black Miata was parked in the circular drive. I pulled alongside the curb and grabbed the papers and a pen and left my phone and purse in the car.

I'd just be a minute.

The double-doored entry was a lovely blend of stained glass and wrought iron. I rang the bell, signed my name and dated the papers, preparing to hand them over. Music played in the house, but no one came to the door. I waited, shuffling my feet, suddenly nervous. A certain amount of adrenaline carries me to the front door but it rapidly dissipates the longer I wait.

As I rang the bell again, I listened to ensure it sounded in the home. It did. No answer. I followed the music toward the back yard.

Walking around to the side of the garage, I noticed the gate was propped slightly open by an oak branch.

"Hello, hello!" I called, loud enough to be heard over the jazz as I inched the gate open, peeking into the yard. Miles Davis played through mounted outdoor speakers. The smell of cigarette smoke wafted toward me. Without considering the consequences of a bad choice, I pushed the gate fully open and stepped into the back yard. I had trespassed, an offense rarely committed and never admitted.

The heavy wooden gate banged shut and latched at the top of the fence. I stood in the back yard, in a deep indentation. Dirt and sod had been dug out, as if to make it difficult for a person to leave through the gate. I pulled on the handle, but the door remained fastened. Glancing up, the latch was at least eight feet up, too high for me to reach without a stepladder. A disheveled young man of about thirty stood on a multi-level redwood deck, smoking, pacing, and muttering to himself. He hadn't noticed me.

At least he was dressed.

The Day Smoking Saved My Life

"Hey, are you Jimmy?" I smiled and waved.

Startled from his reverie, he stared at me, puzzled, as if he'd manifested an alien in his yard.

"Yeah, I'm Jimmy," he said.

"Oh, okay, so, uh, I have some papers for you."

"Why'd you close the gate?" he shouted. "Now we can't get out, bitch. We're locked in here." His tone of voice, the inflection of his speech, calling me a bitch—terrified me. I glanced at the gate with the sickening knowledge I couldn't reach the latch to escape.

Be calm. Think.

"I don't know who they're from," I lied. "But hey, Jimmy, let's look them over and talk about it, see if we can work something out, okay?"

He nodded.

"Is this your parents' house?" I slowly approached Jimmy and the deck.

"Yes."

"Are they home?" I hoped against hope there was a less-intimidating adult in the house, yet I knew the house was empty.

"No, they're in Florida. My sister's getting married."

Oh, that's no good. His parents were at the sister's wedding, but he was here, behind a locked gate, at an empty house in Auburn, Alabama. Behind a very tall privacy fence. I scouted the area: four sets of sliding glass doors led from the house to the covered deck. Featured were a built-in stainless steel barbeque grill, a wine cooler, and beer kegs installed with taps. At the center was a large glass patio table with eight wrought iron chairs adorned with thick cushions. An outdoor fireplace provided a focal point, with a television mounted above, a perfect area for Saturday afternoon football enjoyment. Large concrete planters graced the deck edges, with manicured peach and cherry trees, their stone fruit maturing in the summer sun. There were two lounge chairs and side tables. A water feature adorned the southern edge of the deck: an elephant spraying water over his back. Blooming orchids, in vibrant pinks and purples, graced the perimeter of the fountain. Hummingbirds danced in and out of the mist.

I wanted that fountain.

Silly me. I was struck by deck envy when I should be overwhelmed by worry. I couldn't even call for help. My phone was locked in the car.

Disengaged, Jimmy sat on the north edge of the deck, directly on the redwood, under the shade of an old, well-pruned oak tree, and lit a cigarette. His legs dangled off the edge but did not reach the ground. He was short, only five feet tall. The ashtray overflowed with butts. I stood near him, on the grass, and began scanning the paperwork.

"Okay, Jimmy, now this is a twenty-eight-day petition, meaning you need to respond to this lawyer and the court within twenty-eight days."

"Business days?"

"No, this says twenty-eight days to respond. Weekends count. Do you have a lawyer?"

He lit a cigarette with a match, not a lighter. An idea formed.

"My dad is one. He's got a firm. They help me." He was doing something odd with his fingers, moving them as if playing a keyboard, in time with the staccato music, cigarette clasped in his teeth.

"What does this say?"

I had been reading forward, to edit, if needed. The petition was scary as hell, given I was trapped in the yard with this guy. Descriptive words leapt out at me: violent, abusive, neglect, manic episodes, suicidal ideations, child endangerment, crack cocaine abuse, arrests, methamphetamine, alcoholic blackouts, bi-polar disorder, refusing medication, and involuntary commitments; these words riddled the documentary landscape, each an unexploded landmine.

The Day Smoking Saved My Life

This is bad.

Sidestepping his question, I skimmed to the end of the twenty-page document.

"How about I go inside, through the glass doors, and out the front door? Then I can come around and open the gate?" I offered, hoping to flee this situation and drive off in my car.

"Won't work," he replied. "The alarm's on. The police will come and arrest me. The gate's the only way out."

"Can't you turn off the alarm?"

"Nope. I don't know the code. I'm on supervised house arrest, and my supervisors are away. See," he pulled up his pant leg, exposing an ankle monitor. "You screwed me by closing the gate."

"How are you out here then? Aren't the sliding doors armed?"

"No, my mom had the guy turn it off on those," he said, pointing at a set of doors. "So, I can come out here and smoke. Can't smoke in the house. She loses her mind if I do. Waves her arms around, sprays stuff. Yells."

I would lose my mind if I had to deal with this guy smoking in my house, too. Back to the issue: 1 reasoned I could get out if I had a stepladder. I glanced around for one.

"What do those papers say?"

"She's asking for supervised visitation," I said, figuring this was the least objectionable thing I could say. She'd petitioned he'd have no contact with their young daughter, but I'd allow him to discover that himself.

He stubbed out the cigarette in the brimming ashtray. He reached into the Marlboro box pack for another. He had one left.

"Hey, Jimmy, can I bum a cigarette from you?"

He handed me the remaining smoke and lit it. Last cigarette, last match. He crumpled the empty pack and matchbook.

I drew the smoke deeply into my lungs, exhaled, and set the papers on the deck. My best friend and smoking partner were in Vermont for the summer, so I'd sworn off cigarettes until her return in September, but I needed this one.

"I got more in the house," he said, standing up. "I gotta get another pack and find some matches."

Smiling, I thanked him, then asked if he would bring me a glass of water, too. He nodded, entering the house through a sliding glass door. I set the signed and dated papers on the deck, with a landscape brick on top, and checked my pocket for the car key. I grabbed a cushioned chair from the table and hauled it to the gate. I stood on the chair and sprang open the latch, pulled the gate open and held it with my left hand. I shoved the chair aside and ran to my car. The gate slammed behind me. I was safe.

And lucky. I had trespassed. If I ever wrote a book on the mechanics of investigating, it would include a chapter on the perils of entering enclosed spaces alone, with a strong warning to always read the papers before serving. Lesson learned. This time.

Garbage

I had a haiku, a mantra if you will, for those times when an investigation called for a garbage run.

No cat litter, no
dirty diapers, fingers crossed
there's good evidence.

People know little of the treasures that may be elicited from a trash bag, and I promise you—cases have been won, or at least settled, based on discarded items. One man's trash is the plaintiff's treasure, if you will.

There are rules to gathering garbage. If the can is next to a house, those coffee grounds and soiled paper towels are personal effects, like a water hose, a bird feeder, or a garden gnome. But once the can is moved to the curb for pickup, it's fair game for anyone to grab what's inside. The trick is getting into the bin once it's on the street, but before it's picked up—without being seen. Neighbors love to report suspicious activity, and stealing garbage bags from a can is shady behavior. Someone will report you, if not to the police, who will ignore those complaints, but to the former owner of the garbage.

The contents of a trash bag will tell you much about the subject's habits. Is she a closet smoker? A heavy drinker? A junk food binger? Think about what goes into your weekly trash haul and what the contents say about your lifestyle.

The first time I made a trash run was for a divorce case. A woman suspected her husband of an affair. Diligent scrutiny of his lunchtime and post-work activities proved this true. But in Alabama, like most states, adultery is no longer grounds for divorce. "Irreconcilable differences" is the standard divorce pleading; to me, a benign and unsatisfactory phrase. This marriage, of over twenty years, had run its course. There were no children, no pets, only assets to fight over. We knew her husband had a girlfriend. We needed to know if he was hiding money or spending it on her.

Here's a fact: civil cases are always about money. You'll hear phrases like 'in the children's best interest,' but trust me, it's always about child support and alimony. Money. The person who controls the money wins.

Abigail, my client with the straying husband, knew some of his earnings were not going into their joint account. He was a realtor and worked strictly on commission, so his income fluctuated monthly, but, as he had been in the business for decades, he earned well over a hundred thousand dollars even in a bad year. One day she met a young couple moving into their new home in her neighborhood. Abigail was stunned to learn her husband had been their agent. Normally Abigail and her husband celebrated a home sale with an expensive meal and champagne, but he'd not mentioned this one. Curious, she began to examine bank statements, and those revealed deposits had declined over several months. Their credit card bills showed no unusual activity. She suspected he had a secret bank account and credit card.

Scheduled to leave home for several weeks to care for her dying mother, Abigail asked me to snoop into the suspected hidden accounts. Like other clients in similar straits, Abigail did not pay me out of marital assets. I sent her father my invoices, and he paid them promptly. He didn't like his son-in-law.

Garbage day was Thursday. Through a quick call to Waste Management, I learned the truck scheduled pickups in the neighborhood between 8:30 and 9:30 a.m. According to Abigail, he didn't leave for work until 9 a.m. and often dragged the can to the road in the morning when he went out for an early jog. Experience has taught me it's tricky to pull trash during daytime hours.

Garbage

I suspected her husband would spend nights with his girlfriend while Abigail was away. On the first Wednesday evening, I drove to the house after darkness fell. The street was lined with garbage cans, ready for pickup, and Bingo! He had already pulled the can to the curb. The house was dark, the street clear of neighbors. I pulled in front of the can, popped open the trunk of my car, took two time-stamped photos of the position of the garbage can, and one photo of the house, to chronicle my actions. I grabbed the sole garbage bag and photographed it in my trunk. I was apprehensive about leaving an empty garbage can but hoped he wouldn't notice.

Once in my garage, I set up a video camera in preparation for opening the bag. Chain of custody is important: I needed to show the time and date, and what items came out of the bag. I lined up several black garbage bags on the floor of the garage, pulled on a pair of disposable gloves, unpacked the contents from the bag and placed them on the liners. There were a dozen crushed Diet Coke cans, an empty Styrofoam egg carton, eggshells, a cereal box, and a squashed 1% milk container. There were two apple cores, a rinsed sardine tin, and an empty cracker box. This was the extent of the food evidence. He had thrown away a pair of raggedy shorts and several pairs of socks, an empty toilet paper roll, some used dryer sheets, dental floss, paper towels, and a real estate magazine. The few food items indicated he was eating most meals elsewhere.

Among the refuse, there were several credit card receipts for meals at an upscale Italian restaurant, a steak house, and a sports bar. The amounts on each were well over one hundred dollars. There was also a receipt for TJ Maxx, showing purchases of bath towels and women's clothing totaling over $300, dated after my client left town. I took photos of each receipt, then placed them in a sealable plastic sandwich bag. Abigail would be able to check the last four digits of the credit card and determine if the account was known to her. I put everything else back into the bag, drove to their subdivision, and put it back inside the garbage can, in case he was to come home later and throw something away.

My client stayed away for four garbage cycles. Each week I found more receipts. A deposit slip was in the third garbage bag, and this proved crucial in locating the hidden accounts. Abigail's attorney was able to glean enough information to subpoena the husband's banking records. A settlement was quickly reached in the divorce. Abigail kept the house and her assets. Her ex was on the hook for five years of rehabilitative alimony, primarily because he secreted money in accounts not accessible to his wife and spent marital assets on his girlfriend.

Other garbage runs were not so easy or so clean. Most civil cases I worked on, whether it was a divorce, child support modification, custody battle, or embezzlement situation, involved at least one round of garbage scrutiny. Trash runs were so common, I included several questions on my intake paperwork:

- Do you, or the subject have babies, toddlers, or anyone in the household who wears diapers?
- Do you, or the subject, have cats and litter boxes?

Originally, I thought to ask about dog poop, but it didn't seem anyone was putting that in their garbage cans. Maybe no one picked up dog waste in Alabama. I wanted to ask about condoms, but my husband urged me to let that question go.

"It's the unexpected surprises that make life worth living," he laughed.

Indeed.

If it was a corporate client, we usually had little insider knowledge about diapers or cat litter.

From experience, I assure you there are few things nastier than a dirty disposable diaper or a dump of cat litter in a garbage bag, especially when the bags have been marinating in the heat and humidity of Alabama. Think biohazard. Toxic fumes wafting from melted, runny poop. Visualize flies, worms, and roaches. These bags rode in my car unless I convinced my apprentice investigator son Jacob to steal them. But the bags would still end up in my garage for examination.

Yuck.

Garbage

It became my practice to charge higher fees for garbage runs, a hazardous waste surcharge, if you will. After some practice Jacob and I got good at opening bags right in the can, late at night, shining a flashlight directly into the bags to get a sense of the contents before hefting them into our cars.

Jacob got the task of pulling the garbage of a woman suspected of embezzling money from a Montgomery manufacturing company. Her can was full the first night on the job. He pulled out three bags of dirty cat litter and set them aside. The fourth bag, at the bottom of the can, held household trash, but it also yielded printouts of accounts receivable from the company, marked up with margin notes. The woman had devised a code for the transactions. In the evenings, she would renumber and change invoices to hide the skimming from deposits she and her son were transacting.

From what we learned, the woman and her son conspired to defraud their family's company, and the irony was not lost on me, especially as my son and I worked to expose their fraud while building our family business.

She removed payments from the reports she turned over to the accountant. She deftly made the accounts balance, although the company was selling far more goods and services than was reported. During a routine interview with me, prior to the garbage run, she gleefully pointed fingers at long-term, loyal employees, and accused them of stealing declining inventory. Soon we learned the goods had been properly purchased and the inventory had not declined through pilfering. The woman had siphoned money from the receivables, wrongly thinking she could perpetuate the fraud. Other family members, disappointed with their shrinking dividend checks, requested the accountant launch an investigation, and I was hired. Something was amiss, and we caught her.

My final garbage run, in 2005, came about as an attorney suspected his legal assistant was misappropriating money. In many small law offices, a secretary manages the payable and receivable accounts. They will make deposits, keep track of retainers and trust accounts, and pay the bills weekly, often preparing the checks for the attorneys to sign.

In this office, the secretary was writing checks to herself or cash, forging the attorney's signature, but entering the checks as payment for legitimate bills. She continued this for several months before the attorney realized bills weren't being paid on time, if at all.

This secretary had sent me a lot of work over the years and often referred clients to me. She was instrumental in helping my agency become established and prosper. She was a single parent and my friend. I was sickened when the attorney confided his suspicions to me. My invoices were typically paid on the Fridays after receipt. I never had to chase payment from them.

She was out of the office one afternoon with an ill child. The attorney's wife answered phones and greeted clients. A call came from their insurance company. A premium for their errors and omissions policy was 90 days past due and about to be canceled. His wife saw the payment marked in the register, with a corresponding check number. She began searching for the canceled check but couldn't find it. This led to closer scrutiny of their accounts, and she turned up multiple instances of missing cleared checks and payments made to someone but not to the vendors. They closed their office for a couple of days and gave the secretary paid time off, while they investigated the discrepancies.

The attorney had a private dumpster in the alley behind the law office, and it was emptied monthly. He asked me to come in for a meeting. I assumed it was regarding a new client, but he briefed me on what had occurred. After establishing I had played no role in the fraud, he asked me to go through the dumpster, looking for the "real" canceled checks. His wife had gone to the bank to obtain copies of the missing checks which had been cleared, to learn who had cashed them. It took me an entire day to work through the leftover lunches and discarded cleaning supplies, but I found several of the checks in the dumpster, as well as a worksheet of the misappropriated funds and a list of the bills she had marked as paid on the register yet were still outstanding.

Damning evidence all. The situation distressed me. The secretary was fired, but the attorney declined to press criminal charges against her.

Garbage

Perhaps he didn't want either his colleagues or his clients to know he'd allowed himself to be swindled. He paid me for my time, but he never again sent me work or referred me to clients.

I said nothing of my knowledge of the situation to the secretary, but I distanced myself from her, as I feared our association had tainted my reputation as well. She went on to work for other attorneys. Several years later, I learned she had stolen from the wrong lawyer: she'd been arrested and prosecuted. She spent 15 months in prison.

By then, my garbage days were long over. But I learned a valuable lesson: don't throw anything into a garbage can that could incriminate you. Someone someday may pull your trash bag and expose your secrets to the world.

Life in Wartime: The Custody Game

"Never, ever purchase a house that's down the street from your former spouse."

This is my divorce advice. No matter how much you love the neighborhood, move elsewhere. It's not healthy to watch the activities of your former partner, and you don't want your ex watching you.

Trust me.

In August 1998, two years into my practice, I was introduced to Thomas and Kathy Palmer by their attorney, Edward Williams Jr. Suspecting his ex-wife had a live-in boyfriend, Thomas sought custody of his 9-year-old child. He objected to an unrelated adult male living under the same roof as his daughter.

Thomas and his second wife, Kathy, had been married for two years, and during this brief period, a multitude of issues from Thomas' first marriage had kept them entwined with his ex-wife in court. Now, the Palmers pursued a custody and cohabitation case and needed my help. Thomas and his ex-wife Paula shared joint custody of their daughter, with Paula as the primary physical caregiver. Thomas wanted their daughter in his home, in his care, and vowed to give his ex-wife 'generous' visitation.

Thomas, Kathy, and I met around a conference table in the law office. Their attorney was deliberately absent, leaving me to formulate a plan with the clients. Both Palmers were in excellent physical shape. In her early thirties, Kathy was a raven-haired aerobics instructor at a local YMCA and blew into the meeting wearing yoga pants and a midriff-baring crop top. Her full, surgically enhanced cleavage was on view for all. She apologized for her attire, saying she'd had to cut a workout class short to make the meeting on time. She pulled her hair off her neck, flashing her talon nails, her left hand adorned by a large two-carat solitaire and diamond-encrusted wedding band, poised to catch my eye. I nodded, acknowledging her treasures.

In his mid-forties, Thomas was a commercial airline pilot with sandy hair graying at the temples and a friendly smile. He was dressed in a short-sleeved cotton shirt and pressed khaki pants. His leather loafers were polished and immaculate, his hands manicured, his demeanor calm and professional. The guy you'd trust to fly the plane through turbulent air.

"Are you based in Montgomery?" I was curious. The local airport was small, and the flights were often inconsistent, making connections unreliable.

"No, I'm with Delta out of Atlanta," he replied. "I mostly fly international routes now. The money's better," he glanced at his wife. "And we need more money."

I nodded, wondering why he chose to live in Montgomery rather than Atlanta.

Kathy had brought two young daughters into this marriage, and Thomas had legally adopted them. There was no mention of their biological father. Kathy seemed eager to bring his daughter into their home permanently.

"Do they get along well?" I asked.

Thomas and Kathy flashed ultra-bright smiles at one another. "Oh, yes," Kathy gushed. "They're best friends and sisters." Her daughters, I learned, were six and eleven years old, and Kayleigh, Thomas' daughter, "fit right into the mix."

My skin prickled at this statement. Her words didn't quite ring true. For several years, I had been a single parent, and I never dated men with children. The baggage most kids of divorce carry is heavy and unwieldy; dealing with other kids' issues was unpalatable to me. Caring for my three was a constant physical and emotional struggle. I had unresolved issues with their father and couldn't imagine willingly bringing more problems into my household. Raising children was a lot of work, and the days left me exhausted from routine chores like laundry, cooking, and homework. Arranging visitation with their out-of-state father, splitting holidays between households, and dealing with dark clouds of anxiety and anger were akin to navigating landmines in a war zone. My custodial footing was insecure, and some days were fraught with the danger of losing my teenage kids. I was skeptical about Kathy's description of the perfectly blended situation.

Over the next hour, Thomas, Kathy, and I worked through my initial client questionnaire. They listed their address as 1259 Piney View Drive, Montgomery. Thomas said his ex-wife, Paula Thomas, lived at 1014 Piney View Drive.

"You live on the same street as your ex-wife?" I was stunned.

"It wasn't supposed to be this way," Thomas said.

"She bought a house right down the street during the divorce," Kathy said. "Who does that?"

Thomas cleared his throat. "Well, in Paula's defense, we were supposed to sell our home, and after I'd refinanced it to pay her half of the equity, Paula used the cash to buy a house down the street." He reached over and clasped his wife's hand. "Kathy loved the house, so we decided to keep it."

Kathy rolled her eyes and withdrew her hand. "I do love it, but we have to drive by her house every time we go somewhere."

I wasn't familiar with the subdivision. "Can't you take a different route?" I asked.

"No, it's not possible," Thomas explained. "We live at the end of a cul-de-sac. Coming and going, we have to drive right by Paula's house. Can't avoid it."

My interest was piqued. The Palmers were upset by the proximity of the ex-wife yet had chosen to keep the house on the same street. This was a clear indication of the hostilities swirling around these clients. I made a quick assessment: Paula bought her own house in the neighborhood. I assumed she sought stability for her daughter, allowing her to remain close to her friends, by staying in the same school. Good for her. After my first marriage imploded, I was too financially strapped to do the same for my kids. Likely, Paula had hoped her ex-husband and his new bride would live elsewhere, like Atlanta. Kathy's daughters were now in the same neighborhood, and in the same school, as Kayleigh.

At least one of those girls was living in Kayleigh's former bedroom.

I couldn't imagine a less tenable situation.

"She paid cash for the house," Kathy sneered. "She could have bought anywhere."

So could you, I thought but kept my mouth shut. These were my clients. For better or worse, I worked for them.

During this initial meeting, I learned Thomas paid Paula $1800 a month in alimony and another $850 in child support. I did a quick calculation: $31,800 a year. A lot of money to come straight from his paycheck, and while I suspected they wanted custody of Kayleigh to decrease child support and staunch the outflow of money, I wondered how he could get out from under the alimony obligation.

"If she has a boyfriend living with her, I can likely stop paying alimony," Thomas said. "We have to prove it."

Kathy handed me a file folder containing information about Paula's daily routine, her part-time job, stores she frequented, and the address of Paula's parents. There were few details about the boyfriend. I scanned through them. His name was Brian Beatty. He often wore a ball cap, sometimes drove Paula's car, didn't seem to have a job, and drank Coors Lite beer.

"How'd you know about the beer?" I asked. Kathy shrugged.

Life in Wartime: The Custody Game

"I may have gone through the garbage can."

I laughed. "That's my job. Don't go through her garbage anymore."

We discussed my fees, and Thomas handed me a check for $500 to begin the case. In those days I charged $50 an hour, plus mileage and expenses. I suspected this retainer would barely scratch the surface.

After the Palmers left the office, I remained at the conference table for a few minutes, finishing my notes. As I was packing up, legal assistant Debbie pushed open the door. I pegged her age at sixty, but she was energetic, spritely and expertly managed all the cases in this office. She was a treasure trove of information about legal procedures and clients.

"This is for you," she said, handing me a thick manila envelope. "It's all the court pleadings for the Palmers. These will bring you up to speed. Call me when you have questions, and I'll try to help."

"Thank you, Debbie, for this information, and the referral."

"You're very welcome," she said. "Did Thomas mention he has a first appearance in criminal court tomorrow?"

"He was arrested? For what?"

Debbie pulled a chair away from the table and sat down, eager to talk. "Did you see Kathy's ring?"

"Who could miss it?"

"Well, Paula, the ex, filed a report with Montgomery Police claiming Thomas had stolen it during the divorce. Paula wants it back."

"Seriously? What kind of guy gives his new wife the first wife's ring?"

Debbie laughed. "Well, Thomas did. He says the diamonds were his mother's, and he reset the ring for Paula when they married. Then, a week before he served her with divorce papers, he took the ring to Cronier's to be cleaned. Paula didn't see the ring again until it ended

53

up on Kathy's finger. She had him arrested last week. He was charged with felony theft. The ring is valued at over $10,000."

"Wait, how long ago was the divorce?"

"Well, the divorce was finalized in April 1996. Thomas and Kathy got married 31 days later, after the 30-day waiting period expired. But they've stayed in court, trying to resolve issues, ever since.

"That's crazy. He already had the new wife lined up?"

"Maybe. They're vague on the dates of when Thomas and Kathy met, but he had been flying routes to San Diego for a year and spending longer layovers there before he filed for divorce. I'm sure you'll get all the details."

"Oh, I can't wait," I sighed. "What's going to happen in court tomorrow?"

"Well, Eddie will file some motions and kick this down the road a bit, along with the two other open court issues happening with these people. The custody and cohabitation cases are the newest rounds of court filings."

"Why not settle the ring issue? Certainly, Thomas could pay Paula, say, half the value of the ring and move on. He's probably paid more than the ring is worth to Eddie and court fees by now."

"Oh, but Susan, settling the case is beside the point. These folks will rip each other to shreds until someone backs down. Thomas has deep pockets, which translates to lots of billable hours." She winked. "Eddie has his eye on a new sailboat. I'd like hardwood floors in here, to replace the carpeting."

She stood, pushing the chair back under the table. She pointed to the envelope. "Happy reading."

The game was mid-play, and I'd been asked to join the team. I picked up the heavy envelope and left the office.

Life in Wartime: The Custody Game

While in Montgomery, I stopped at the bank to deposit the retainer check, then walked across the parking lot to an independent living facility to see my mom. The receptionist said she was playing dominos in the activities room. I observed my mother for a moment: she was dressed impeccably, her hair styled, nails manicured, lipstick freshly applied. She wore her diamond ring and her pearls. She looked good, but she was in the early stages of dementia, and I knew rough times were ahead. The ladies spotted me and reluctantly halted the game for a few minutes, while I chatted with them until bored, they turned their attention back to the game.

I made a quick stop at the grocery store, then headed home. The kids were already there, and Peter would be home soon. It was time for homework and dinner. Work on the case would commence the next day.

In the morning, I checked the office answering machine. The Palmers had called four times since our meeting, urging me to contact them. The kids were in school, Peter at work. I'd already vacuumed. The washing machine and dryer were running. I brewed a fresh pot of coffee and carried a cup, a notepad, and the case background information out to the glass table in the sunroom. Summer mornings were lovely out there. The room was glassed in on three sides. It faced west, over hundreds of acres of protected forest. The afternoon sun blazed through the pine and oak trees, making this room unbearably bright, but the mornings were comfortable.

Debbie had mentioned three ongoing cases. I knew about the ring and felony arrest case, and I was hired to work on the custody and cohabitation case. The third filing was an unresolved issue from the divorce about the division of personal assets. According to the case action summary, Paula had designed and ordered a set of custom-made drapes for the marital residence. They were iris and gray silk and cost $1,750. *For curtains?* There were photos of them in the file. At the last court hearing, the judge lost his composure and ordered Thomas and Paula into mediation to decide the custody of the draperies. Would they even fit any of the windows in Paula's new house? I could only shake my head and wonder.

These were my clients.

The phone rang. It was Kathy Palmer. We were, as they say, off to the races.

"We called you four times yesterday, but you didn't call us back," she said when I picked up the phone. "We paid your retainer; we expect you to speak with us when we call."

Here we go.

"Did you see him at the house last night?" she asked.

Kathy had the voice of a drill sergeant, commanding and loud. The serenity of my sunroom was disrupted by 8:35 am. I had barely opened the envelope to familiarize myself with the Palmer situation when Kathy called, expectant of results. I hadn't even formulated a plan for the day, much less an outline for working the case.

One of the most critical aspects of private investigating is understanding your client's motivation, the reason they've retained a PI. Oftentimes, the client has an entirely different agenda from the reason they give you or their attorney. Based on our meeting, I suspected this situation was more about money than the child's welfare. Kathy was tired of $3,000 leaving her household and going into the ex-wife's account every month and wanted the money to work to her advantage. I took a deep breath and ventured into the case.

"Tell me everything you know that leads you to believe Paula has a man living with her."

Over the next eleven months, until the day in court when she turned on me, I came to know Kathy Palmer as well as I could understand another human. She was anxious, often irritated, and prone to sudden outbursts and mood swings, but she could also be friendly, engaging, and, I believe, genuinely interested in solving the question of whether Brian Beatty was cohabitating with Paula Palmer, a situation that could cost Paula her monthly alimony check.

Life in Wartime: The Custody Game

"I leave the house every weekday morning at 5:15, as I teach a 6 a.m. aerobics class downtown. Many mornings, the light is on in her garage. It isn't the house light, but the automatic light that comes on when the garage door is opened and stays on for five minutes. We think she's taking her boyfriend back to his car before she wakes up Kayleigh for school.

"This same light also comes on around 9:30 at night, an hour after Kayleigh's bedtime. We've seen her leaving the house in the evening, and then again in the morning. Is she picking him up, taking him home? Or back to his car?"

"You tell me: Have you ever followed her, to see where she takes him?"

I jotted a question on my notepad: Was Paula leaving her daughter home alone? For how long? Given Kathy said she left early every day to teach a class, she was leaving her daughters by themselves when Thomas was flying. She couldn't accuse the ex-wife of neglect if they did the same. I would address this later. One battle at a time.

"I tried following them a couple of times, but she filed a report with the police, saying I was stalking her," Kathy said. "They came to talk to me, gave me a warning, so if I see her driving, I go in another direction."

"That's why you don't have his tag number, right?" I asked. "You've described his car, but have you put him inside it, or seen the tag number?"

"No, I haven't seen him in the car, but it has been parked in her driveway."

"How do you know the red Toyota Corolla is Brian's?"

She paused for several beats. "Kayleigh told us it's his car, her mom's boyfriend."

"What else has Kayleigh told you?"

"Um, not much… I mean, we're not allowed to question her, the judge's order, it's in the court records." I waited for her to speak again.

"When are you going to get started?"

"I'm working now," I said. "Every time we speak, I'm on the clock, like your attorney."

"You charge for phone calls?"

"Kathy, I charge for everything. Just like your lawyer." I thought of something else. "Yesterday, as I was leaving your attorney's office, Debbie handed me a large envelope of all the prior court pleadings from your cases, your discovery, and I charge for the time it takes me to read through it."

"Why? I don't understand why. You could ask me or Thomas." I explained I needed to know what had led them to this point. She elicited a promise I would do some drive-bys through the neighborhood that day. For some reason, she thought this would bring the case to a swift conclusion. However, at the end of this 11-minute conversation, which I billed as a quarter-hour, I had no new information, except garbage pick-up on their street was on Wednesdays. I looked at my notes: Brian Beatty was the boyfriend, he was White, about 45 years old, and drove a red Toyota Corolla. As insignificant as this seemed, it was more information than I started with in many cases. I was relieved his name wasn't John Smith, William Martin, Bob Roberts, or some variation of commonly held names. Something irritated me about Kathy. I decided to do some fieldwork to move this case forward. Before I left the house, I called my friend and attorney, Jacqui Austin. I needed to know what evidence I needed to prove cohabitation.

"Where does he receive mail?" she asked.

My first stop was the civil court counter in the Montgomery County Courthouse. There was a public-use computer there so anyone could look up cases by name or Social Security numbers, either by specific counties or through a statewide search. The database at the time was rudimentary, but in the two years I'd been a working PI, this information portal was a crucial tool for information gathering. Many people don't know court records in most states are open to the public; otherwise, why pay me for information?

I plugged in the name Brian Beatty and his age range as 40-50, selected Male from the list and did a statewide search.

The computer gave me listings for several Brian Beatty's. I eliminated two: one was Black, and from Birmingham, and the other had a birth date of 1923. I jotted down the case numbers associated with the sole remaining subject. Brian Christopher Beatty. His birthday was November 19, 1954, which would make him 44 on his upcoming birthday. There were twelve case listings linked to his name, eight of these were in the Montgomery civil court system, which included, to my immense delight, a domestic relations file with subsequent modifications.

Be still, my beating heart. A divorce file is a treasure trove of information, an investigator's dream come true.

He also had two criminal charges: Public Intoxication and Breaking and Entering, both accrued within the past three years. Paydirt. Aside from two traffic citations, he had been sued by banks, and I suspected these were lawsuits over bad debt, likely stemming from business deals gone awry and credit problems from his first marriage.

While I was on the database, I checked out Thomas, Kathy, and Paula. Aside from the multitude of case filings stemming from the divorce, Paula had two traffic tickets. Thomas had the criminal arrest for theft of the ring. I already had the arrest record from Debbie, but I didn't have Paula's traffic citations.

I handed my list of case numbers to the civil records clerk and requested the files. She raised her eyebrows when she saw the list of eight cases for Brian Beatty.

"Do you need all these files today? You know we charge a quarter a page, right?"

I assured her I did and showed her my checkbook. "I'm going to read them first and decide what needs to be copied." This search would be pricey, but this was why I never worked on a case without a retainer. She agreed to bring the case files to the Clerk of the Criminal Court office, where I could use a carrel to study the files rather than stand at a counter.

While I waited for the civil cases, I retrieved copies of the traffic citations and the two criminal court records for Brian Beatty. There are obvious reasons why we should avoid traffic tickets, keeping our insurance rates low is one, but here's my thinking: I want to be invisible to prying eyes. I don't want anyone to find my records, my date of birth, or my Social Security number. Traffic tickets stay on your permanent record. They contain your full name, date of birth, address, and, in Alabama, like many states, they contain your Social Security number, which is a vital piece of information to a licensed private investigator. I was friendly with the clerk in this office, so I was able to pull files on my own, photocopy the records, and pay when I was finished.

Brian Beatty had two tickets in the past year: one for speeding, 57 mph in a 45 zone, and another for not wearing his seatbelt, which stemmed from the speeding incident. Paula had two tickets for speeding in the past four years. I noted the dates and times and would research them later, to try to determine if she had Kayleigh in the car with her when she was caught speeding.

The civil clerk eventually brought the requested files to me. But they came with a warning:

"The Judge sealed a portion of the testimony in the divorce case," she said. "The information pertains to the two teenaged daughters of the parties." She looked at me. I nodded, understanding. "I didn't remove that section from the file, but I put the pages into an envelope and stapled it directly on the folder. You can't look at them."

"How bad is it?" I had to ask. "Were there allegations of abuse? Sexual abuse?"

Life in Wartime: The Custody Game

She opened her mouth to say something, then caught herself. "All I can say is this: Mrs. Beatty got complete custody of their daughters. He lost all rights to them, with no visitation." She turned and began to walk away before I could respond.

A bombshell. Wow. Brian Beatty lost all rights to his daughters in his divorce case. Why? Perhaps this tidbit would assist Thomas in securing custody of his daughter. Curious as hell, I fingered the sealed envelope but didn't dare break the seal. Instead, I read the case from the beginning, marking sections of the file for photocopying. I made a note of the ex-wife's home address as well as the four or five addresses Brian Beatty had provided the courts: his parents' address, his business address, and others. There was no doubt I would visit the former Mrs. Beatty at some point. Brian could not see his daughters, but he was on the hook for $300 a month in child support which, I noted, he hadn't paid in eleven months. A court notice had been sent to one of the addresses listed but returned as undeliverable. His driver's license was about to be suspended for failing to pay child support. He listed his occupation as a realtor.

Close to three hours later, I emerged from the courthouse, bleary-eyed, with hundreds of pages from the Beatty divorce proceedings, which read like a bad television drama. Beatty had turned a routine divorce into a spectacle of bluster and bravado while acting as his own attorney. He had provoked the judge repeatedly and caused much pain and anguish to his wife and teenage daughters, by forcing them to testify in open court, while cross-examining them.

The cloudless sun seared my eyes despite the dark prescription sunglasses I always wore. My head hurt, and I hoped like hell I hadn't gotten a parking ticket. I'd blown the 60-minute meter and hadn't bothered to leave the courthouse to buy more time. Ugh. The downtown parking enforcement officer kept track of cars. You weren't supposed to stay longer than one hour in a specific space, and she marked tires with chalk. I walked quickly, carrying an armful of papers. I spied my car. No tickets. Whew. She must have taken the day off.

Brian Beatty's background came into focus, aside from a vague description, I had no idea what he looked like, but I knew where I could find a photo. Armed with the traffic citations, I drove to the Alabama Driver's License office downtown and parked in the free lot. I pulled two forms from a rack near the counter and filled out requests for the driving abstracts for both Brian and Paula. I had their full names, dates of birth, and driver's license numbers from the tickets. The abstracts contained the photos from their driver's licenses, complete driving histories, and their Social Security numbers.

In those days Alabama didn't require licensing for private investigators. That would come later. But I had a business license, which many agencies recognized as official proof I was indeed an investigator and had a legitimate right to obtain records. So, thirty dollars later, I had DMV photographs of Brian and Paula and copies of their driving records. I then drove to the auto tag agency on Atlanta Highway and the Eastern bypass to pull Brian's license tag number and vehicle information. For $5.50, I could positively identify his car. I had what I needed to begin building the case, starting with a timeline.

I was assembling the puzzle, beginning with the edge pieces.

There was a drive-through coffee shop in the middle of the parking lot. I ordered a latte. I had hours of work ahead and lunch would slow me down.

Fortified by a large coffee in the cup holder, I drove to the Prospero Point subdivision, off Taylor and Vaughn roads. This was considered an "elite" area of Montgomery, but this distinction shifted through the years, primarily as the racial composition changed and White flight pushed new neighborhoods to the east. Many Alabamians claim to be racially blind but let a family of color move into the community and watch the for-sale signs pop up like crabgrass. The area was a maze of cul-de-sacs, and it took a bit of navigation to locate Paula's home.

Surveillance was going to be a nightmare. This was an active mid-to-upper middle-class neighborhood. Cars in driveways, gardeners,

Life in Wartime: The Custody Game

basketball hoops, dog walkers. Everything pointed to active and observant residents. Despite what we've seen on television, surveillance is difficult, whether in the suburbs or the city. Try it sometime. Hang out too long on a street and someone will spot you, and either approach or call the police about suspicious activity.

Paula's house was a neatly maintained one-level ranch with an attached two-car garage. It was a light-gray stucco, and the roof shingles appeared new. There were three sets of windows facing the street, framed with black shutters. The blinds were drawn, the curtains closed, keeping the sun out and the secrets in. The lawn was freshly mown, the concrete driveway clean, with no oil spills or weeds growing through cracks. There were four windows at the top of the double garage door. They were too high to get a close look inside, to see if cars were parked there, but a light shining through would be visible to passersby. There was a single solid metal door on the side of the garage. The backyard was enclosed by a six-foot-tall, wood privacy fence. The houses sat on quarter-acre lots. I continued down the street to check out Thomas and Kathy's home.

The Palmer home was a two-story brick and mortar that stood out among the neighborhood of single-story, stucco structures. Built at the end of a cul-de-sac, the house sat in the middle of a half-acre lot, double the size of any of the neighboring yards. The parcel was surrounded by a black wrought iron fence, and a motorized gate spanned the entrance of the circular driveway. The house was grandiose compared to the other homes in the area, large and ostentatious. The layout would make sense on acreage, but it was too big for the lot. There was a keypad, speaker, and camera system. The property was meticulously maintained, with perfectly manicured hedges and a lush, green lawn with no dead spots. I felt massive house envy.

Scanning the street for a niche to hide in, I continued by Paula's house, snapping a quick date-and-time-stamped photo as I passed. At the stop sign, I turned right, then right again onto the next street, and counted down five houses on the right. I pulled alongside the curb. The lot directly behind Paula's was undeveloped, which meant I could try to do some surveillance from the fence line. This was the only place to watch her house at night. There was a For Sale sign in front of the lot. A dashboard thermostat registered an outdoor temperature of 98 degrees. I pulled a scrunchie off the gear stick and wrapped my hair in a messy chignon. I stepped out into the muggy air, locked the car door, and gingerly made my way to the back of the lot.

Dandelions, chickweed, and bitter chamber formed tangles along the ground, perfect for tripping a walker, hazardous in the dark. Snakes came to mind. The ground was uneven, with fallen branches covered in kudzu, I stumbled and nearly lost my footing several times. Trees grew together in rangy clusters: thin pines mixed with oaks covered in Spanish moss, which meant no-see-ums. Mosquitoes buzzed my face and landed on my arms and legs. I could endure those critters. But no-see-ums were insidious and took hours to burrow into your skin, biting, burning, and itching. The spaghetti-strapped, knee-length sundress and sandals I wore provided no protection from those near-invisible beasts. I pushed through several large spider webs, shuddered with revulsion, frantically pushing the silken strands off my face and arms.

I reached Paula's privacy fence and realized it was too tall to see over. I walked along the uneven ground by the boundary line until I found a rise in the dirt that gave me enough height to look over the barrier. Most of the yard was covered by a large, multi-level deck. There was a barbeque grill, lounge chairs, a table, and a yellow umbrella to block the sun. Flower beds of white roses and bright pink perennials landscaped the treeless yard.

The back of the house stretched in a line, from the garage at one end to the primary bedroom at the other. There was a roofed-over sunroom, much like mine, off the family room, and a large bay window highlighted the dining area. There was a kitchen window and an opaque-glass bathroom window. Except for the primary bedroom windows, none were covered with blinds or curtains. There were no windows at the back of the garage, making it impossible to tell if there were cars parked inside. Despite this, the vacant lot provided the ability to watch. It was about as good as anything would be with this case. I reminded myself to bring bug spray and wear hiking boots.

Life in Wartime: The Custody Game

Driving home, I called Kathy to ask about their weekend visitation schedule with Kayleigh. I wanted to watch the house when the girl was home with Paula. Ideally, I'd see Brian there as well. She said Kayleigh would be with her mother the upcoming weekend and offered to sit in the woods with me. The idea had some appeal. But I declined. It was best she stayed clear of surveillance activities.

"How was court today?" I asked. "Was Thomas cleared?"

"Nothing happened," she said. "The judge continued the case for three months."

I smiled. It looked like Eddie might get that new sailboat.

After dinner and homework, showers, laundry, and the general chaos of three teenagers, I went out to the sunroom to work on the Palmer case. Due to a shortage of bedrooms, Peter and I kept the computer on a desk, and this room was my office. I'd already blown the $500 retainer in what amounted to one day of work. I typed up an invoice and tallied my expenses for the court records, mileage, and the time I'd spent on the case, and printed it out to mail to the Palmers. I turned to the pile of courthouse documents and began reading them slowly, noting addresses and making a to-do list. I began to piece together a timeline and a case report.

Brian Beatty used several different addresses for his court dealings, from his pre-divorce marital house to various work addresses, but he listed his parents' home as his primary residence. He said he lived with his parents during his divorce but was furious when legal documents were delivered to this house. "The process servers upset my mother," he complained to the judge.

I'd be upset, too, if I had a forty-year-old son living with me, ducking court papers. Beatty was pro se, meaning he represented himself, too cheap to pay an attorney, and too arrogant to realize he needed one.

Sadly, this scenario was familiar: I'd been tied up in court since 1994 by an ex-husband who represented himself, demanding full custody of our children. Every two months I had to attend a court hearing, 350 miles away. I had an attorney on retainer; there had been psychological evaluations, mediation sessions, and court fees.

These expenses accrued steadily. After four years, little had been resolved. In 1996, I'd had to petition the court for permission to move, with the children, to Alabama when Peter's job relocated us from Florida two years into our marriage. While my ex-husband contested the move as a hardship to him, the judge gave approval.

When their father and I separated in 1989, I declined to seek alimony or child support. I wanted the kids and the dog, and to be left alone. This worked for five years until Peter and I married. Within a month, I was served with a custody petition. Once in court, the judge was angered that my ex-husband, a well-educated and professional man, had not provided any financial help and ordered him to pay child support. He pled poverty, provided little income documentation, and was ordered to pay $235 a month, a meager sum compared to the income he was capable of earning. The money, when it came, was a drop in the bucket and didn't cover the health insurance premiums Peter paid for the kids. One Friday a month we had to drive four hours to Tallahassee, halfway to their father's apartment in Tampa, for their weekend visitation, then drive again on Sunday afternoon to pick them up. It was fair to say we were mentally, financially, and physically exhausted, but we'd tried, with limited success, to maintain an atmosphere of lightness and fun.

In custody cases children are pawns on a battlefield.

Money that could have been used to improve our quality of life went directly toward legal fees. My mother, who helped Peter and me shoulder this financial burden, occasionally suggested I turn the tables by simply giving up primary physical custody of the kids.

"He doesn't want them," she said. "He's doing this to torment you." In the meantime, their father moved from pillar to post, failed to hold a job, lived with girlfriends, ate free meals at political rallies and church functions even though he didn't vote or attend religious services. This was a man who once had a bright and shining future.

Life in Wartime: The Custody Game

And there I was, late on a Tuesday night in August, pouring through court records, working on a custody case that hit too close to home. I could usually sideline my worries while working, but Brian Beatty's court documents triggered deep emotions, shrouding me in anger and depression.

Thomas Palmer objected to Brian living in the same house as his daughter, and he didn't yet know what I'd found. He'd flip out when he learned of the sealed court documents.

I assumed Beatty was a freeloader, sustained by the alimony and child support paid by Thomas, unfailingly, every month.

Was Beatty a real estate agent? I'd check his licensing status. Court notices returned as undeliverable indicated the addresses he'd used were vacant. My mind drifted to the documents I was prohibited from seeing.

What had Brian Beatty done to his daughters? Was Kayleigh at risk?

It was nearing 11 pm. The kids were settling down. Peter had gone to bed. I had to make a garbage run. I enlisted my eldest son, Jacob, to come with me. "Here, you drive," I said, handing him the car keys. At sixteen, the chaos and confusion of the custody case, the move to small-town Alabama, and, I suspected, loneliness, weighed heavily on his shoulders. The once funny, witty child had become quiet, withdrawn, hollowed. These had been unnecessarily difficult years.

It was 26.3 miles to Paula Palmer's house. Jacob drove expertly, quietly following my directions. He turned on the radio as if to ward off yet another conversation about skipping school and academic difficulties. Exhausted, I didn't press the issues and relaxed as he drove. The Palmer neighborhood was quiet, with garbage bags placed along the curb of most homes. The neighborhood forbade the use of trash cans, and residents were required to put garbage into heavy, HOA-approved, black plastic bags for weekly pickup. Paula's house was dark. There was no bag of trash for us to grab.

Early the next morning, I called Kathy, just as she was leaving home. "Check for a bag of garbage," but I knew there wouldn't be one at the curb.

Several hours later, I'd set up file folders and processed all the paperwork I'd gathered. There was no mention of Brian's relationship with Paula, nor did he use her address for any legal correspondence. Brian Beatty was arrogant, but cautious not to link himself to Paula's house, although Thomas believed they'd been a couple for at least two years.

Proving cohabitation would not be as simple as showing he used Paula's address as his own or that he slept at her house. We needed a better plan.

Several packets of legal papers for service arrived over the past few days. I opened the FedEx packages and scanned the paperwork. They were bad debt and collection filings. The addresses were all residences, and I plotted them on a map: papers for a man in Coosada, a fleabite town in my county; one in Montgomery, a third in Vestavia Hills, a suburb of Birmingham. A legal secretary had called the day before about divorce documents to be served in Clanton, midway between Montgomery and Birmingham. I returned her call and said I'd pick them up shortly.

I'd spend the day driving Alabama roads, serving papers, and working out a strategy for the Palmer case. I needed fresh air and sunshine to shake off the gloom enveloping me.

Friday night, at dusk, I returned to the vacant lot, dressed head to toe in black, my hair secured under a ball cap. Peter had coated me with bug spray before I left home, and I sprayed myself again once I got out of my car. Equipped with binoculars, a film camera with night vision, and a telephoto lens, I hoped to be able to capture some activity in the house. I had a flashlight, fresh batteries, and a bottle of water. I'd be judicious with the water but brought some tissues just in case I needed to relieve myself.

Life in Wartime: The Custody Game

I hoped to God I wasn't in the woods long.

My concern was that Paula and Kayleigh were away for the night. My fingers were crossed they'd return home, and Brian Beatty would be with them.

The house was dark, illuminated solely by a fixture hanging over the kitchen sink, and a night light in the bathroom. I crouched near the fence and waited. The sounds of the night grew loud: katydids, grasshoppers, and crickets provided a soothing rhythm for my taut nerves. I closed my eyes and breathed into the music. Thankfully, it wasn't a rowdy, raucous cicada year. It was impossible to hear anything above their mating calls when those buggers emerged, every decade or so, from the dirt to procreate. Nature entertained me for a while, with the occasional 'who-cooks-for-you' call from a barred owl, rustling feathers from a nearby nest, and a sudden, frantic squawk. Worried about snakes and whatever else might be lurking, I didn't lean against a tree, although I wanted to; the other evening, while on the deck, Peter and I watched two Timber Rattlesnakes slither down the oak closest to us.

I recalled the evening we were watching television with the kids, and I saw movement on the Oriental rug near the boys. Bedlam ensued when we realized it was a snake: Michelle shrieked and stood on the couch, the boys were alternatively fascinated and terrified. I yelled, Peter was curious about the snake, and all of us propelled into motion, anxious to find it, to move it outside. We pulled out the stove, then the refrigerator, checked the closets and cabinets, showers and tubs, and looked under beds and through all the bedding. Horror, then anxiety prevailed when, after we had searched the house, we didn't find the snake, or its entryway inside.

"It's a red, yellow, black snake," Peter said. "But it's the safe one."

So he said.

A few years later, when we gutted the kitchen for a renovation, we thought we'd find the remains of the snake, but we didn't. The joys of living in the woods.

I thought about all the things I'd rather be doing. It turns out nearly anything is better than sitting alone watching a house.

At 10:41, lights flashed abruptly against the house as a car pulled onto the driveway. *Please be them.* I pulled the camera from the ground, ready for action. I lifted the binoculars to my face as a bright overhead light came on in the kitchen, and there they were: Paula, Kayleigh, and Brian. I hoisted the camera, and adjusted the zoom, but could barely make them out. These wouldn't be great photos. The flash was off, but the night vision was on. A piece of tape hid the red light. Snap. Snap. Photos. Time and date stamped.

Through the binoculars I watched Brian open the refrigerator and walk out of the kitchen into the sunroom with a can, perhaps a beer. I cautioned myself to be still. He sat on a couch and turned on the television. Lights came on in the primary bedroom, then the adjoining bathroom. I assumed Paula was putting Kayleigh to bed and would join Brian.

But she didn't reappear. Eventually, the bathroom light went off, and the bedroom light dimmed, replaced by blue light coming from a television in the primary. Paula had gone to bed. Brian finished his drink, set the can on the coffee table, and turned off the sunroom television. I watched him move through the house, turning off the kitchen light, leaving only a nightlight for guidance. I wondered if he would leave the house, but he didn't. By midnight, the bedroom television was off, and the house was dark. They were in for the night. I went home to shower off the bug spray.

After three Wednesdays of no garbage, I investigated the dumpster behind the boutique where Paula worked. The container was behind a strip mall, and I suspected Paula was putting her household garbage into it, rather than leaving the bag at her house. The dumpster was unlocked, and the HOA-approved black bag sat on top of flattened cardboard shipping boxes. I grabbed my camera and snapped a quick photo of the dumpster, then the bag, then threw it in the trunk and headed home, to set up the video camera to record the exploration. I

Life in Wartime: The Custody Game

was unsure how I would bring anything into custody, but I would damn sure try.

Kathy called while I was driving.

"Were you by the dumpster?" she asked.

"Why, where are you?" I was shocked. "Are you by the boutique?"

"Yes," she said. "I was driving by..."

"Bullshit," I thought.

After several pointed questions, Kathy admitted to having taken Paula's garbage not only from the curb but from this dumpster as well.

"When?"

"Before we hired you," she said. "But not since."

I didn't believe her.

"Don't go near the garbage can or dumpster," I reminded her.

"But I want to help you," she said. "You have a cool job. When our case is over, I want to work with you."

I rolled my eyes. A cool job. I wish I had a dollar for each time I'd heard this. People watch television shows and think there's something glamorous about this job. Two years in, and I'd yet to find the charm. Talking about the work was much more fun than doing it. I decided to confront her.

"Kathy, when was the last time you took garbage from the work dumpster?"

"I don't know," she said. "Maybe a week or two ago?"

"And what did you find?"

She was silent, thinking of a way to answer that wouldn't make me angry.

"A canceled check," she said. "Paula paid Brian seven hundred dollars."

Okay, this was big. "Wow, really? What did you do with it?"

"I have it," she said. "It's in a safe place. Should I give it to Eddie? Will this help our case?"

Thinking carefully, I told her to simply hold onto it. "Put it in a baggie. Mark the date you found it. Keep it in a safe place until I figure out what we can do with it."

Truthfully, I had no idea if this was evidence. Kathy had found it in a bag of garbage in a dumpster behind a business. It didn't matter if Paula gave her boyfriend money, not really. But we were trying to build a case, one piece of evidence at a time.

"Did you find anything else, anything to prove it came from Paula's house, like a piece of mail addressed to Brian?"

"No, some beer cans, kitchen garbage. Nothing else."

"Okay. Make a copy of the check, front and back with the endorsement, and give the copy to me the next time I see you. Make sure I can see whatever is on the back clearly. Let me figure this out."

I didn't know what we could do with this check. If he had deposited it into his bank account, I would have his information, and Eddie could decide if it was worth trying to subpoena Brian's bank records. But if Brian had cashed it, I wouldn't have learned anything new because I already had his driver's license number. Why Paula paid him $700 was pure speculation on my part. I decided to make regular runs to the boutique dumpster on Wednesdays.

Kathy offered to follow me home, to help me go through the new bag of trash. I declined, citing a busy schedule. Once in my garage, I set up the video camera, pulled on a pair of disposable gloves, and began emptying the contents, one item at a time. The bag was full of Diet Coke and Coors Light cans, eggshells and toast crusts, a half-eaten sandwich, and orange and banana peels. There were tags from

Life in Wartime: The Custody Game

two new dresses purchased from the upscale Parisian department store. One was priced at $390, the other at $310. They weren't even marked down. *Must be nice*, I thought, digging through coffee grounds and soggy paper towels. I pulled out a tampon applicator. Ewww. Disgusted, I gingerly sifted the rest of the trash. I saved the clothing tags and pushed the crap back into the black bag. Ripping off the disposable gloves, I went inside to the half bathroom off the laundry room to scrub my hands. I looked at myself in the mirror as I washed. This was not how I had envisioned my adulthood.

The glamorous life of private investigating. I rolled my eyes.

The Palmer case crawled at a snail's pace, frustrating for me, maddening for Kathy and Thomas. Twice I consulted with Eddie, their attorney, and Debbie, his assistant.

"Keep going, you'll get us there," Eddie said. Debbie was more circumspect: perhaps Paula and Brian were guarded because they knew Kathy and Thomas were plotting to petition the alimony and custody arrangements. While I felt Brian Beatty's ex-wife would be an illuminating source of information, the attorney thought I should wait a while longer before approaching her, even though it had been, and continued to be, a contentious and spiteful divorce.

"She might pick up the phone to tell him there was an investigator asking questions," Eddie said. "Which would blow our case. Focus on other areas."

When I explained the Palmers, particularly Kathy, were pressuring me, the attorney laughed.

"Get a secretary to manage them," he said. "Or ignore their calls. Build a solid case. They'll keep paying you."

It made sense to postpone a visit with the ex-wife, but the little bit of intel I'd gathered wasn't adding up to what we needed. Work tasks like surveillance and garbage runs slid to the margins simply because I felt guilty for billing for scant results. I didn't know how to crack the case open. How could I prove he lived with Paula? It seemed he did; apart from his parents' home, none of the addresses contained in his divorce file were valid. He had no utilities in his name. Nerves were frayed all around. There was no clear path toward a conclusion.

When I was a child, my father, a sailor, skilled navigator, and raconteur, told me stories about the Sargasso Sea. "The Doldrums," he explained. "Where there's no wind. Ships founder and men die.

"The eye of the hurricane, Susie, is like The Doldrums. When the sun shines through thunderheads, the rain slows to a trickle, and the wind dies. You think the storm is over, but it's just toying with you, taking a break. It's the calm before the outer wall slams into you and knocks you on your ass."

Truer words were never spoken.

Brian Beatty had provided numerous work addresses in his court filings. I'd driven to each and found them vacant. I had verified his parents' home address, driven by, several times late at night and pre-dawn mornings, attempting to find the red Corolla. Their house had a two-bay carport, with no garage in which to stash a vehicle. A month into this investigation, and I hadn't found his car. He was inside Paula's house the night I'd spied from the vacant lot, but I'd yet to see him anywhere else. I agreed with the Palmers' suspicions that he parked elsewhere, with Paula driving him into her garage and quickly closing the door. I drove ever-widening circles to locate the car. There were numerous clusters of strip malls and medical offices in the area, and I cased those frequently. On at least two occasions, late at night, I confess to killing the lights on my car, pulling onto Paula's driveway, and standing on the doorjamb of my vehicle to look through the garage door windows, attempting to see his car. Even if it had been there, I was trespassing, and I'd never have been able to use that evidence. Lawyers called illegally obtained evidence fruit from the poisonous tree, and to admit to law-breaking would destroy my credibility, in the sense that bad news travels much more quickly than good. Frustrated, I needed something to break open the case. I was mentally and physically exhausted.

He'd claimed to be a realtor, and, if that were true, he had to be licensed by the state.

The licensing board office was tucked in a commercial area on Carmichael Road. Two women employees worked behind a counter and greeted me pleasantly. My cover story was that I'd worked a few years prior with an agent named Brian Beatty and wanted to find him again, but the contact information I had was outdated. Within minutes, his folder was produced, and I had a copy of his complete licensing history. He had been an agent for over a decade but switched companies frequently. He had a broker's license, so technically, he could work independently, but his current broker was the local affiliate of a national real estate company. His parents' address was his permanent residence. He'd been with this firm for nearly a year.

But was he earning money? That $700 check from Paula came to mind. Was that a loan? I asked the women if they kept records of sales commissions.

"Why, no," said one woman. "We don't have any way to track that information."

"Does your office receive complaints made against agents?"

"Yes," the other woman answered. "We have a contract investigator who determines the merit of complaints, and then we act administratively if we need to."

There had been no grievances against Beatty. I made a mental note to get onto the state bid list, investigating complaints might be a good way to grow my income. I drove to the real estate company and looked for his car, but it wasn't there. I parked and went into the office, to pick up a brochure of their listings. Sitting in my car, I skimmed through the sales sheets. Beatty had two listings: one was a residence, a starter home in an older neighborhood, and the other was a large tract of land in East Montgomery. His cell phone number was listed. And right below it was Paula's.

Late the next afternoon, I took my daughter to an orthodontic appointment in Montgomery. Just two months into braces, this was a routine check-up to document the gradual progress of teeth straightening, tighten the wires, and replace the rubber bands that held the braces snugly against her teeth. Michelle had chosen purple bands that day and she smiled at me, to show them off. "Ibuprofen for discomfort and soft food," Dr. Dunn suggested after she'd briefed me. I'd made a pot of chicken soup that morning specifically for Michelle.

My phone rang as we left the office. It was Thomas Palmer.

"I hate to ask, short notice and all, but I was just driving home, and I noticed Beatty's car in Paula's driveway," he said. "Kayleigh has a violin lesson at 4:30, and I wonder if you could see if he's driving her?"

"Does Paula usually stay for the lesson?"

"It's an hour, so she drops Kayleigh off, runs errands, then circles back for her."

"Do you want me to hang around? To see if Beatty picks her up?"

"If you don't mind."

Pulling out the street map, I located the address. It was just off Carmichael, three minutes from the doctor's office. Michelle pulled the camera bag from the trunk and put it in the back seat, within easy reach. We drove to the teacher's street.

It was a quiet residential neighborhood, with houses built in the mid-1960s, cinderblock and brick. The trees were large, the sidewalks wide. We spotted the teacher's house and continued to the end of the block. I made a U-turn and parked alongside the curb, five houses down on the opposite side of the street. Several cars were parked on the road, so we weren't out of place. Far enough away to not be noticed, but close enough to see, and photograph, who was driving Kayleigh.

We were six minutes early. Michelle began her homework assignments. I readied the camera. At 4:28 p.m., a red Toyota Corolla turned onto the street. A man's arm leaned out the car window. I snapped a photo. Brian was driving. The phone rang.

"What do you see?" Thomas asked.

"He just drove up. Kayleigh's getting out now," I said, as a young girl exited the passenger door. "Hold on." I dropped the phone. Michelle closed her notebook. I captured several shots of Kayleigh, violin case in hand, walking to the front door, knocking, and entering the house. Brian honked once, waved, then backed out of the driveway, drove to the intersection, and made a quick left turn. I followed him, picking up the phone from between my seat and the console.

"Hey, Thomas?"

"I'm still here," he said.

"I'm following him," I said. "I'll call you back." I handed the phone to Michelle.

"Mom, what are you doing?" Michelle asked.

"We're going to follow him for a minute, see where he goes." I glanced at my daughter and nodded, handing her the camera.

"Okay, photos of the car. Get the plate number, and him, if you can. There's more film in the bag when you need it."

Another car had pulled onto Carmichael, separating me from Brian. That was fine. It's always better to keep a little distance, not crowd your subject. Traffic was building. Workdays at the Air Force bases ended at 4 p.m., and the roads were congested for several hours. Brian made a left onto Perry Hill Road. The light turned red, I followed, checking the mirrors for cops. I was three cars behind him, but at least I hadn't lost him. He approached another intersection and made an abrupt left turn into a shopping center just as the light turned yellow. The car ahead of me stopped.

"Oh, come on!" I yelled, slamming my hand on the steering wheel.

"I'm watching him, Mom. He's by the pet store." Michelle rummaged through the gear bag for the binoculars, then adjusted them.

"He's going into a barbershop."

The light finally turned green, and nine northbound cars cleared the intersection before I could make the left. The strip mall was not a popular one; the lot was speckled with cars. I parked three rows away, which provided a great sightline of the Corolla. Michelle took a photo of the car, but she couldn't see the tag. I circled the lot so she could photograph the tag, then parked in another spot. Eighteen minutes later he came out of the barbershop, his ball cap in hand. He stood by his car and made a phone call. Michelle took two photographs of him.

It was getting close to the time he'd need to pick Kayleigh up from her lesson. He got into his car but didn't start the engine. The minutes ticked by. It was 5:25, but he remained parked.

"Shouldn't he be picking up the girl?" Michelle asked. "Should we go back to see what happens?"

The answer was yes, but I was torn. Should we watch Brian or return to the violin teacher's house? We remained in the lot, eyes on Brian. At 5:41, a champagne-colored Nissan Maxima pulled alongside the red Corolla.

"Take some pictures, that's Paula."

Michelle shot photos of the car, then of Brian exiting his vehicle, locking the door, and walking to the passenger door of the Maxima. Kayleigh got out of the front and slid into the back seat; Brian took her place in the front. Paula pulled out of the parking lot and headed to the light at Perry Hill Road. She turned left. We followed.

The boys had called numerous times that afternoon, first Danny, then Jacob, curious as to when we'd be home. Michelle phoned Peter to update him and suggest they all have the soup for dinner. We were working and would eat later, she said, proudly and professionally. I smiled.

Life in Wartime: The Custody Game

Anxious for news, the Palmers had phoned three times since we'd left the violin teacher's neighborhood, in pursuit of Brian. They wanted live-action updates, but conversations during active surveillance were too distracting, so Michelle managed the phone and camera while I drove. From a distance, we followed Paula's car to Vaughn Road, then turned left onto the Eastern Bypass. She pulled into the entrance to the Olive Garden restaurant. We watched them enter the restaurant. Michelle snapped photos. It was 5:54.

I couldn't believe our luck. I could finally put the three of them together. This was fun.

"Hungry?"

"Yes, but my mouth is sore, Mom," she said, wiping some saliva on a tissue.

"Oh, sweetie, I know it is, but we'll find something good for you."

Michelle and I entered the restaurant behind a party of six, just as Brian, Paula, and Kayleigh were led to a table to the left of the host station. We were seated several tables from them.

"Soup, salad, breadsticks," I told Michelle. "You can have a Coke, but no special orders. We need to get back to the car before they do, to see where they go." I pulled out a bottle of Ibuprofen from my handbag and shook out two pills into her palm.

Dining alone with Michelle was a treat for me. She is my only daughter, the youngest of my three children. Smart, determined, and confident, she was often overshadowed by the chaos and calamity of her adolescent brothers. We enjoyed our meal, and she caught me up on middle-school gossip. I kept a surreptitious eye on my subjects while we chatted.

Covertly, I studied them. Paula was elegant, as well as beautiful. She was a striking figure in a beige linen dress, regal, like a runway model. Her hair was professionally colored in shades of honey and cream, her makeup expert, her nails manicured. This was not a woman who washed dishes or cleaned bathrooms. She wore tasteful, expensive jewelry. I was ashamedly envious of this woman, yet I knew I'd never pull off wearing that linen dress in 90-degree heat. It would have been a sweaty, wrinkled mess on me.

Kayleigh was the same age as Michelle, gawky and plain, a duckling, but she had the genetics to become a swan. She wore a smocked sundress and sandals; her dirty blonde hair cut in a shoulder-length bob. One day soon, Kayleigh would be a knockout like her mother.

In sharp contrast to the women, Brian resembled an aging frat boy. He was dressed in a washed-out Crimson Tide tee-shirt, taut over a beer gut, Bermuda shorts, and scuffed Bass Weejan loafers with no socks. Despite the haircut, he wore that ball cap I'd seen in the parking lot. He was unshaven, a stubble of gray beard and an unkempt mustache that held remnants of his dinner. He looked like he'd been doing yard work all day and hadn't bothered to shower or change his clothing. He drank two beers with a spaghetti-and-meatballs entree and chowed down on several baskets of breadsticks.

What did Paula see in him? This man was uncouth, the antithesis of Thomas, who wore composure like an expertly tailored suit. Thomas and Paula must have been a strikingly attractive couple, but their new partners were puzzling: Brian was a bum. Kathy was loud and brash, an exhibitionist romping through town in aerobics pants and crop tops. She was enhanced, through surgical procedures, and had just recovered from a round of liposuction on her thighs, which, I'd learned, was major surgery. Try as she might, Kathy turned heads, but she was not a beauty. I thought it would be daunting, as a second wife, to be compared to Paula. I was curious as to who had ended that marriage, Thomas, or Paula? Both had a particular sophistication but their current partners, Kathy and Brian, seemed less polished, less ideal.

Nearing the end of their meal, the server handed Brian the dinner check. He gave it to Paula. She took several bills from her wallet and placed them on the table. Brian ate the remainder of Paula's soup and salad, then slid Kayleigh's plate of lasagna over to his side of the table. When she began to protest, Brian reached over and stroked Kayleigh's face, an oddly intimate gesture. She recoiled from his touch. I was certain Paula had seen that interaction, but she dug into her purse. I thought of the sealed court documents, again wondering if he'd molested his daughters.

Michelle and I finished our meals, and I settled our bill while she used the restroom. We returned to the car before our subjects left the restaurant. Paula handed Brian the car keys and slid into the passenger seat. Michelle took photos. I allowed two vehicles to pull out of the restaurant behind them, while closely watching the Maxima. Brian turned left on Vaughn Road, driving toward Paula's house, rather than to his car, still parked at the Perry Hill Shopping Center. I followed.

Kathy had left six messages while we dined. I'd left the phone in the car so I wouldn't be interrupted while in spy mode inside the restaurant. I called her.

"My daughter and I just had dinner with them at the Olive Garden," I said.

"What?" she yelled. "At their table?"

She must think I'm an idiot. I shook my head.

"No, they were three tables away."

I explained they were driving back to Paula's, but that I couldn't risk being seen in the neighborhood.

"Do you think you can get a photo of them pulling into the garage?"

Kathy said she'd try. I followed the Maxima to the first turn into the subdivision and watched them make the right. I continued down Vaughn for a bit, then doubled back to the shopping center, and took another snapshot of Brian's Corolla. Kathy later called to say she'd taken a photo of the three of them pulling into Paula's garage. I didn't ask how. I didn't care. We'd had a breakthrough. Finally.

Each week I found bits of evidence Brian Beatty was living with Paula and her daughter Kayleigh. September slipped into October and then into November. I had stopped trying to catch Brian in the subdivision when a neighbor spotted me parked along a curb one too many times and called the police. According to Kathy, the police officers came to the street and questioned people about a gray and white sedan. My car. Thankfully, the woman hadn't gotten my tag number. I didn't gain much by watching the house anyway. Although I frequently rotated cars, using Peter's and my mother's, I had simply driven one too many times onto Piney View Drive.

I continued watching him drive Kayleigh to her after-school activities while Paula worked. There was a pattern to the weeks. Mondays meant court-ordered psychological counseling for Kayleigh, who was occasionally joined by her parents. Paula declined to allow stepmom Kathy to join the family sessions, but Thomas pressed to have Brian participate. Paula downplayed the relationship with a curt, "I hardly see him, we're just friends."

Despite this statement, Brian was a fixed presence in Kayleigh's life. On Monday afternoons he picked her up from school and dropped her at the counselor's office. He took her to the Tuesday violin lessons, then Paula picked her up, and the three met for dinner. I came to know all their regular restaurants, although I never dined with them again. Brian took Kayleigh out for ice cream after Thursday's Girl Scout meetings. Kayleigh spent Wednesdays with her father, Kathy, and stepsisters, so I had those nights, and every other weekend, off.

I continued the Wednesday garbage runs to the dumpster outside the store where Paula worked. Through trash, I learned she was making a bid to purchase the boutique, and I found a partial copy of her financial records, which included several pages of bank statements. There were more dress tags from Parisian and expensive women's and men's clothing purchases from the Nordstrom store in the tony Buckhead area of Atlanta.

Twice, I found monthly billing records from Brian's cell phone provider in Paula's household trash. I identified calls to and from Paula's phones but didn't dissect the other numbers. The billing address was his parents' home.

Life in Wartime: The Custody Game

While these bits and pieces added up, there was still no direct proof of cohabitation.

In mid-November, I met Thomas and his attorney Eddie, for a status conference. I presented the evidence I had gathered to date and handed each man a copy of my draft report, with a breakdown of my time and expenses and copies of the photos I'd taken since August. While I could put Brian with Paula and Kayleigh, we simply didn't have enough proof to support a legal filing to stop alimony based on cohabitation or to change the custody arrangement. I'd hoped they would drop the investigation, but Eddie urged me to continue. I handed Thomas my latest invoice. He grimaced.

Again, I asked permission to interview Brian's ex-wife, to learn what was in those hidden documents, but Eddie urged patience.

"Can you subpoena those sealed records?"

He explained he could, once they filed a new case, but said the judge would seek to protect Brian's daughters and keep the records sealed.

"You'll have to get that information from his ex-wife," Eddie said, "but not yet."

Kathy, Thomas, and I had frequently hashed over our suspicions as to why Brian couldn't see his daughters. Thomas was especially frustrated about this as he sat in family counseling sessions each month and couldn't ask direct questions about Brian, for fear of alerting Paula to the investigation. We were caught in a loop, like the Greek god Sisyphus, doomed by Zeus to eternally push a boulder up a hill, only for it to fall back down. I fixed my gaze on the tattoo on Eddie's wrist, the infinity symbol, but my mind connected the ouroboros, the image of the snake eating its tail: [2]

We were either pushing boulders uphill or eating our tails. Thomas was concerned about his own daughter's safety, but he had to remain silent.

As well-heeled as the Palmers seemed, the incessant lawyer fees and my bills were taking a toll. Kathy made comments about my charges and angled for a discount. I shaved time off my billing, but this case was so time-intensive, I'd turned down work from other attorneys, and I feared they would use other investigators. When I wasn't working for the Palmers, I was often on the road, serving papers throughout the state.

Shortly after this meeting Kathy called, asking about our Thanksgiving plans. Her daughters were spending the holiday weekend with an aunt, so she and Thomas would be alone.

"We don't cook," she said. "But we can bring wine."

We invited them to share the holiday with us. It was our year to have the children, which meant we could enjoy a long weekend, without driving the kids back and forth to Florida to meet their father. I thawed the turkey, went to the grocery, prepped potatoes, made the cranberries and pies. My mother would not join us. The dementia had progressed, so even minor changes to her routine were upsetting. She no longer recognized my sons, although she flirted shamelessly with my husband. She was anxious when she was away from her apartment. A month earlier she had ridden the Eastdale Estates bus to her dental office for an appointment. During the routine cleaning, she punched the hygienist, her two-carat diamond puncturing the woman's cheek. I was called. I apologized, my mom was banished from the office, and I secured the diamond ring in her safety deposit box. To minimize her stress, I decided Michelle and I would visit her the day before, to accompany her to the Eastdale Estates holiday luncheon.

Life in Wartime: The Custody Game

The shit hit the fan on November 25, 1998, the day before Thanksgiving. I wish I had read my horoscope for the day. It may have said:

'This is a good day to lock the doors and mind your own business. You have no control over your life, so don't even try.'

Michelle and I drove into Montgomery that morning, a couple of hours ahead of the noon luncheon. I had a few items to pick up from the grocery store, make a bank deposit, and, since it was Wednesday, a bag of garbage to grab from the dumpster. I chose to make the garbage run first and drove behind the strip mall. I opened the trunk of the Intrepid, reached inside the dumpster, and yanked out the bag.

Suddenly, a car pulled alongside me. A red Corolla. I saw Brian and his stupid ball cap. Seized with fear, I held the bag, frozen in place, staring at the man.

"What are you doing?" he asked. He remained in his car, door closed, window open.

"Nothing," I said. I threw the bag in the trunk and slammed it shut.

"Who are you?" he asked. "Why are you stealing garbage from the dumpster?"

I didn't answer. I climbed into my car and put it in drive, turning the wheel to the right. But he moved to block me, I put the car in reverse and backed away from him, panic blooming. When I gained a foot or two, he'd move to hem me in, a chess game played with cars as pawns, the parking lot a game board. After several maneuvers, I'd extricated the car and made a fast run to the exit. I blew a stop sign and turned right onto the Eastern Bypass. Brian was behind me. Rather than head to the Atlanta Highway, toward my mother's apartment, I ran a red light, made a quick right onto I-85, and, off the ramp, quickly exceeded the 55-mph speed limit, blasting by other cars.

I frantically scanned the rear-view mirror and saw the red Corolla approaching.

Motherfucker.

He was in pursuit. It took him mere moments to catch us. I realized how foolhardy this was, speeding on a highway through Montgomery, my daughter in the car, chased by a man I had been spying on for months. I zoomed by the next two exits and hoped to get off at Mitylene and wend the eleven miles back to town on Wares Ferry Road, a slower road but with less traffic. If I couldn't get off there, I'd have to wait to the Tallassee exit, and I didn't have any phone signal out there.

He was directly behind us now and gaining on my bumper. Suddenly, he accelerated as if to hit me, a disaster at this speed. Barely checking for other cars, I pulled into the right lane. I exhaled. Lucky. Brian was ahead of us. I dropped my speed to 45 mph and fell back into traffic.

Then he dropped his speed and pulled alongside my car. And he eased behind me again.

This was nuts.

"The girl is in the car with him," Michelle whispered. She had to repeat it before it registered with me. I reached behind Michelle's seat and pulled out my purse, dropping it on her lap.

"Get my phone, call 911," I said, as calmly as I could. "Tell them we are being chased, and we are afraid for our safety."

She dialed and, in a measured, professional voice, explained we were being pursued by an unknown man on I-85 northbound. She recited the exit we had passed, to fix a location. She gave the make and model of our car and pulled the registration out of the glove box to read our tag number to the dispatcher. She described Beatty's Corolla but said she did not know the driver. She was put on hold.

Life in Wartime: The Custody Game

He was half a car length behind us. I increased my speed and drove, again, much too fast in traffic. The dispatcher said there was no assistance nearby but was trying the Alabama Highway patrol.

We were on our own. I told Michelle to disconnect the emergency dispatcher. No one was going to save us, and really, what could they do? How could I explain why he was chasing us?

I saw the sign for the Mitylene exit one mile ahead. There was a cement mixer slowing for the turn-off. I accelerated to pull in ahead of him, barely missing the front end of his rig. He laid on the horn, and slowed to a crawl, blocking Brian as I coasted to the light at the end of the exit ramp. I looked both ways, there were few cars and no police officers. I made a quick left, then ran the light, and made a second left, back onto the highway, opting for the faster road back to town.

We lost him. I returned to the Atlanta Highway exit, minding the speed limit, hidden in the middle of southbound traffic. Michelle watched for the red Corolla through the passenger-side mirror. He was gone, for the moment.

Several blocks away, at Eastdale Estates, I switched the Intrepid for my mother's LeSabre. It was 11:15, and we had 45 minutes to make a quick grocery run before the luncheon. I didn't want to risk Beatty finding us.

"So, I guess he knows who we are," Michelle said.

"Yes, you're right," I sighed. "By the way, you were great with the dispatcher. That was scary. I'm sorry you had to experience this."

She shrugged her shoulders. "It's all good, Mom, but let's not tell my brothers, because my dad might find out. We need to keep this secret."

She was right. Later, both Thomas and Kathy urged me to file a police report against Brian, especially as Kayleigh was in the car. But I couldn't officially put this incident on record. My parenting skills were already under a microscope.

Southern Lies and Homicides

Back at home, Michelle lost herself in the tasks of domesticity. She dusted the furniture and set the formal dining table with the good lace tablecloth. She arranged a bouquet of flowers as a centerpiece. We bought two sprays of chrysanthemums and roses after the car chase. I always brought flowers to my mother, who appreciated the gift of bright colors. She watched as Michelle clipped the stems and arranged them in the cut crystal vase that had always graced my family's holiday dinners. I snapped a photo of my mother holding the flowers, with Michelle's arm around her waist. A good memory.

I sauteed onions, garlic, and celery for the stuffing as the pies baked in the oven. The boys were supposed to clean the bathrooms and vacuum the floors, but sounds from their room indicated they were playing video games. I moved from one task to the next, fighting to overcome the pervasive anxiety triggered by the morning's events. I half expected Brian Beatty to ring the doorbell, having gotten my tag information. Or the police to drive up the lane—to arrest me for reckless endangerment. There was no end to my worries, but one thing was clear: this had to be the end of the case; a relief, yet a disappointment. I'd failed Thomas and Kathy and dreaded our Thanksgiving get-together.

The bag of garbage sat in the trunk of the Intrepid, hidden in the garage. I didn't notice the phone ringing, until Danny brought me the cordless. "Mom, it's for you. It's Peter."

"I'm going to be late today," he said. "The VP is in town, and he's taking Bo, Tom, and me out for a drink."

"What?" I pushed the pan off the burner. "Why is he here?"

The VP lived in Denver. Just prior to Christmas 1995, he closed the Gainesville, Florida laboratory, firing dozens of employees and prompting Peter's transfer to the Montgomery, Alabama facility, along with five other employees. Now, three years later, before a holiday again, he was in town and taking the IT guys out for a drink. I searched the catch-all drawer for my hidden pack of cigarettes.

Life in Wartime: The Custody Game

Like I said, I should have read my horoscope that morning and just stayed home. Change, destruction, rebirth. The snake eating his tail. Ouroboros. We were going to start over, once again.

"Kelso, Washington," Peter said. "That's where we're going. Wherever Kelso is."

Kathy and Thomas arrived in the early afternoon with a platter of bakery cookies, a case of wine, and a Christmas card. "Your check's inside," she said. "For your recent invoice." I set the envelope next to the computer.

Over a glass of wine, we discussed the coming move. "What kind of work do you do?" Thomas asked Peter. There was so much chatter in the kitchen, they took their wine outside to the deck. I banished the kids to the living room while we finished the food prep.

Kathy was agitated, her mouth twisted in a grimace. "You're our investigator; you can't leave. We've paid you so much money; we'll sue you if you don't finish the case."

"What? No," I said. "Kathy, I'm compromised now. There's nothing more I can do."

"What about court? You're going to testify, right?"

"I don't have much to testify to. Brian driving Kayleigh to appointments, some stuff found in the trash." I drank some water, willing myself to slow my drinking. "At our last meeting, Eddie told me to keep working because we can't yet prove cohabitation."

"You can't leave until the case is finished."

"The kids and I will probably stay until the end of the school year," I said. "The case will be over by then."

"Maybe, maybe not," Kathy said, refilling her wine glass. "We want you to file a police report about the car chase yesterday."

"Kathy, we've been over this. I'm not going to file a report, and you know why."

"You must. Kayleigh was in the car, and she could have been hurt."

"My daughter was in the car, and *she* could have been hurt," I said. "I get it, but I can't risk losing my children." Our conversation was terse, uncomfortable. I began to mash potatoes, Kathy carried food to the table. Peter and Thomas came back inside. Peter carved the turkey while Thomas refilled our wine glasses and summoned the kids.

"As soon as you give me your CV, I'll get it to the contracting officer," Thomas said to Peter. "I'm hopeful he can find a good slot for you."

That made me smile.

Over dinner, we talked about how we met our spouses. Kathy and Thomas said they met on a flight from Los Angeles in late 1996, exactly two years ago, when Thomas was deadheading back to Atlanta. Kathy had the seat next to him.

"It was shortly after Paula filed for divorce," Thomas said. "I'd gotten the papers a few days before. They were a punctuation mark on a failed marriage."

"So, you really are newlyweds, aren't you?" I asked.

"Yes, it was love at first sight," Kathy gushed. "I knew, right there on the flight, I wanted to spend the rest of my life with him." They married once the divorce was finalized. "Why wait? He wanted to adopt my girls, so we began our beautiful journey together."

"And we've been tied up in court ever since," Thomas said, knocking the tines of a fork on his wine glass. "Cheers, to new friends."

"Cheers, to good friends in low places," Peter said. We laughed; the earlier tension was gone.

Life in Wartime: The Custody Game

After we'd eaten, the guys said they'd clean up the kitchen before dessert and coffee. Kathy suggested we examine the bag of garbage I'd grabbed the day before.

"I finally get to see this," she said happily. She'd brought a glass of wine with her.

We arranged the video camera on a tripod and placed plastic bags on the ground. As afternoon segued into early evening, the weather turned wet, cold, and windy as a front pushed in. We shivered in the unheated space. The bag was light, and once opened, revealed crumpled sheets of notebook paper, filled with handwritten notes. I smoothed each page, scanned the text, and put them into order.

"What's this?" Kathy asked.

"A bombshell."

Paula had outlined a custody petition. She accused Kathy of physically and mentally abusing Kayleigh. She sought to strip Thomas' parental rights, and to prevent Kayleigh from having any contact with her stepmother and stepsisters.

"She wants Thomas to have supervised visits, with no sleepovers."

"Oh, my God," Kathy said picking up the pages after I photographed them. "Oh, fuck her! Fuck Paula."

Kathy's anger was fueled by too much wine. I took the glass from her hand and set it on a worktable. I read the complaint aloud. In it, Paula stated Kathy used multiple ways to discipline Kayleigh when she was insolent or wouldn't do her homework or chores. Paula cited dates when she claimed Kathy tied the girl to a chair in a bathroom until she apologized for her behavior. Kayleigh would, at times, remain in the bathroom 'for over an hour before she would apologize appropriately enough to be released.' Meals would be withheld from Kayleigh if she wasn't 'friendly' or 'cheerful' toward her stepmother or stepsisters. A deadbolt was installed on the exterior of her bedroom door, to prevent the girl from leaving the house. Kathy was called the perpetrator and Thomas the co-conspirator because he condoned the abuse.

"What does this mean?" Kathy asked.

"Paula is suing you," I said. "These are notes for a petition, for her lawyer to file, if they haven't already."

"When will we know what's happening?"

When you get served papers, I thought, but this was too harsh to say. "Let's finish going through the bag."

Kathy clutched a handful of papers and marched into the house to show Thomas. Moments later, Thomas joined me in the garage. Peter followed.

"That goddamn Eddie, and goddamn you for listening to him," Kathy screamed. "I told you we should have filed, but he said, 'Wait, wait, wait.' Now, this has happened. This is your fault." She threw the papers at her husband's face.

"Enough!" Thomas snapped. He turned his back to Kathy and faced me. He was trembling with rage. He pointed to a paragraph. "This isn't Paula's handwriting. It must be Brian's."

"Hey, let's go inside, it's freezing out here," Peter said, hoping to defuse the situation. "There's fresh coffee and pie, and those cookies you brought. Let's go inside to warm up."

They followed my husband while I tidied the garage. In addition to the abuse claims, Paula cited instances when her privacy had been invaded. I was going to be roped into this mess. Brian saw me take this bag of trash. He would assume I worked for Thomas and Kathy. There was no question these claims could put us in criminal court. As I was about to enter the kitchen, I had a chilling thought:

Neither had denied the allegations.

The next morning, I opened the card Kathy had brought and removed the payment for my recent invoice. The check was odd, issued by a California bank, not drawn on the Montgomery credit

Life in Wartime: The Custody Game

union they usually used. A Los Angeles account, opened in 1993, was jointly held by Thomas Palmer and Kathy Knight. Yesterday, they said they'd met two years earlier, on a flight. How, then, had they opened a joint account five years ago?

If they lied about this, what else were they lying about?

Two weeks passed, and I avoided my clients. Other work poured in, taking me throughout Alabama, a typical end-of-year flurry as attorneys cleared their desks. Thomas took the papers to Eddie, who maintained his wait-and-see attitude. The lawyer agreed I was compromised but urged me to keep working, to somehow find proof Brian was living with Paula. But Eddie finally gave me the green light to interview Brian's ex-wife, to discuss those sealed records.

Late one afternoon, I was returning home when Michelle and Danny called, worried.

"Mom, there's a man parked in the cul-de-sac," Danny said. "The bus driver yelled at him for blocking the road, and the guy told Mr. Jerry to kiss his ass." He giggled.

"It's the man from your case," Michelle added, careful not to say the man who chased us. He's in a red Toyota."

He found me. And now my kids were home alone.

"Should we call the police?" Danny asked. "I can get his tag number."

No, and no, I told Danny. I spoke calmly to minimize their fear, and mask mine. "Are the doors locked? Is the dog outside the house?"

When they answered yes, I told them to sneak out the back door and quietly go through the woods to our neighbors TJ and Christl Sumner. "Lock the door behind you."

"Mom, he's ringing the doorbell," Michelle said. "Where are you?"

At least ten minutes away. "Go quietly. Go. Now." Michelle disconnected the phone.

There was no sign of Brian when I arrived twelve minutes later. I raced up the hill to the house to see if he was there, then back down the driveway to Sumner's Lane. Danny and Michelle were eating cake at the kitchen counter, surrounded by four dachshunds, talking with TJ, an older gentleman who loved us better than family.

When I was alone with Michelle, I asked her if it was Brian Beatty.

"Yes, Mom," she said. "I recognized him. I was so scared."

After dinner, he returned. Peter answered the door, and Brian asked to speak with me.

"She's not here," Peter said.

"Yeah, sure," Brian slammed a set of papers into Peter's hand. "Tell her she's been served," he said. "I'll see her at the deposition." I watched him from the dining room window, an unshaven man wearing a ball cap, a ragged sweatshirt, and worn shoes. "Asshole," I whispered.

They wanted to know what evidence I'd gathered.

Kathy and Thomas were served as well, though not by Brian. We would be questioned individually, under oath, by Paula's lawyer. Eddie agreed to represent me, then delayed the depositions to mid-January, instructing me to stay on the case. I couldn't risk going back to Piney View, and I couldn't send anyone else there either. I was stuck.

One day, close to Christmas, I had an epiphany.

A local car dealer allowed me to test-drive one of his trucks on a Friday afternoon. He hired me occasionally to watch his ex-wife, whom he loved madly. Bobby made a copy of my driver's license and insurance card, handed me a key, and said he needed the truck back by nine the next morning. It was a new black Ford 150 with a gray interior. I tucked my hair up into a ball cap and assumed a new identity.

A house sat directly across the street from Paula's. I knew from Thomas the homeowner was disabled and unable to work. His living room window faced Paula's garage. I quickly approached the door, carrying a duffel bag of equipment. George Brown Jr. was expecting me.

He and Paula had a history of disputes during the brief time she'd owned the house across the street. Mr. Brown and his wife frequently held Sunday afternoon get-togethers for members of their extended family and their church. It was not unusual for visitors to park along the curb, up and down the street. Paula objected to cars in front of her house, but rather than speak with George about this, she filed complaints with the HOA board, and often called the police, claiming the visitors were making too much noise, or preventing her own guests from visiting. She was disagreeable, even when George and his wife brought her a homemade pie and tried to work out a compromise. She slammed the door in their faces.

"I think she doesn't like Black people," George said.

In less than ten minutes, we'd set up the tripod and video camera, focused on Paula's driveway and garage door, and I'd shown him how to change the tapes. Curtains hid the camera; tape covered the red recording light. The date and time stamps were on, but he would mark each tape when he changed them every four hours, on a continuous 24-hour basis, for the next week. I provided enough cassettes to carry him through to the following Thursday, when I would meet him at 10 a.m. in the Wetumpka Walmart parking lot. There, we would exchange the recorded tapes for 42 new ones, with a check for $175, made payable to his wife, so the earnings wouldn't affect his disability status. He wouldn't watch the tapes; I'd pay my kids to watch them. I hadn't briefed my clients. I was taking a gamble. We shook hands.

My next stop was to visit Brian's ex-wife.

Maryann Beatty owned a modest home in a working-class neighborhood of Montgomery. The house needed a coat of paint, but the lawn was mowed, the flower beds tidy. An older model car sat in the driveway, a hubcap missing. She wasn't expecting me.

She was a slight woman with a hesitant smile and a weak handshake. I briefly explained why I was there, and she reluctantly invited me inside. "My girls will be home in an hour, and I'd rather they didn't see you."

She summarized the story: she was an elementary school teacher, and Brian couldn't keep a job during their marriage. He was a 'house husband.' She'd had to work extra jobs to keep money trickling into their bank account.

"There was never enough money, not even for basics," she said. "When we had big expenses, like car repairs, or a new refrigerator, he'd ask his parents for a loan. They loved the girls, and always helped, but knew he'd never repay them. They still help us." She shook her head, tears in her eyes. "He was content to let everyone else support him."

She'd filed for divorce when she learned he was having an affair. He coerced her to take him back, which she did.

Then, their eldest daughter tried to kill herself.

She was fourteen. She swallowed a bottle of aspirin and left a note. She said her father had been molesting her since she was eleven. But she refused to tell this story to a social worker at the hospital and later recanted the claims he had abused her. She denied writing the note. The psychologist who treated her reported the girl was "deeply traumatized." While she suspected there had been sexual abuse, her client was unwilling or unable to discuss the situation in the few therapy sessions they'd shared.

Brian maintained his daughter felt rejected, angry, and hurt when he had the affair. He denied any inappropriate behavior with her.

Life in Wartime: The Custody Game

While the allegations were addressed in closed court proceedings during the divorce, the child would not speak with the judge. Nor had she spoken with her father since the suicide attempt. The younger daughter was unable to either confirm or deny the claims. Maryann could not force her daughter to speak about the abuse, and because her daughter was uncooperative, she chose to not pursue criminal charges, believing both daughters had been damaged enough.

That's what was in the sealed divorce and custody records. A restraining order remained in place. He was not to contact his ex-wife or his daughters.

Where there's smoke, it doesn't mean the fire is nearby, but... I wanted to vomit. This was the man who spent every afternoon alone with Kayleigh Palmer.

"Tell the truth," Eddie said. "Depositions are fishing expeditions, for the other side to find out what we know."

Eddie had agreed to represent me during my testimony so I wouldn't need to hire a lawyer. He winked and charged me one dollar, because he'd include my legal fees in his billing to Thomas and Kathy. I'd be charging them for my time as well.

"Don't offer anything, but if asked, tell them," Eddie continued. "If you fail to disclose any information here, we can't admit it as evidence when we go to trial."

Eddie said when, not if.

We completed the fourth week of video recording, and I halted the operation. George Brown Jr. proved diligent and dependable at maintaining a steady, unbroken flow of 24/7 surveillance. We had gathered substantial evidence to prove Brian Beatty was, indeed, living with Paula Palmer. He was with Kayleigh and Paula on subsequent Tuesday nights, and we saw all three of them enter the garage in Paula's car and stay there for the night. There was footage of Paula leaving her garage at nine-thirty on some evenings, and returning within 18 minutes, with a second person in the car. Sometimes, she didn't immediately close the garage door, and we could clearly see Brian and his ball cap get out of the Honda. There were many mornings, around 5:30, when the car pulled out of the garage, sometimes with Brian driving, and Paula would return home to get Kayleigh ready for school.

Later, after Kayleigh left the house, Brian would return, parking his red Toyota inside the garage. We caught him raking leaves, washing his car, getting the mail from Paula's mailbox, bringing in bags of groceries, and mowing the lawn once in mid-January. He was there each day when Kayleigh got off the school bus, and her mother was at work.

Brian Beatty was Paula's house husband.

Months of work finally coalesced. I was relieved to see the finish line.

The deposition was held in Eddie's office on January 19, 1999. Debbie, Eddie's assistant, greeted me warmly, and offered coffee. It was a wintry morning, and a warm cup would have been great, but I was jittery from too much caffeine, raw nerves, and exhaustion. I waited while Kathy was questioned. Thomas had to cover for another pilot, so his deposition was rescheduled.

"Who's Paula's attorney?" I asked, hoping it was someone I'd worked with. "How long has Kathy been in there?"

"Paula has an attorney from Birmingham, a new lawyer." She mentioned his name, but it wasn't familiar. Kathy had been in the deposition for two hours.

"Brian Beatty is in there, asking questions," Debbie warned. "I've heard Kathy yelling, so he must be pushing buttons."

"Why is he here?" This chilled me. Since the day when he sat in my cul-de-sac blocking the school bus, my kids had seen him in the neighborhood several more times, but as far as I knew, he didn't come onto my property. Our woods were dense, and there had been times I felt uneasy, like someone was watching me, lurking behind the trees.

"He's Paula's legal advisor," she said, shrugging her shoulders. "Go ahead and take a seat," Debbie said. "They'll break soon, then bring you in."

Nervously, I sat and waited. Within fifteen minutes, the door to the conference room opened, and Kathy stormed out. She grabbed my arm and pulled me outside.

"You can't say anything," she said. "Don't tell them anything, just say you don't remember."

"Kathy, we need to get the evidence on record." I spent hours writing a comprehensive case report with copies of the evidence and my invoices. I was prepared to thoroughly discuss the case.

"You can't show them the evidence. They'll arrest you." She'd been crying. Mascara had run under her eyes, her makeup was streaked, her nose red, her hair disheveled. She was a wreck. Something had happened in the conference room. I fished a tissue from my purse and handed it to her. I reached over to smooth her hair, but she pushed my hand away.

"They're coming after us," she said. "They're going to have us all arrested, including you. Don't tell them anything. Please."

Debbie stuck her head out the door. "They're ready for you, Susan," she said and handed me a plastic bottle of water with a big smile. "You'll do great," she said.

Kathy followed me into the conference room. The lawyers conferred in whispers, and Eddie dismissed Kathy, excluding her from my deposition. Paula's attorney introduced himself, then handed me his business card. Paula, outfitted in a stunning plum-colored wool suit and pearl-white silk blouse, resolutely ignored me. Brian, dressed in jeans and a sport coat over a tee shirt, smirked.

"You know you're working for the wrong side." He reached across the table to shake my hand, but I ignored the gesture.

A video camera rested atop a tripod. I sat next to Eddie, who held the remote control for the camera.

He introduced me, opening the deposition.

"Why were you retained by Thomas and Kathy Palmer?" he asked.

"They had concerns about a man who appeared to be living with Paula Palmer and her daughter Kayleigh," I said.

The questions were standard fare: they wanted dates and times, and the results of my investigation. Eddie handed each person a copy of my case report, which was a chronology of details, with an inventory of the items I'd found in the garbage runs. I recounted the times Brian drove Kayleigh to appointments while her mother worked and discussed the dinner at the Olive Garden. I described how Kayleigh visibly flinched when Brian brought his hand to the girl's face. I spoke about the sealed records in the Beatty's divorce file, and how the former Mrs. Beatty explained the sexual abuse allegations their eldest daughter had made, and though she'd later declined to discuss her claims with police investigators, Brian was legally restrained from seeing his daughters.

Paula would not look at me. I watched as each person flipped through the extensive report. Paula, composed, smug at the beginning of my testimony, grew tense as I spoke: fists clenched and white knuckled, jaw taut, body rigid.

I completed my testimony by explaining I'd been compromised by the car chase and the placement of video surveillance in the neighbor's house. This news shattered Paula: she slammed her fist on the table, and keened; a high-pitched, shrieking wail that brought Debbie running into the conference room. Paula fled to the restroom; my testimony halted.

Both attorneys retreated to Eddie's office to confer. I was alone with Brian, bracing for his reaction.

"Well done," he said, nodding his head. "Videotaping from the neighbor's house. An interesting twist."

Alert, on guard, barely breathing, I didn't say a word. The deposition resumed once Paula recovered her poise. I reviewed the information obtained from the tapes. When I finished, I apologized silently to George Brown Jr., hoping like hell Paula and Brian would leave him alone, but knowing they wouldn't. I hoped he didn't lose his disability. George had helped me prove cohabitation, which could cost Paula her alimony.

"You violated our right to privacy by recording us," Brian said.

"We're going to sue you," Paula whispered. "And the neighbor, too."

Eddie cleared his throat. "Now, folks, before you file any lawsuits, let's be clear. Mrs. Lehmann followed the law," he said. "The neighbor set up the camera to observe what was happening around his property, which is perfectly within his rights. He happened to capture Ms. Palmer's driveway in the process." Eddie shrugged his shoulders. "And Mrs. Lehmann bought the information."

His dismissiveness sucked the air from the room. Brian looked to Paula's attorney for affirmation. The attorney nodded. The final questions circled back to the day before Thanksgiving and the trash I'd taken from the dumpster. I described taking the bag and the subsequent eleven-mile, high-speed pursuit by Brian, with Kayleigh in his car. Eddie distributed copies of a notarized statement I'd written about the car chase. I read it aloud, placing it onto the record. I did not mention my daughter.

"Did you find some specific papers in a trash bag?" Eddie asked.

"Yes, I did," Eddie gave them photocopies of the handwritten statements alleging the abuses Kathy had inflicted upon Kayleigh. They took a few minutes to review the papers.

"Have you shown these documents to either Kathy or Thomas Palmer?" Paula's attorney asked.

"Yes, I have."

"Did either Kathy or Thomas Palmer deny the charges?"

All eyes fixed on me. I hesitated, aware of the consequences of my response.

"No, they did not."

My testimony cast a dark shadow on all four adults. Kathy had known it would. That's why she didn't want me to testify.

Thomas was deposed several days later. Once his testimony was complete, the two attorneys urged Thomas and Paula to forego additional legal actions and reach a settlement.

"There will be no winners here," Eddie said. He insisted Thomas drop the pursuit of a custody or cohabitation case to halt alimony payments to Paula. Her attorney suggested they set their "hostilities aside to work together for the best interests of Kayleigh." They insisted Kathy and Thomas halt all surveillance activities. Both Kathy and Brian agreed to attend family counseling sessions. Formal letters of understanding were drafted and signed.

I was encouraged when Thomas called with news of this settlement arrangement, though given the toxic cloud surrounding these people I doubted détente would be sustainable. I completed my final invoice and boxed the evidence to drop off at their house.

A plea deal was reached in the criminal case against Thomas. He had the ring appraised and paid Paula half the value of his family heirloom. This case had taken eleven months to resolve, and Thomas was finally out of criminal court jurisdiction. Kathy was furious that Thomas had to pay Paula for the ring. Thomas shrugged it off and wrote a check.

And that, as they say, was that. All the effort we'd put into the case; the time, the money, the personal risk—yet nothing had really changed for my clients.

Life in Wartime: The Custody Game

But because of the Palmer case, the dynamics of my family life had improved. Peter was hired by a contracting firm to provide information technology services to the Air Force. His starting salary was double what he had earned at the environmental engineering firm. We remained in Wetumpka, Alabama, and didn't have to pull up stakes to move across the country. We invited Thomas and Kathy to dinner, to thank Thomas for Peter's new job, but Kathy snubbed me. She felt betrayed by my testimony and declined the invitation. She never spoke with me again.

Debbie called several months later.

"You won't believe this," she said, her voice bubbling with excitement. "Guess who's been arrested?"

One Saturday afternoon, Kathy was driving Thomas and her daughters to a restaurant on the Eastern Bypass when she spotted Paula's car traveling in the opposite direction. Brian was behind the wheel. Paula and Kayleigh were passengers. Inexplicably, Kathy hung a U-turn and sped through traffic to catch up with them. Once behind the Honda, she began honking the horn and flashing the headlights. Brian braked abruptly, and Kathy slammed into the back end of the car.

Infuriated, Brian got out of the vehicle, yelling at Kathy. He grabbed her ponytail. She lunged at Brian, screaming. Paula got out from the passenger side of the Honda as Thomas retrieved a golf club from the trunk of Kathy's car. Traffic halted around them, bystanders gawking. Kathy punched Brian in the face as Thomas hit him in the back with the golf club.

The police arrived as Paula pulled a pistol on Thomas.

Several days later, as Kathy taught her early morning aerobics class, Montgomery police officers entered the studio and arrested her. Thomas, wearing his pilot uniform, was cuffed, and taken into custody as he was about to board the flight to Atlanta. Paula and Brian had filed criminal charges against Thomas and Kathy.

So much for détente.

Eddie declined to represent them. I never worked another cohabitation case.

Chicken Feathers

Recently, we watched a home improvement show in which the designer built a chicken coop that was a replica of the featured house. Peter and I agreed we wouldn't be discouraged from buying a home with a coop, but we weren't certain we would want to fill it with hens. But maybe? This minor conversation about poultry housing led my thoughts on a journey through the role chickens have played in my life.

My paternal great-grandfather led his first wagon train to the Western United States when he was twenty-one years old. After many successful crossings, he opened a poultry hatchery in Charles City, Iowa, with one of his uncles.[3] This became a keystone Waller family business. His daughter-in-law, my grandmother, Anna Waller, whom my mother often described as "meaner than a rattlesnake," was known to feed her chickens in the mornings while wearing a nightgown, high-heeled slippers, a fur coat, and diamond rings. Once, after feeding the chickens, she noticed a diamond missing from a setting. She instructed the hired man to kill all the poultry to check their entrails for the diamond, which was never found. Anna would also remove her rings and earrings while enjoying dinner, wrapping them in napkins. These, too, were often lost, but the story of the chickens brings me here.

It's become quite fashionable for suburbanites to keep chickens. I suppose it's the allure of fresh eggs that encourages folks to build coops and keep poultry. Some birds are exotic and pretty, but most chickens I've seen look like, well, chickens.

I have an acquaintance I'll call Abby. She lives in Utah, in a bucolic setting on the outskirts of a city. She has a few acres of land, and one summer, she had a chicken coop built and began keeping the birds, primarily because she wanted fresh eggs every day, for herself as well as for her daughter's family. Until I visited Abby, I didn't know one had to teach a chicken how to lay eggs, and they require special diets, but both statements are true. Abby bought a rooster to increase her flock. A neighbor objected to the noise, so Abby shared the fresh eggs to mollify the woman.

Before long, a fox discovered the hen house, and while Abby had the coop fortified, and erected better fences around her property, the hens were still getting killed. Abby got herself a Great Pyrenees puppy, to protect the henhouse against marauders. Then she thought the puppy was lonely, so she brought home a littermate to help guard the chickens. The pups had to mature a bit before they could be guard dogs, so she rented a neighbor's German Shepherd for a few months. Then someone left a goat on her property, tied to the fence, and one goat led to two and then to ten. Again, the same neighbor objected to the noise and, no doubt, the smell, so Abby shared her goat milk with the woman. One day I asked Abby how she was enjoying the fresh eggs and goat milk, to which she laughed.

"I have spent nearly thirteen thousand dollars to have a few fresh eggs," she said. "And now I have a farm."

It's a slippery slope when you build a chicken coop.

Over the years, through my work, I've had occasional encounters with hens and roosters, chicken coops, and poultry processing plants. But this one story stands out above many.

One late afternoon in early spring 2002, I traveled to rural Troy, Alabama. I had divorce papers to serve and was told the woman would either be at the townhouse or the country estate. Thinking I needed to impress this woman into opening the door for me, I drove my husband's E-300 Mercedes Benz sedan, a gorgeous teal machine with a beige leather interior. He must have been out of town. The sunroof was open, music blasting as I followed a truck in the direction of the country estate.

Chicken Feathers

Gradually, I became aware of the billowing clouds of something white surrounding the truck, then flying around my car, and finally inside the car. Something tickled my face. Horrified, I realized the Mercedes was filled with chicken feathers! Quickly I closed the sunroof and backed off from the truck, which I realized was hauling chickens to a nearby processing plant. Shortly it turned off onto a different road, and I continued to the country estate.

Pulling into a church parking lot to inspect the damage, I checked myself first in the reflection of the car windows. Delicate white chicken feathers were stuck to my hair and covered my long-sleeved black tee shirt and jeans. Feathers clumped in the back seat, on the dashboard, and on the headrests. It would take me hours to get the car clean. Brushing feathers out of the way, I got back into the car, checking myself in the rear-view mirror. A hairbrush through my hair and swipe of lipstick; I was ready to deliver some divorce papers.

A metal gate stood partially open at the driveway. Turning off the highway, I got out of the car and pulled it wide enough to allow the Mercedes to pass through. The driveway was a worn path, weeded between vehicle ruts; dirt surrounded by pine and oak trees, untrimmed and encroaching the passageway. The house was to my left. I looked for the front door.

Stopping the car at the end of the drive, I was immediately surrounded by a pack of dogs, scrawny, barking, baying, jumping to the car windows. I laid on the horn but had little hope of attracting anyone as there weren't any vehicles within sight. I managed to shoo the dogs away and got out of the car, papers, and pen in hand, as well as a small taser. I knew the taser wouldn't be much protection against an attacking dog, but we arm ourselves with the equipment we have.

Struggling through a yard gone to dirt and weeds, redolent with manure, I approached the front porch, which was overgrown with wild vegetation. There were more dogs on the porch, but these were ill and starving; several raised their heads, two managed a faint tail wag. In all, there were at least twenty dogs in the yard; all eager to see me, hoping for salvation, or at least a meal.

The screen door hung from a hinge. I nudged it open with a knee, then rapped on the wood door, unnecessarily, as there was no one home.

Bad as this scene was, the cruelest feature was the sway-backed mare tied to a porch rail: fly-infested, with yellow, goopy eyes and the most pitiful bearing I'd ever seen. Glancing around the yard, hoping for a shed with some food, or a hose for water, I saw a chicken coop.

The coop was dilapidated and broken as if the starving dogs had managed to break it open and seize the chickens. Indeed, I saw a beak, several feet, and tufts of bloodied feathers surrounding the ground around the henhouse.

What happened here? Stunned, I carefully made my way back to the car, dogs flanking and tailing me. Sickened by leaving these animals in such dire straits, I picked up my phone to call the county sheriff. There was no cell service. Surprisingly, none of the dogs followed the car down the drive to the road. Pulling through the gate, I got out and pushed it closed, but there was no latch to secure it. Turning to the bushes I threw up, tears flowing from my eyes.

I was torn. Should I try to find the woman first or go to the sheriff's department? It was just after five p.m. Directions indicated the 'city house' was twenty-five minutes away. I wasn't certain where to find the Pike County Sheriff's department, so I continued to the woman's other residence. Fooled once by the term *country estate* I was skeptical about the house in town.

Searching for the address, I found myself in a campground, with concrete pads and picnic tables. I looked for a house number. Most spots were empty. I must have come to the wrong place. The early generations of GPS car systems were often woefully inaccurate.

A compact trailer sat on a pad, with a beat-up Honda Civic parked in front. The number on the lot sign corresponded with the address. Angry and disgusted, I wasn't going to brook any nonsense from this woman. I parked behind the Honda, then approached the trailer. A window was open, and I heard Oprah rallying her faithful audience.

"Hey! Can you help me?" I yelled into the window. "I need some help." I stood at the bottom of the trailer steps and waited. Within moments a bolt was thrown, and the door opened by a hard-50-ish woman with a mess of overprocessed magenta hair, a stained tee-shirt, and too-tight cut-off shorts. She carried a fluffy white hen in her arms. A small poodle, freshly groomed with pink bows and painted toenails ran down the steps, growling. The woman followed the dog, who circled my legs, sniffing.

"What do you need, hon?" she asked as she stroked the fluffy hen. "How can I help?"

"Are you Mrs. Johnson? Edith Johnson?"

Her face clouded with apprehension.

"I've got divorce papers for you," I said, and thrust them at her. Confused, she may not have known whether to take them or run back inside the trailer. She kept both hands on the chicken.

"Take them, don't take them," I said, dropping the papers to the ground. I was furious. "You've got thirty days to respond." I marched back to my car and sped away.

Back at home, I called the sheriff's office. I spoke with a deputy and filed a report against the woman, for animal cruelty and neglect.

Shortly after 10 a.m. the next morning, my office phone rang. It was the legal secretary who'd sent me the divorce papers to serve.

"I take it you found Mrs. Johnson," she said. "Because she said you left the gate open, and her Thoroughbred horse was hit and killed by a neighbor's truck. She wants your contact information so she can sue you."

"What?"

It took a moment to explain the situation I'd found at the country house. Shortly afterward, I received a call from an investigator from the Pike County Sheriff's Office. She asked a few questions, then told me she had returned from Mrs. Johnson's 'country estate.' She had called for the animal rescue service to take the dogs into custody, and she was preparing an arrest warrant for Mrs. Johnson. The horse, she said, would need to be euthanized, as would many of the dogs. I answered a few questions, and she said she'd contact me if necessary.

A day or two later I received another call from the legal secretary.

"Mrs. Johnson called this morning," she began. "She said she suffered a broken leg because you pushed her out of her trailer and down the stairs onto the concrete. She said she was going to have you arrested for assault."

We shared a laugh over this story. I didn't say I wished I had assaulted her.

Many years and thousands of miles later, when Peter and I prepared to sell our beautiful Mercedes, I opened the glove compartment and pulled out the leather book with the owner's manual. A white chicken feather was pressed between some pages. I put the feather in my wallet.

In late December 2017, I met with Laura Waller Butts in Milledgeville, Georgia, along with two appellate lawyers from Atlanta. I had not seen Laura since 2007 when we had completed an unsuccessful evidentiary hearing to remove her son Robert from death row. During those years Laura had buried her youngest son, learned to breed pit bulls, and built a chicken coop. She was mostly sober and learned to find pleasure in caring for her animals.

Days before our visit, the governor had signed Robert's death warrant. The clock was ticking. His legal team launched a last-ditch effort to save his life.

As we left the trailer, I pulled out a business card to give to Laura. A white chicken feather was stuck to the back. She took it into her hand and traced the pattern with her finger. We smiled through our tears, two battle-hardened friends, and hugged each other tightly.

The Hoover Affair

There were only two check-out lanes open in Winn-Dixie. I was in the wrong one.

"I should've known," muttering as I eyed the pile of brightly wrapped food items the woman ahead of me was buying. Nothing but junk. Garbage.

"I think I need to rent that carpet cleaner," the woman ahead of me said to the cashier, waving her checkbook at the machine. "How much does it cost?"

I looked over at the woman, then at the red and silver carpet cleaner. *Don't rent it, lady—You don't know where it's been.*

I decided to mind my own business.

As I pushed my cart toward the other lane, I heard the woman say, "Let me borry your pen, darlin,' and get me the carpet cleaner!"

Janice and Bobby hosted a barbecue and bonfire on their property most Saturday nights. Our daughter Michelle was close with Stevie, their youngest child, and the girls often spent weekends together. Peter and I had a standing invite each Saturday, and we went over a few times, but we were never comfortable sitting on logs, drinking beer, balancing sagging paper plates on our laps, talking with people whose accents were so thick we needed a translator.

"Nod and smile," Peter advised. "Consider this good people-watching experience, Miss Private Investigator," he teased.

On those nights, we sat together in front of the fire and listened to the small talk. I studied the guests, but I was particularly fascinated by the interactions between Bobby and his neighbor, Nancy.

Nancy was cute and sexy, especially when compared with Janice. While Nancy was tanned, fit, and blonde—professionally blonde—I doubted Janice had ever given a thought to her appearance. She dressed in raggedy shorts and washed-out tee shirts with tennis shoes. Her long hair was often dirty and badly in need of a trim. *The barn needs a coat of paint*, I thought, unkindly, the first time we met.

Janice had confided that Nancy's husband, George, was a drunk. She rolled her eyes when she told me. Hmm. I'd never seen Janice so much as sip a beer, but I'd seen her own husband sloshed. By the third bonfire evening, Peter and I shared a bottle of wine with no expectations of stimulating social conversations.

Bobby finished grilling hamburgers as the sun went down over the surrounding forest of pines, redbuds, oaks, black walnut, and tulip poplars. The adults filled their plates, as teenagers grabbed food and vanished into the house, with Janice running back and forth between the kids and the guests like a scullery maid.

Bobby and Nancy settled in for the evening, together, in front of the bonfire, drinking beer and smoking cigarettes. They didn't eat. They passed a cigarette back and forth, sharing it companionably. She slipped her hand through his arm. They whispered, they smiled, they were tender with one another. Occasionally, Bobby looked around, to see if anyone was watching. More than once, he caught me looking.

Bobby and Nancy were in love.

"Do you think Janice knows they're fooling around?" I asked Peter as we drove home. I considered raising the topic with my friend, but I couldn't think of a decent way to do it. I mean, what do you say? Hey, Janice, I noticed your husband making out with your neighbor the other night. Is this new behavior or standard procedure?

We decided I would not say anything; she wasn't my best friend. Either Janice knew about the affair and was keeping her mouth shut-

The Hoover Affair

or she didn't. During my investigative career I'd worked plenty of divorce cases to realize people will ignore, or overlook, adultery. Some people don't want to turn their lives upside down with a divorce and division of assets. I've spent days, nights, and logged hundreds of miles gathering evidence against a no-good cheating spouse only to have my client thank me, pay me, then tuck the damning pictures and report away to maintain the status quo—behavior that baffles me.

I've also had clients so infuriated with their cheating partners they scorch the earth with their rage, leaving nothing but smoldering embers and destruction in their wake.

This I understand.

Shortly thereafter, we stopped going to the bonfires, much to our mutual relief. Saturday night became Sushi night. Michelle made many new friends, but she and Stevie still had an occasional Saturday night sleepover.

My office phone rang. It was Janice. She asked if I wanted to take a walk. We arranged a hike through the hills in my neighborhood.

Janice showed up several hours later, with her dirty hair pulled back into a ponytail. She wore a rumpled tee shirt and an old pair of shorts. Her face was swollen and puffy from crying. I tried some cheerful chit-chat as we walked the heavily forested roads. She was sullenly monosyllabic. Finally, as we were about to climb the killer hill on Buck Ridge Road, she came out with it:

"Bobby's having an affair with Nancy."

The hill was steep, and I was breathing hard. Janice struggled up the hill, as tears poured down her face. Neither of us spoke. Once we reached the summit, I placed my hand on her shoulder. We stood there for a few moments, winded.

"Why do you say that?" I flashed on the couple sharing cigarettes in front of the bonfires. I was relieved I wasn't the one who had broken the unwelcome news.

"Late one night last week, I woke up. Bobby wasn't in bed, so I went out to the kitchen to get some water. I didn't turn on any lights. I went into the breakfast room, stood in front of the glass doors, and looked out onto the backyard. There were lights on in his office. I thought about checking on him, why was he up so late? A voice in my head told me to wait and watch."

She quieted, staring into the deep woods. Her fists were clenched.

"So, I waited. I sipped the water. After a while, the office door opened, and Nancy came out—she was wearing a fucking nightie. A nightie! They stood in the doorway, kissing, hugging, giggling, like a couple of horny teenagers! Then she walked back to her house."

Janice sobbed. She sat on the edge of a boulder alongside the road. I perched next to her. A stream burbled cheerfully behind us. She took a deep breath before continuing.

"Bobby stayed in the office. I ran back to our bedroom, and pretended to be asleep when he came in. He went straight to the shower, then came to bed."

I draped my arm around her shoulder—a moment of silence came and went. Off in the distance, a woodpecker tapped a rhythm into a tree.

"God, Janice. Have you said anything to him?"

"Nope, not a word. He flew out the next morning." She stood up, and we continued down the road. It was an afternoon to be outside, to keep walking.

Janice said Bobby had called earlier that morning. He said he'd had to work on a job site through the previous weekend but planned to be home Friday afternoon. She hadn't seen Nancy since that night coming out of the office. George, Nancy's husband, said she'd driven to the beach with some friends. Suspicious, Janice drove out to the airport and found Nancy's sedan parked next to Bobby's truck in long-term parking.

"Did you take photos of their cars?"

"Yes, I did."

I was impressed with her sleuthing abilities and suspected she had plenty more to tell me.

"Hm. So, what have you found out?"

She sighed. "Well, at first, I couldn't find the extra key to the office door. He keeps one hanging on a hook by the refrigerator, but it wasn't there. I looked everywhere and finally found it taped underneath one of his dresser drawers."

I was impressed by both his determination to keep her out of the office, and her resolve to snoop.

Once inside the office, she logged onto the computer and studied the business expenses for the past few months. She gathered the statements for his banking and credit card accounts. She'd made copies of all the financial records she could find, highlighting the suspicious transactions that pointed to the affair with Nancy. Then, she began digging into their emails. She said there were hundreds of messages between Bobby and Nancy. She printed every single one.

"By the way, he's not at a job site this week. He's on vacation!" Janice said. "The asshole's in Cancún. With her. He took eight days off from work. I haven't been to Mexico. Bobby and I haven't gone anywhere without the kids, hell, since we had the kids. But there they are, in fucking Mexico! He bought her ticket, too. First class."

"Cancún? Holy shit!" This was a serious relationship, if they were vacationing openly together. "Do you know how long they've been seeing each other?"

"You mean fucking?" she asked. "They started seeing each other a year ago, maybe longer. They've had lunches, dinners, and trips together. He buys her shit from high-end stores all over the country. Perfume. Jewelry. Silk underwear. Nighties. He's never bought me anything pretty. I can't remember when I last got new underwear, and it came from Walmart. And there are notes and cards and gifts she's given him."

Her shoulders were pulled back, her head held high, eyes wide open with rage. She had crimson in her cheeks—anger was a better look for her than depression.

"I'm going to find out exactly, to the penny, how much money he's spent on her. Tens of thousands, I'm sure."

I smiled and nodded. Janice was ready for battle. She managed a slight grin, and that, too, was a better look than sorrow.

"It's good you've discovered the financial stuff. He's spending marital assets on her. Money that should go toward college tuition for the girls, right? Or taking you on a trip to Mexico?"

"Oh, sure," she said, rolling her eyes. "He never thinks of what I need. I'm driving a shitty thirteen-year-old minivan, but he gets a new truck every year."

That minivan was a mess of chipped paint, dirty upholstery, and near-bald tires.

"What about his cell phone? Have you looked at the records?"

"I've downloaded the billing records for his cell phone, too. Most of the calls are between Bobby and Nancy." She paused, lowered her voice. "I need your help."

"What can I do?"

"Well, I need you to keep talking with me, to keep me sane. I can't tell anyone else about this, okay?"

"Absolutely. Give me a dollar when we get back to my house. Then our conversations are privileged, okay?" Janice nodded. "Call me whenever you need to talk."

The Hoover Affair

I agreed to store her records and help her get photos of the two together. We discussed his cell phone records, and she said Bobby had a landline phone in the office. Janice suspected he used that phone to call Nancy, but I told her records of local calls aren't kept by the phone company. Janice wondered if she could somehow record those conversations to learn when and where they planned to meet.

I sighed. This was where the legality of investigations becomes tricky, and I explained the ground rules. "Let's talk about recording calls, okay?"

Janice nodded.

"Alabama is a one-party consent state, which means only one person in the conversation is required to know the line's being recorded. Got it?"

"Yes," she said. "Well, actually, no."

"Okay, so 'one-party' means I can call you and record the conversation, and I don't have to tell you I'm recording."

Janice nodded.

"And if someone were to call and leave a message on my answering machine, it's fair game because the caller knows he's being recorded. But let's say, hypothetically, you want to record all the calls Bobby makes or receives from his office line. That's a bit trickier."

"Why?"

"Well, it's not a phone line you or your children use, right?"

"No, it's a dedicated business phone line, inside Bobby's office."

"If you don't work for Bobby, you don't have any reason to use the office phone. You don't have a right to record those conversations, but if you did, the recorded phone calls would not be admissible in court, and you could get into trouble for recording the calls."

We walked in silence as Janice tried to absorb the information.

"I'm actually his business partner, I'm on the incorporation papers as the treasurer," Janice turned to me. "I want to know what they're planning. I want to record the calls."

"Are you actively involved in his business? Do you work in the office, or answer the phone?"

"No."

I stopped walking and stood in front of her. "I'm not telling you this, understood?" Janice nodded.

"Okay, you can buy a device to automatically record both sides of the conversation. Go to Radio Shack; they sell them for under forty bucks. You'll need tapes and batteries, too. You'll have to listen to the tapes and check the recorder every day."

"Will you show me how to set it up?"

"Nope. I won't touch it. To record this way is illegal, and I'm not going to get anywhere near it. Now, remember—those tapes are not admissible in court, right? They can't see the light of day. You cannot ever tell anyone you made the recordings, especially your attorney."

"I want to know when they're meeting, so I can take pictures, put together evidence. Can you help me?"

I could and I did. Over the next several months, Janice and I built an ironclad case that included about a hundred photographs of Bobby and Nancy together, as they met up for lunches and dinners, afternoons and evenings on his bass boat, and random make-out sessions in his truck. There were motel rendezvous and trips out of town. We captured every shred of evidence we could find.

Surprisingly, I never again saw Janice angry or lit up with rage. She grew sadder, withdrawn. She listened to those tape recordings every morning when Bobby and the girls were gone. Janice obsessed over their liaisons, their sheer audacity. She brought me boxes of photocopied account statements, with highlighted transactions she suspected involved Nancy, all carefully notated. There were hundreds of emails, all painstakingly printed and catalogued by date. I had generated stacks of photos from their numerous trysts during my surveillances.

This project took up so much of my time, I had little left for work that paid my bills. After several months, wearied by Janice's inability to move forward, I suggested we had enough evidence, excluding the tapes, for her to give her attorney, to get the divorce underway. I never asked her for payment, yet she never offered to buy me lunch or a tank of gas, much less reimburse any of my expenses. She was a woman obsessed, mired in a self-made purgatory. Her mental health concerned me.

One day, I'd had enough. I told her: File the papers. Pursue a divorce. Take the steps. Make yourself healthy. After hundreds of conversations about Bobby and Nancy, I was bored and exhausted. I needed some paying customers.

I knew she'd retained a lawyer because he was one I'd suggested—one who routinely sent me clients. He thanked me for the referral when I stopped by his office to pick up a batch of papers to serve one day.

"Has she filed?" I asked.

"Not yet," he said. "But I'm sure you'll be serving the papers."

I groaned. He winked. I smiled. He was right, of course.

The days went by, and soon, the weeks turned into months. Michelle and Stevie weren't hanging out much. I didn't hear from Janice. Other cases, other clients, and other aggravations filled my time.

One Saturday evening, Peter and I were home with Michelle. We had finished our dinner of takeout sushi and retreated to different parts of the house. The phone rang. I didn't move off the couch. Michelle came out of her room a few moments later, the cordless extension in her hand.

"Mom, can I go over to Stevie's tonight?"

I was considering a second glass of wine. I had settled into a good book, music played throughout the house, and there were no surveillances to run. Both of my sons were out, working or with friends. I didn't feel like driving. Janice's house was a mile away as the crow flies, but there was a forest, a narrow road full of hairpin turns and lurking deer, multiple ravines, and a stream in between our homes. It took at least thirty minutes to drive there and back, and that's only if I didn't get stuck in a conversation.

"No, not tonight, sweetheart."

She pouted. "Mom, please? I'm so bored."

"Then clean your room."

"Mom! Stevie said they're having a bonfire tonight, and you can come too."

"Nope, not interested. I'm not going anywhere."

"But please? Her sister isn't home; she's spending the night at a friend's. Stevie is bored, too. She doesn't want to be by herself. She thinks there's ghosts in her house."

"No."

My fourteen-year-old daughter thought she could pique my interest by mentioning ghosts. A supernatural hook usually worked, but the pull of a second glass of wine was stronger.

"You're no fun."

"I know, dear. I'm your mother. Incidentally, your room is a disaster."

"Please? I promise I'll clean it tomorrow if I can go tonight."

The Hoover Affair

I opened the book. "Nope. If you're so bored, you can clean your room. Tonight is a *perfect* time for you to clean your room. And don't throw everything into the closet. Clean. Actually clean."

"Ugh." She stomped off to her room and slammed the door.

As expected, within a few minutes, she emerged from her room looking for Peter. I heard him say no—she stormed back into her room. I chuckled to myself.

I didn't see Michelle again that evening, but a barrage of phone calls punctuated the next several hours. As I was about to drift off to sleep, I heard the sound of the vacuum in her room. Pleased, I fell asleep.

My cellphone rang at exactly 7 a.m. Sunday morning. I sighed as I groped blindly for it. It couldn't be good news, not this early in the day. I peered at the caller ID: Janice.

"Hey, good morning," I mumbled. "What's happening?"

"Were you sleeping?" Janice asked. She sounded wide awake.

"Yeah, it's early. What's going on?"

"I need the name of a good criminal defense attorney."

"Now? Why?"

"Because Bobby shot and killed George in our breakfast room last night."

I sat bolt upright. "What?"

"Stevie and Bobby and I were eating pizza last night after everyone went home." She hesitated, as if to steel herself for the next sentence. "Then George showed up. He was drunk, and started yelling at Bobby, accusing him of having sex with Nancy, everything. He barged into the house, through the sliding glass doors. Susan, he was screaming and crying and saying all kinds of crazy shit about Bobby and Nancy.

Then Bobby grabbed his shotgun. He ordered George to leave. George lunged at Bobby and… and Bobby shot him."

Janice stopped. I heard her breathing, deeply. Then, a high-pitched whisper, "He died on the floor, my God, Susan, on the floor next to the table. Right there."

"In your breakfast room?"

"Yes. Right in front of us."

"Oh my God."

Peter stuck his head out from under a pillow and silently mouthed what? I held my hand up. Stop. Don't talk. I simulated shooting a gun with my thumb and index finger. I placed my hand over the mouthpiece. "Bobby killed George," I whispered.

"Nancy was right there, too. She'd followed George to our house. She saw it happen, from outside and ran in once George was shot. I called 911, and the sheriff's department came, and the paramedics, and an investigator. They were here forever, taking pictures, asking questions."

"Was Bobby arrested?"

"No, but the investigator said he should talk with a criminal lawyer."

"Are the cops still there?"

"No, they finally left at about four this morning, when the coroner came to get George's body," she said. "I mean, he was lying there for hours, bleeding all over the floor. There was blood and brains on the walls, and all over the table. They tracked blood all over my new carpet, you know, I had it put in a couple of months ago. I thought they'd never leave. It was a fucking mess!"

"Oh, God, Janice, Janice. This is awful." Stunned, I asked about her daughters. "Did Stevie see what happened?"

The Hoover Affair

"She was right there. Sitting right at the table when Bobby shot George. A ringside view. So, yeah, she saw it all. Once the cops came, two of them questioned her. Then we told her to go to her room and stay there."

Stevie had witnessed the murder, and this distressed me more than the news of George's death. Goosebumps crawled my neck and arms. That Michelle could have been there terrified me.

"Oh, Janice, so awful this happened," I was out of bed, pulling on a robe. "Do you want me to pick her up, to bring her here for a while, until things calm down?"

"No, she's sleeping. I just checked on her. She'll be fine."

I doubted Stevie would be fine.

"All right, but she's welcome here. Anytime." I stood in the bathroom. "How are you going to clean the mess? They have those companies, you know, to clean up after shootings. I've got a card for one, I can find it."

"Oh, it's all clean," she said. "I just got back from returning the carpet cleaner to Winn-Dixie. It took some work, but I got all the blood out."

"You rented the carpet cleaner from the grocery store?"

"Oh, yeah. I wasn't going to use mine to get George's blood, and uh, stuff, out of the carpet. That's too gross. I'd never be able to use it again, if I knew his blood and guts had been sucked into it."

We hung up shortly after this. There was nothing left to say.

I walked down the hallway and nudged Michelle's door open. She was sound asleep. Her room was spotless. We had narrowly avoided something horrible.

Michelle never asked to spend the night at Stevie's house again.

A few days later Janice and Bobby stopped by to pick up the boxes of evidence we had gathered and placed them in Bobby's truck. He had scraped together $100,000 to retain an attorney, by pulling equity from their home. Their criminal defense lawyer had prepared a sworn statement, which Bobby handed me. This was an agreement to not speak with anyone, including law enforcement, about the affair, without the defense attorney present. I took the affidavit but did not sign it. I needed to talk with my own attorney.

Motive.

Homicide investigators would be looking for a reason George entered the home enraged and why Bobby had shot him to death. Those boxes contained plenty of damning information and would have provided a treasure trove of information to investigators.

Fucking poetic, I thought as they drove down the lane and out of my life. Not only did they vacuum up George's remains, but they also scrubbed clean all traces of the affair. Our evidence disappeared.

Just like it never happened.

My attorney advised me to tear up the statement and ignore the defense lawyer. She admonished me to not say a word to anyone, unless I was approached by police investigators, then I was to call her. The police never contacted me.

Two years later, a Grand Jury returned a 'no-bill' after hearing the details of the shooting from investigators and carefully drawn testimony from Janice and Nancy. The dead man, George, was portrayed as a raging alcoholic who had attempted to attack Bobby and his family during a blackout rage. The jurors declined to indict Bobby for shooting George as this appeared to be nothing more than an unfortunate stand-your-ground situation.

The Hoover Affair

A month later, Bobby filed for divorce from Janice. The evidence we gathered to document Bobby's infidelity was long gone and no longer applicable anyway unless she wanted to tell the investigators Bobby and Nancy had been having an affair when George was killed.

For two years, she stood by his side, believing Bobby had wanted their marriage to work.

Bobby and Nancy were married shortly after the divorce was finalized.

Years later, after our daughters were in college, I saw Janice in a Montgomery coffee shop. She had lost weight and cut her hair. Her face was tired and sad. Bobby had bought her a small house in Montgomery as part of the divorce settlement, and she had gone back to college, to become a teacher. She lived alone; the girls visited her but considered the house in Wetumpka, where she'd raised them, to be their home. I thought of all that had happened, and how she had protected her husband, through thick and thin, against all evidence to the contrary.

One evening, I dashed into Winn Dixie to pick up a few things for dinner. Peter and I were empty-nesters, and meals were easy. As I stood in line, I felt someone staring at me. Looking around, I saw Bobby watching me. I looked away quickly, with no acknowledgment. As I walked out of the store, I saw a woman loading a carpet cleaner into the trunk of her car. I thought of Janice cleaning her carpet, anxious to put her house in order, while Bobby got away with murder.

Since then, grocery store carpet cleaners and I have become completely, thoroughly, and irreconcilably... divorced.

Fool Me Once

Eventually, your client will lie to you.

This is the one absolute truth in this line of work.

In early 2001, I had a client I'll call Mike Thomas. At the time, he was in his late 50s and owned a small business. His wife was having an affair and he had proof, but he needed it documented by an investigator. He wanted a divorce, but didn't want to be on the hook for alimony or a financial settlement. He wanted to keep his business intact. He said he got my name and number from an attorney I knew.

We met at his business. Mr. Thomas was a thin, impeccably dressed man who wore his graying hair nicely coiffed. He pulled a shoe box from a shelf behind him. He counted out $2,000 in twenties and stuffed it into an envelope, which he handed to me. I noticed his nails were well-manicured and buffed to a shine. I glanced at mine. I needed a manicure. His cologne was recognizable, Old Spice, but it wasn't overpowering.

"Watch her good at lunchtime," he said. "She's with her boyfriend then, and she's with him after work." He handed me several photos of his wife. I pegged her to be in her early 50s. Her hair was cut short, an uncolored brown. She looked like a woman who had slipped easily into middle age, with mousey hair and more than a few pounds overweight. She didn't seem to be in the throes of a love affair.

His wife was a government employee at Maxwell Air Force Base in Montgomery, Alabama. In those pre-911 days, I could get onto military installations with ease; these days, it's much more difficult.

"Keep eyes on her and let me know when you're watching." He said she typically took her lunch break from 11 to 12. "Call me when you've got eyes on her."

I drove by their residence and noted the beautiful landscaping that highlighted the otherwise nondescript home. There were several types of roses in bloom, with lush azalea and butterfly bushes, accented by rock gardens. I assumed she was the gardener as his nails were too clean, too perfect. Even when I wear gloves, I damage my nails when planting and weeding. Mr. Thomas didn't look like he spent any time outside.

He called me early the next morning. "Watch her good," he said. "She's acting funny, like she does when she's meeting him."

Once on the base I parked outside her office building. I eyed her car and chose a space across the lot and down several spots. I was close enough to other cars to blend in, but there was enough distance so no one would really notice me if they walked to the nearby cars. I turned around in the driver's seat, to watch her office behind me. I snapped one or two placeholder photos, dated and time-stamped, in case we needed evidence for court, but also to prove my location and work time. I had the video camera placed on the dashboard tripod, a new tape inside, the switch flipped to standby but ready to record. The gas tank was full and ready for whatever Mrs. Thomas had planned for lunch. My car was a surveillance vehicle. I could see out, but the windows were tinted to within a hair's breadth of being legal. This gave me a bit of privacy.

At exactly 11 a.m. I flipped on the video camera and positioned it to face the back window as she walked, alone, out of her building and over to her car. I readied to follow her. Mrs. Thomas wore dark blue polyester pants, with a brightly multicolored top, and a pair of worn brown flats. She unlocked the car, but rather than climbing into the driver's seat and driving off to meet her beau, she opened the door behind the passenger side, reached in, and brought out a flowered tote bag. She locked her car and crossed the parking lot to a picnic table nicely shaded by two large oak trees directly in front of my car. Perfect.

I quickly attached the zoom lens to the camera. She opened the tote bag and brought out a can of soda and several plastic containers.

Mrs. Thomas set the table with a paper doily placemat, followed by a paper napkin and some plastic cutlery. *Maybe her boyfriend is joining her*, I thought optimistically. But she set the table for one diner, not two. She unpackaged her food: a sandwich, a fruit salad, and a bag of potato chips. She daintily opened the chips and placed the food on the plate in front of her. She bowed her head and folded her hands as she blessed her food. I quietly groaned.

Her prayer finished, she raised her head and pulled a paperback book out of the tote bag. For kicks, I zoomed in on the title, *To Love Again* by Danielle Steele. She read as she slowly ate her lunch. Just before noon, she put the book and the plastic containers back into the tote bag, finished her soda, threw away the trash, put the tote bag back into her car, then returned to her office building.

Other people had come and gone from the building during the hour, but none had greeted Mrs. Thomas, who seemed so engrossed in her book she barely nibbled at her food.

My client called three times within that hour, to make certain I was watching her. He seemed puzzled she was dining alone, and speculated her boyfriend must have taken the day off.

"Do they work together?" I asked.

"I don't know," he said. "That's why I hired you."

As agreed, I returned to the base later in the afternoon. At exactly 4 pm, she left the building, got into her car, and drove straight home. I hung around the neighborhood for the next hour or so, waiting to see if she'd leave. Mr. Thomas called several more times. I assured him she was home, her car parked by the side of the garage. I left when I saw Mr. Thomas pull into the driveway.

This continued the same way for the next several weeks, although on rainy days she would go to a Wendy's restaurant near the base entrance for lunch. Like every other time, she sat alone, reading her paperback books while she ate. The client called constantly, and he began to insinuate I was doing something wrong. I was already feeling insecure about this case. Was I missing something? Why couldn't I catch her with the boyfriend? I never once saw her speak on her cell phone. I brought in my son Jacob to pick up some of the afternoon surveillances in the hopes he'd have better results. He didn't. Mrs. Thomas went to work. Mrs. Thomas ate alone. Mrs. Thomas went home.

The miles racked up on my car. The ongoing surveillance took hours at a time. My patience was thin.

"Are you certain you have the right woman?" Mr. Thomas asked periodically.

"Yes." I watched Mrs. Thomas. She was a ringer for the photos he had provided.

"I'd heard you were good," he said. "But they must have been mistaken."

I rolled my eyes.

On one Friday afternoon at 2:30, he called me to say she was going to Biloxi after work, "with her sister, or so she says. Now's your chance. You'll get her this weekend."

I looked at my watch. I briefly considered going to Biloxi, a one-way trip of 250 miles. My college kids were coming home, and we had plans that did not involve the Mississippi casino town.

"Uh… do you know where she's staying in Biloxi?" There were a handful of large hotels and casinos and plenty of smaller ones. "If I lose her on the highway, do you have any idea where she would be staying?"

"No, but I hired you to find out," he said. "She's supposed to pick up her sister, but she's having chemo treatments, so I don't think that's true. I know she's going with her boyfriend."

Fool Me Once

I really wanted to quit the case, but he paid well, and in cash. I was on my third retainer. My clients were usually a bit more circumspect about paying my fees; while this one made rude comments, he did not balk at giving me more money.

"You know, this is pretty short notice for me to be going out of town," I said. "I haven't seen any indication of a boyfriend at all…" Mr. Thomas cut me off.

"If it's money you need, swing by the store, and I'll give you plenty for the weekend," he said. "You need to catch her."

Making the eight-hour round-trip drive held no appeal, especially not for this client. I often traveled for casework, but I needed time to work out a strategy, to pack a bag, gather money and equipment. I would look strangely out of place as a woman alone in Biloxi; I would rather take my husband with me.

I told the client I wasn't going. After some blustering on his part, we worked out an agreement.

He gave me the sister's address. I followed his wife from the base to her sister's house in downtown Montgomery. I shot photos of Mrs. Thomas and another middle-aged woman, wearing a head scarf, as they loaded grocery bags and a suitcase into the car. I followed them to the I-65 South entrance. Then, I drove several car lengths behind them on the highway for the next hour or so.

At the second Evergreen exit, I pulled off the highway and found a restroom and a cup of coffee, then I turned around and drove north. I had done what I said I'd do. Mrs. Thomas had left town with her sister and headed toward Biloxi. I called the client. He was churlish.

"I'll bet she's meeting her boyfriend in New Orleans," he said. "And you're going to miss it. All this money I'm paying you, and you're not catching her. I think you're just stringing me along."

New Orleans? What happened to Biloxi? I bit my tongue and hung up the phone. I went home.

The next morning, I was drinking coffee and enjoying the sounds of a house filled with my family when my office phone rang. I thought to let it go to voice mail, but I answered it anyway. A man introduced himself. He'd gotten my number from one of my former clients, a woman who'd been in a bit of a jam I'd helped resolve.

"My wife's having an affair," he said.

Oh, brother, I thought. "Really? How do you know this?" I couldn't muster much enthusiasm.

"Oh, I've got photos and motel receipts. I need someone else to put it together for court."

Although I was intrigued, I told him I was busy, I couldn't take on his case.

"Oh, come on, Susan," he said. "It would be easy. My wife is rendezvousing with her boyfriend at lunchtime, and then some days after work, at the Red Roof Motel in Prattville. This is the easiest job you'll ever work."

"I'm already working a case at those hours," I said. I knew I could manage another lunchtime case, and it wasn't far from the base, but I didn't want to. He continued talking about his wife and her boyfriend.

"… she's with him this weekend…"

Something tickled my brain.

"Do you know who the boyfriend is?" I asked.

The man laughed. "Well, yes, his name is Mike Thomas, you may know him."

Suddenly, the pieces fell into place. I'd been used by my client to keep eyes on his wife while he shacked up with his girlfriend. He had paid me well, at the very least.

Fool Me Once

I didn't take the new case, easy as it would have been. It was simply a conflict of interest. A few days later, I quit the case and ignored a flurry of phone calls from Mr. Thomas.

A year or so later he left a message. "My wife is really having an affair this time." He wanted to hire me again. I never called him back.

My Final Divorce Case, Part One

Monday, February 14, 2005

The day found me on the couch, bored, and at the tail end of a nasty flu. It was Valentine's Day. My husband was working in Washington, DC. It was also our wedding anniversary, but there would be no celebrations on this day. I recalled happier V-Days: son Danny's birthday, cupcake baking, gift giving, happiness. Danny was in the Infantry now, in Germany, destined for Iraq. Too little activity, too many days alone left me depressed. Tired of reading, weary of being sick.

How do you go from a house filled with noisy, active kids to this kind of quiet?

The cell phone rang. I glanced at the caller ID—it was a law office. I considered letting it go to voice mail, but I answered, my voice and croaking. The attorney had a friend who needed some PI work done.

"Sure, have him call me," I said. "And thank you for the referral."

"I'll be handling the divorce, so all evidence should come to me," he said. "And thank you."

Several minutes later, a man named Chad Sandhill called to discuss his situation. I unwrapped a cough drop and popped it in my mouth, then got up off the couch and walked down the long hallway to my office. I grabbed a notepad and pen and returned to the couch in the living room while he told me his story.

His wife had been acting strangely over the past several weeks. She did not come home from work most evenings; rather, she made excuses—late meetings, going out with friends—and did not get home until late night, or early morning, either long after the kids were in bed, or before they got up for school.

Chad and Elizabeth Sandhill had been married for fifteen years, and they had three children together. Elizabeth had one son from a previous relationship, recently graduated from high school. Chad raised this boy as his son; he did not know Chad was not his father.

I asked him if he planned to divorce his wife. Sometimes, people want to know if their spouse is cheating and have no intention of taking a case all the way through to divorce. Chad said his wife had "a history of extra-marital affairs," and he was disgusted with her behavior. "She always promises to change, but she doesn't."

Chad denied dalliances of his own, but briefly outlined a handful of Elizabeth's affairs, the ones he knew about, during their fifteen-year marriage. He suspected she had been fooling around with another guy when they were dating. He said her behavior, and his, followed a specific pattern: she'd cheat, he'd find out, they'd fight, patch things up, start over. The previous affair was with a married co-worker. A reckless choice. The affair cost the man, a school administrator, his job, and she was fired from her teaching position as well. "All of our children were damaged. His kids found out because his wife told them. Our kids all go to the same school, and his kids told our kids. It was a real mess."

"You may want to speak with him, and possibly his wife, before this is over," he suggested. I made a note of the man's name. "After this happened, she cried and promised to go to couples' counseling. She went to church with me and the kids. She came home from work and spent time with all of us, cooked, helped with homework. She was a part of the family. We did stuff together with the kids on the weekends, and we were a couple again."

Elizabeth made it through one counseling session and never returned. "She couldn't relate to the counselor," Chad said, an undertone of anger in his voice.

My Final Divorce Case, Part One

"If she's had multiple affairs over the course of your marriage, why pursue a divorce now? Why is this time different?" All sorts of warning bells were dinging in my head.

Chad said he was tired of being treated like a doormat, and he wanted custody of his children. He verified he had retained Phillip as his lawyer. He hoped to avoid alimony and didn't want to be ordered to give her half of his 401k. He wanted to keep the house.

I popped another cough drop in my mouth.

"If I do this and find out she is having an affair, we will document what we can and prepare for court. But here's what you need to understand…"

"What?"

"These cases are grueling and expensive, and they can turn dangerous for me and my crew. If we get you the leverage you need to keep the kids, the house, and your 401k, then you need to promise you'll go through with the divorce, you won't take her back."

"Take her back? That's never going to happen!"

"Hang on a sec," I hit the mute button on the phone and slipped it into the pocket of my robe. My throat was dry from talking despite the candy. I surveyed the living room. Used Kleenex littered the floor. Disgusted with myself, I picked them up, made my way to the kitchen, washed my hands, and put a kettle on the stove to make a cup of tea. I sat at the counter before pulling out the phone to continue the conversation.

"Sorry. I'm not well yet," I cleared my throat. "You need to understand what happens during these cases. This is not like on TV detective shows. These cases are rough for the investigators. We'll turn ourselves inside out following your wife, as we build a case. If we make it through without getting caught, your wife will get served divorce papers. She'll know then you've hired me, and we've got her with a boyfriend, not just once, but multiple times. She stands to lose everything—kids, house, lifestyle—maybe even be ordered to pay child support—and she'll try to get you to drop the case. She'll cry, beg, and plead and, at some point, try to reconcile with you, by making promises, such as agreeing to return to church and the marriage counselor. Like she's done before, right?"

"I guess so, but this time I have a lawyer. I intend…"

"I know what you intend, but the moment you sleep with her, or say you'll give her another chance, all our evidence disappears. Poof, it will be gone.

"And the beautiful case we've built goes right down the drain. All the money you've spent is gone. And, if that happens, I will not work with you again."

The water came to a boil. I poured it over the teabag. I made my way back to the couch in the living room and pulled a blanket over my lap.

"Why not? If I'm paying you, what difference does it make to you?"

"I'll be compromised," I coughed. My throat hurt. I took a small sip of scalding tea. "Once she knows what you've got on her, you might as well throw the case in the trash. She'll figure out who I am, and my cover is blown." I eased off the couch and into the kitchen again.

"But what if she doesn't find out who you are? Will you come back to the case then?"

I filled a glass with water and sipped it, trying to clear my throat. "Look, Mr. Sandhill, Chad, these cases take a lot of time to build correctly. Catching her once with another guy is good, but we need to establish a pattern, a relationship. She can explain away one indiscretion, but the more often we catch her with a boyfriend, the more iron-clad the case becomes. I will put my soul into building your case, but only once. Understand?"

"I think I do." He was quiet. "So, catching her once is not enough, right?"

"Right. She can explain it one time. An indiscretion. Our goal is to build a case to shame her, one her attorney can't poke holes in. It's

My Final Divorce Case, Part One

tougher than on TV. Things happen. Sometimes, the spouse gets spooked, feels paranoid, and behaves. I come up empty-handed, which is no good for either of us. I'm going to rely on you to assist me with information, to help me catch her."

"I'll do whatever you say, I promise. I left a check for you with Phillip, your standard retainer of twenty-five hundred dollars. Is that enough?"

In those days, my retainer was fifteen hundred dollars, but I didn't say a word. The retainer would be just the tip of the iceberg. These cheating spouse cases were expensive to work correctly.

"Thank you. Your reports and invoices will go through your lawyer, okay? It'll be best if we don't meet."

"Yes, fine," he said. "Will you be feeling well enough to get started tomorrow?"

I visualized the FedEx envelope that had been sitting on my desk for a week. "I've got to drive to Lineville tomorrow, to serve some papers. We can start the day after."

"I'll call and let you know what she's doing."

"Okay, good," I said. "Listen, I'm sorry you're having this trouble. But seriously, please don't waste my time, or your money."

He promised he wouldn't take her back, no matter what.

And so began my final divorce case.

The Road to Nowhere

On February 15th, 2005, I had to drive north to Lineville to serve subpoenas to the owner of a cabinet shop. I'd had the flu and hadn't worked in a couple of weeks. But the sun was shining, the temperature was in the low sixties, and I felt I'd been released from a dark cave. I cranked up Sirius Disorder on satellite radio—the Stones were playing. I flew out of Wetumpka on Highway 9 with Mick and Keith. I was happy.

According to my mapping program—GPS was not a commonly available service in those days—it was seventy-nine miles from my house to the cabinet shop. I'd had a leisurely morning at home, doing some light housework and playing a few computer card games. I left the house at noon and expected to arrive at the cabinet shop at about one-thirty or so, after lunchtime.

Too many times, I'd shown up at one of these small manufacturers only to be welcomed by a locked door, at which point I'd have to hang around a little town and wait for folks to return from their lunchtime exodus. I also didn't want to get there too late in the day, for fear of missing employees who might leave mid-afternoon. I always had to perform a weird time calculus before I left home to serve papers—when would I be most likely to find a person, especially one who may not want to be found? It's an easier question to answer when serving someone at a business. Finding people at home, sometimes a hundred miles away, is always trickier. I lose money if I don't find someone the first time. Distance, time, and cost are all factors I consider before setting out to serve papers. Time is money.

Occasionally, someone will ask why I don't call ahead and make sure the person will be there. *Call ahead? Really?* I answer sarcastically.

"Because people are *thrilled* to receive legal papers?" I never give anyone an opportunity to duck service if I can help it.

A midday arrival was what I'd planned. I thought even with a bit of a delay, I would be back home by four at the latest. Peter was away, and my daughter wouldn't be home until six. I planned to take her out for dinner. The day was completely mine. Well, almost.

There was little phone coverage on that rural highway. The towns were small, separated by acres of pine and oak trees. Azaleas bloomed in deep fuchsias and pinks. There were few cars, and I maintained a steady sixty-one mph. My mind flitted casually as I moved along in my pretty Volkswagen Jetta. The sunroof was opened several inches to allow fresh air in, but not enough to mess my hair. I had bought the brand-new car two years earlier, when I realized I wasn't hauling kids around anymore. The Jetta was a dark gray, four-door sedan with black leather seats. It was a beauty. I washed it by hand every week.

I had just crossed under U.S. Highway 280 and stopped at the traffic light in Kellyton. I sat there, the only car at the intersection, and realized this was the first red light I'd caught. I glanced at my watch— I was making excellent time. The light changed. I took off. I was a few miles from the town of Goodwater.

A flash caught my eye. Then a jolt, and a loud, booming thump.

The car shuddered and groaned.

What the hell?

Something big flew off to the left.

Slamming the brakes, pulling to the side of the road. Skidding to a stop just off the pavement.

Oh my God, oh my God, oh my God.

Fuck.

Breathe.

The Road to Nowhere

Think.

I turned off the radio.

What did I hit?

I Clenched the steering wheel.

A person? A kid?

Oh my God.

A hairline crack ran across the windshield. The hood was crumpled. My heart pounded with terror. *What had I hit?* I unlatched the seat belt, pulled on the door handle. But it wouldn't open. I pressed my shoulder into the door that wouldn't budge. I jammed the window button. The motor whined. The window remained closed.

I'm trapped.

Trembling.

Breathe.

Slow breaths. Yoga breaths.

I slammed my left shoulder into the door again, rocking the car. No dice. Slow breathing, counting the inhalations and exhalations. *Calm. Focus. Assess the situation.*

A tuft of animal hair stuck to the crumpled hood. Blood splatters mixed with dirt on the windshield.

A deer. I've hit a deer.

The highway was deserted. Woods to the left, across four highway lanes. A dead deer would be lying in the road. A wounded deer would have disappeared into the woods to die. I took my phone out of the console—one signal bar. A call would fail.

Thoughts raced as panic rebuilt… I had to get out of the car.

Several vehicles blew by, one with the horn blaring, fading into the distance. A pickup truck slowed down. but when I waved, ridiculously through the heavily tinted glass, he sped off to the south.

The car might look abandoned. Drivers put the flashers on when they needed help. *Flashers, flashers, where are they?* Just as I reached for the owner's manual, I saw the big button right in front of me. I pushed it. The hazard lights flashed on the dashboard, flicking, flicking.

Maybe someone will stop... If they're blinking outside.

I thrust my right leg over the gearshift into the foot well of the passenger side. Moving carefully, I hoisted my body into the seat. I didn't want to either hurt myself or rip my pants. That would figure. I hoped like hell the passenger door would open.

Another wave of panic...

What if I'm trapped? What if the door won't open?

And then this: *No one knows where I am.* The worst thought yet. A tear rolled down my face. *Don't cry.*

Please, please. I pulled on the handle.

The door opened.

Relief washed over as I got out of the car, stood on the pavement, and examined the car. The hood was crumpled, the left front fender was smashed. The panel over the front left tire was damaged, and the driver's door badly dented. Surprisingly, the door window hadn't broken with the impact. The left headlight was shattered and bloody. Another clump of deer hair hung from a shard of glass. Aside from the hairline crack, the windshield was amazingly intact. The flashers blinked in the back and on the front passenger side.

There were two bars of cell signal. I dialed my husband. He answered on the third ring.

"Hello, darling," he whispered. He was in a meeting in Washington, DC.

"I'm in trouble. I've had an accident," I said, as evenly as possible, struggling to keep panic out of my voice. The phone went dead. I looked at it. There were no bars. Great. Fucking cell phones.

Trying to find a signal, I walked around the car. I opened the passenger door again and stepped up onto the door frame, thinking some height might help with the signal. After an agonizing five seconds, three signal bars appeared on the phone. As I dialed Peter, he called.

"Bad cell area?"

"I'm standing on top of the car," I exaggerated. A brief rundown of the details included the part about not being able to open the driver's side door.

"Are you alright?" he asked gently.

"Yes, I'm okay."

"You're not hurt? Is your neck okay?"

Turning my head from side to side elicited only the usual tightness, a reminder of a long-ago car accident.

"Did the airbag deploy?"

I bent down and peered inside. "No, it did not."

"How fast were you going?"

"Fifty-five or so. I was coming into a town and about to start slowing. The bag should have deployed, right?"

"Maybe. But only if you were hit within the sensor areas. Can you start the car?"

"I don't know."

"Is there steam coming out from the engine?"

"No."

"Look under the car. Do you see anything leaking, like oil or fluid?"

"Hold on." Placing the phone on the roof of the car, I stepped down and bent to look under the car—nothing.

"No signs of oil or fluids."

"Good. That's good," he paused. "Do you think you can try to start it?"

"I, uh… guess so. But I'll have to crawl over to the driver's side."

"Oh, darling, I'm so sorry. Where, exactly, are you?"

"I'm about fifty miles north of the house, on Highway Nine, just past the intersection of Kellyton and 280. I was headed to Lineville."

"I don't know where Lineville is."

"About fifteen minutes north of the turn-off for Lake Martin," I said.

"In the middle of fucking nowhere," he laughed.

"Yep." I smiled.

"I'm going to call the insurance guy," Peter said. "Try to start the car, and I'll call you back, okay?"

"Yes."

"I love you and wish I were there. I'm glad you're okay. It could have been a lot worse."

I left the phone on the roof of the car. I hoped the additional foot of altitude might allow the cellular tower to find it.

Squirming back into the driver's seat, I put my foot on the brake and turned the key. The engine started. It ticked over quietly, with no funny noises.

Equal parts relief and terror washed over me. I put the car in drive and lifted my foot off the brake. The car inched forward. Nothing seemed wrong with the engine or wheels. I turned off the engine, climbed out of the car, and grabbed the phone off the roof. I waited.

Minutes ticked by. Cars and trucks passed. An occasional horn honked, the sound of airbrakes on a semi screamed by. No one stopped to ask why a middle-aged blonde woman stood by the side of a highway next to a car with the flashers on.

This was solid proof of a suspicion I'd long held.

Southern hospitality is a myth.

Peter called and said we didn't need to have a police report for the insurance claim. I told him the car started right up, with no hesitation. He asked if the tires looked okay, and if the wheels or axle appeared damaged. I told him about moving the car a few feet—with no unusual noises or behavior.

"Drive home," he said.

"Really?"

"Yes. If the car is drivable, go home. You're scheduled for a repair estimate in Montgomery tomorrow."

My body tensed at the thought of driving home. "I think I'm pretty close to the next town, Goodwater," I said. "How about I find a mechanic and have him look at it?"

"Oh, okay. That's a great idea."

Back in the driver's seat, belt fastened, I drove for a few minutes, slowly, well below the speed limit, and rolled into the fleabite town of Goodwater. After a minute or so, I spied an auto body shop and pulled into the driveway, tires crunching on gravel.

The place had once been an old gas station with two service bays. The pumps were long gone. I opened the door and peeked in—the office was dark. The smells of motor oil, old food, and years of cigarette smoke scented the room. The desk was cluttered with papers, an ashtray filled with butts, stained coffee cups. I walked through a doorway to the work area. A man worked under the hood of a pickup truck.

"Hello," I called.

He looked up.

"Hi," I said. "Hi... um, would you mind looking at my car? I've had a bit of an accident, and I'm worried about driving it back to Wetumpka." I slipped into my southern voice and stretched the name of the town as I said it: Wee-Tum-Kah. Perhaps he'd help if I sounded like a native.

He wiped his hands slowly with a rag. "What happened?" I told him the bare details as we went outside. He whistled as he walked around the Jetta.

"Yes, ma'am, she got pretty banged up." He took a grimy 'Bama ball cap off his head and wiped his face with the dirty rag. "I saw you up there on the highway, standing there, aside your vehicle."

But didn't stop to see if I needed help? Asshole. Screaming felt right, but I managed to be polite. I said it must have been a large doe.

"Yes, ma'am. I see the hair she left. You didn't see her, though?"

"No, she must have run off into the woods."

"Do you know which way she went?"

As if that really matters. I visualized the accident. "I was headed north. I think she came from the woods on the east side and ran right in front of me until we collided on the driver's side. She must have gone into the woods on the west side."

He pulled a cigarette out of his shirt pocket and lit it. "I'm gonna go back up there and go see if I can find her," he said. "That would be some good meat."

The Road to Nowhere

I'd nearly been killed, and he was thinking about dinner.

"How are you going to find her?" I asked.

"I'll look for the buzzards. They'll lead me right to her."

"Ah." I was suddenly weary and done with this man. "So, what do you think? Do you think the engine is okay to drive home?"

"If you was my wife, I'd tell you to park your car and get another ride home," he said. "Where's your husband?" He looked me up and down. "You got one?"

"He's away on business today." Creeped, I stepped toward the door, away from the man.

"This car ain't safe to drive. You can leave it here and we'll get it fixed up for you. Call someone to come pick you up."

"Hmm." There wasn't anyone to rescue me. My children were fledgling adults: Jacob was at college, Danny was in Germany. Michelle was either in school or at work. Our best friends were in Vermont. There was not a single person who I could ask to drive out to Goodwater, Alabama, to pick me up. I wouldn't leave my car there. And this guy hadn't bothered to stop to help me.

"I'll take my chances." I smiled. "Thank you."

Without another word, I climbed back into the driver's seat, took a deep breath, and started the engine. With odd, metallic grinding noises—sounds I may have imagined—the Jetta eased into a 180-degree turn, headed back to Wetumpka.

Stopping in Goodwater had been a waste of time. The car seemed fine. It was a quiet ride home, the radio off, me white-knuckled and vigilant until the Jetta was parked in the garage.

The damage to the car was cosmetic. A day later, in a loaner car, I drove to Lineville and delivered those papers to the cabinet shop. The owner had known to expect the papers. "What took so long?" he asked. "Did something happen?"

"Yeah," I said and shrugged. "Something happened."

I gave the auto body shop the finger as I drove by. Both times.

My Final Divorce Case, Part Two

Wednesday, February 16

I would try to find Elizabeth this evening.

My day began with taking the badly damaged Jetta to the insurance adjuster and picking up a loaner car. "You're lucky you weren't killed," the adjuster said as she pulled a clump of deer hair out of a windshield wiper, then declared the car could be fixed. She handed me the keys to a loaner. I picked up some groceries, then drove back to Wetumpka, to Phillip's law office. The receptionist handed me a folder containing photographs, along with a copy of the Sandhill's auto tags, and the retainer check. Chad had found a matchbook from a Montgomery bar in his wife's truck, the Pure Country Lounge, and had made a photocopy of its cover for me. He thought she went there, or perhaps to the Doodle Hoppers bar, to meet men. The bars weren't familiar to me. I thought of bringing my eldest son Jacob to help look for Elizabeth but decided to work alone that evening.

Shortly after 8 p.m., I put a thermos of hot tea, a notepad, and the equipment bag in the rental and set out into the night. I began with a sweep of Wetumpka, hunting Elizabeth's truck, then drove into Montgomery.

Oddly convenient, both bars were in the same strip mall, one anchoring on each side of the building. They had been restaurants in previous incarnations. A nail salon and an insurance office filled out the other storefronts.

Parking was going to be a problem. With only a single entrance and exit, the parking lot was jammed with vehicles and people. I could not drive through to spot her truck. I'd have to commit to a walk-through. Raucous music—Skynyrd?—spilled out the open doors, the same music played in both bars. These were the meat markets for single, and not-so-single, middle-aged folks, the older version of the college pick-up bars I'd known in 1970's Tallahassee. Rowdy people on the prowl. Here, men and women stood outside the bars, on verandahs, and throughout the lot, smoking cigarettes and drinking beer, sizing one another up. Talking shit. It was a crowd of White men in baseball caps, jeans, and boots. The women wore identical outfits of skin-tight jeans, push-up bras, heavy cosmetics, big, teased hair, and fuck-me pumps.

The air was heavy with perfume and cigarette smoke, obvious even through my post-flu head cold.

Without wading into the bars, I knew I was in over my head here—a lone woman hanging around in the lot, checking out vehicles, trying not to be seen. There were no empty spots to park my car. Fortunately, this was a neighborhood of strip malls and parking lots. People were parking and walking the blocks from the bars. I spied two empty spots in a lot across the street and drove cautiously around the pedestrians. I pulled in with a clear view of the party.

There was no point going inside the bars to look for Elizabeth that first night. My goal was to find her truck, after which I would be able to positively identify her. I'd already seen several women who could have been Elizabeth. Chad described her as 5'5" and 130 pounds with dark brown hair highlighted with blond. He said her hair fell somewhere between her shoulders and her waist. "It's usually in a ponytail," he explained. She was 37 years old.

After a bit of people-watching I walked the perimeters of the nearby lots, trying to stay out of the pools of streetlights. I ventured into the alley behind the lounges. There were several trucks parked back there, but I didn't see a gray Ford F-350 with a vanity plate that read "Liza." One man spoke to me as he headed toward the entrance. I felt others watching me. I wished I had an invisibility cloak. I wished Peter were with me. I wished I had a girlfriend or two to accompany me, so we could have a beer and fit in. I had considered bringing Michelle but remembered she had gone through school with the eldest Sandhill son. They had been in the marching band together. They were friends. Elizabeth might recognize her. Besides, what daughter goes to a bar with her mother? Who else could I have called? I had a couple of girlfriends, but they had young children and needed to arrange babysitters in advance of a night out. My best friend refused to work with me. She liked the stories but didn't like the work. Aside from backup assistance from Jacob, Peter, and occasionally Michelle, I usually worked alone.

I hadn't planned very well. Dressed in old, baggy jeans, sweater and tennis shoes, my hair pulled back into a messy chignon held by a purple scrunchy. A week of the flu left me pale with a nose rubbed raw by Kleenex. My face was bare, without even a dash of lipstick to give me some color. It didn't dawn on me I might have to go inside the bars and look around. I blamed this lack of foresight on the trauma of the collision with the deer.

After completing a circuit of the parking lot, I returned to my car to wait. By 10:20 p.m. I was convinced she wasn't going to show up, at least not in her vehicle, so I decided to go hunting elsewhere in Montgomery.

I spent the next hour driving through the parking lots of other bars, restaurants, and lounges, looking for her truck. I checked out the lots around some of the motels. By a quarter to midnight, I did a drive-by of Pure Country and Doodle Hoppers again. The crowd had thinned and the few who remained were drunker and louder, beer bottles in hand. I didn't see her truck, so I pulled the plug and headed back to my house.

I checked my phone. The client had called several times, to see if I'd found her. Her truck was not at her office. She had not come home.

Thursday, February 17

The client said Elizabeth stumbled in at 3:35 a.m. He said she would be attending their son's soccer game that evening. After I finished the Lineville service, I drove over to the Prattville nursing home to check on my mother. I found her already in bed, fully dressed in slacks, a blouse, a sweater, and shoes. I took her shoes off and spoke quietly to her. I asked if she'd eaten. She said she never missed a meal, but I knew better. She had grown thin this past year. The demon dementia had stripped most of her short-term memory, including the ability to use a fork or spoon. I then asked if she wanted me to help her get into her nightgown. "I'm already wearing it," she said. "I'm in bed, why can't you all leave me alone," she said, clearly not recognizing me in the late afternoon. Sundowning, it's called. Dementia patients often become more confused as the day draws to a close. I opened an extra blanket and placed it over her legs, then turned off the overhead light and quietly left her room. Heart heavy, I went home to complete the service paperwork, feed the dogs and cats, catch up on emails, and turn the lights on. I fixed myself a sandwich and watched the national news before heading to the downtown football stadium, where the Wetumpka High School soccer games were played.

I saw Elizabeth's truck as soon as I pulled into the parking lot. I drove by to verify the vanity plate, and snapped a photo, to begin the case documentation. I smiled to myself, momentarily relieved because I'd found her, yet barely keeping the creeping anxiety at bay. The night could bring all sorts of challenges. I parked carefully, selecting a dark area, away from lights, but near enough to her truck to watch her movements. Close enough to other cars and the exit, to blend in yet make following easier.

The soccer game was well into the second half when I arrived. It would end shortly. I had topped off the gas tank in the rental car earlier in the day. A full tank of gas is always the first order of business when I start surveillance. I checked my equipment, making sure the date and time were correct on both the still camera and the video camera. Night vision was enabled on both, and the flash features were turned off. There was tape over the red-light indicator on the video recorder, which was mounted below the dashboard. No one would notice a little red light emanating from this car and get nosy. The radio was set on my favorite satellite station and played quietly in the background.

Elizabeth was easy to recognize. I flicked the video camera on. She walked out of the stadium alone but was soon joined by a man near her truck. They stood together, talking, as the lot emptied of cars and

My Final Divorce Case, Part Two

families. There was something familiar about the man... ah, Jerry. A local business owner and assistant coach on several youth sports teams. I had worked on a divorce case for his sister the previous year, and I knew his marriage had recently foundered. Jerry had custody of his sons. His parents lived down the road from me. I often saw them waiting for the boys to get off the school bus in the afternoons.

Elizabeth stood close to Jerry. He reached into his pocket and pulled out an envelope. She took it, and slid it into her purse, then leaned in and kissed him on the cheek.

Bingo. My timing could not have been better. They continued talking. Touching. I didn't see his children, so I assumed they'd left with their mother. Both Elizabeth and Jerry were free of children. Unencumbered.

The school bus with the visiting team pulled away from the curb. A handful of cars remained in the lot. The stadium lights clicked off as I snapped a couple of photos of Elizabeth and Jerry. A few stragglers headed to their vehicles. I started my car and pulled out of the stadium. It was a risky move, but I did not want to be directly behind her when she left the lot. Of course, if she chose to leave at precisely this moment, I'd have to scramble to keep up. I quickly turned down a side street, then immediately doubled back and parked behind a church directly across from the stadium, where I could clearly see her truck, and his. I wanted to catch them going someplace together. I looked up Jerry's home address in the Elmore County directory. Jotted it down, just in case.

All investigations should be this easy.

I trained the binoculars on her truck. She closed the door and started the engine. She pulled out of the lot, behind Jerry's truck. I eased in behind them down Bridge Street. Which way would they turn? Left, or right?

Jerry's home was to the left, over the Bibb Graves bridge. Elizabeth's house was to the right, in downtown Wetumpka. She could have walked to the stadium in the same amount of time it took to drive, because of all the one-way streets. He turned left. So did she. They both drove over the bridge.

I had allowed a car between me and Elizabeth, but, as my luck would have it, the driver stopped as the light turned yellow. I stopped, too, but kept an eye on her truck as she made a left onto Commerce Street, and out of my sight. His truck continued south on Bridge, toward the highway. I opted to follow her. I turned left, then made another quick left onto Court Street. A third left put me onto the one-way East Bridge Street, where her truck was parked in front of her workplace, a real estate office. Lights blazed inside the building. Hers was the sole vehicle, making it too obvious for me to park there. I circled the block, but didn't turn down Court, instead I turned left onto the next street to park near the drugstore, where a handful of other cars would provide cover. The pharmacy was the only business on the block that stayed open at night.

Her truck was still parked in front. I passed a few minutes, taking a couple of photos, and shooting a little video, stalling to see if she'd get back in her truck and drive off. After a bit I got out of my car and walked down the sidewalk, intending to peek in the window. A risky move, as she could emerge from the building at any moment. Feeling awkward and out of place, I took the chance and walked past the storefront. The windows were dark. There were no lights on inside, yet her truck was parked out front. Had someone picked her up in the 30 seconds it took me to circle the block? Where was Jerry? Did he double-back to pick her up? Wouldn't I have seen him? Thoughts nagged at me.

Was Jerry a red herring?

Damn it!

I returned to the car. Waited for a few minutes, idling. I snapped a few photos again of her truck parked in front of the dark office. I realized her truck had been left, so I drove by Jerry's house. There were lights on inside, but I couldn't tell if he was home, as he had a large garage, and the door was closed. I drove back to the real estate office. The truck was still there. The lights were still off inside the building. I drove home. I called Chad and told him what happened. He had gone home with his children when the soccer game was over. They had dinner, homework, and baths to get through. He sounded tired and harried. At that moment I missed the work of running a family. I told him about Jerry.

"He doesn't seem likely," Chad said. "She likes married men, and he's divorced. He's too available. They're just friends."

I wasn't so sure. "Look, this is what I saw," I said. "I watched him drive south on Bridge, like he was headed home. I didn't see him come back downtown."

"Did you check the back of the office?" Chad asked. "Her boyfriend was probably waiting back there for her."

Crap. There was a back door to the office? Why hadn't that occurred to me? I was an idiot.

He said he would keep watch on her truck so I could go home.

"Chad, if you watch the truck, fine, but don't tell me, okay?"

"Why not?"

"Because you can't ever admit you left young children home alone in the middle of the night."

Chad called early the next morning. Elizabeth had come home around 4 a.m.

"She was asleep when I left the house," he said. "But I went through her truck, and I found a piece of paper in an envelope with directions on it."

The directions were to Kilby Lane, in Montgomery. I said I would check it. He said the junior high dance was that evening, and Elizabeth was supposed to chaperone, as their daughter would be attending. The girl would go to a sleepover at a friend's house after the dance.

"So, if your daughter's not coming home tonight, there's no need for Elizabeth to stay for the entire dance, is there?" I asked. "She could duck out at any time."

We agreed I would sit surveillance at the dance and have Jacob on site as a second pair of eyes in the event she took off and we needed to follow her.

That afternoon I followed the directions Chad had found in Elizabeth's truck. The street name had recently been changed from Kilby Lane to North Chase, which was right off the Northern Bypass and Federal Drive in Montgomery. There were two hotels there, a Comfort Inn and a Days Inn. A Waffle House, a gas station, and convenience store sat less than a block away. It was less than a mile to the Gunter Annex of Maxwell Air Force Base. This was a curious development.

Jacob arrived at the Wetumpka Community Center a few minutes before I did. He called me on a walkie-talkie. Cell service would be spotty if we headed out of town.

"I've got the truck," he said as I parked under a tree across from the front doors. I saw his car, then her truck. He was parked close to an exit. I faced the car in the opposite direction. Either way, we would have her when she left.

"Good," I said, and began to cough. "Did you see her?"

"I think so. She helped her daughter out of the truck, and they went inside." He described her clothes and said he took a few photos with the video camera. "You're still sick, huh?"

"Yeah, I'm not great. This cough is awful. I can't shake it."

It began to drizzle at around 8 p.m., and the temperature remained a steady 42 degrees. It was the kind of cold that seeped into your bones and made it hard to do surveillance and stay warm. As we needed to keep our profile low, we could only occasionally run our engines to generate a bit of heat.

Jacob and I waited. And waited. Vehicles meandered through the parking lot. Children arrived late for the dance; others were picked up early. Elizabeth's truck remained.

"Hey, mom," Jacob called me on the walkie-talkie. "Do you think she hauled ass with someone else?"

It was close to 9:30, and the place was beginning to clear out just ahead of the scheduled end time for the dance. We decided to wait. People loaded up and left. Within minutes, the crowd thinned down to a handful of vehicles, but we continued to watch the Ford. Jacob might have been right. She could have left with someone, gone out a back door to a waiting car, much earlier in the evening.

We stayed until the community center went dark and the very last people left. Her truck remained.

And it stayed there all weekend.

Saturday afternoon, February 19

Chad called and said he had heard from Elizabeth.

"She said she's in Birmingham," he said. "But I don't believe her."

"Birmingham? Why would she be there?"

"She said she has a friend named Penny who is in the hospital, and she needs to spend the weekend with her."

"Huh? Do you know Penny?"

"No, she doesn't have a friend named Penny, and especially not in Birmingham," he said.

"Did she say when she'd be home?"

"Maybe Sunday night, maybe not until Monday."

"Did she take the Greyhound bus?"

We laughed. We both knew her truck was still parked at the community center.

She returned home sometime on Monday, while the kids were at school and Chad was at work. She surprised everyone by staying home that evening. Peter suggested she was a little weary after spending the weekend on her back.

Tuesday evening, February 22

Shortly before 8 p.m., Jacob spotted Elizabeth's truck in the Comfort Inn parking lot on North Chase Boulevard in Montgomery, the area I had scoped the previous Friday. I instructed him to stay with the truck until I could arrive on the scene. He shot some photos of her truck along with a few minutes of video to establish her location.

The parking lot was busy. People pulled in and went to their rooms. Others parked and walked to the office to check in, and then to their rooms. We waited. Jacob gathered tag numbers and photos of all the vehicles on the premises. We watched the arrivals. He documented the vehicles, and I watched the people. No one matched the boyfriend we imagined.

We still hadn't seen her by 1 a.m. The client said if we didn't have anything by then, to take one more date/time-stamped photograph and suspend the surveillance for the night. Two investigators for five hours apiece amounted to an expensive evening. We'd already eaten through the initial retainer and were now on a straight weekly billing cycle. Jacob snapped the final photo, and we headed our separate ways.

Chad called early the next morning to say she returned home at 3 a.m.

Wednesday evening, February 23

Chad called at 5:30 pm. Elizabeth would be working late and wouldn't be home for dinner. *Nice of her to call*, I thought. I was out serving papers, so I arranged for Jacob to check out the two

My Final Divorce Case, Part Two

Montgomery motels, beginning at approximately 7 p.m. I would join him when I finished.

Jacob arrived at the Comfort Inn at the scheduled time. He called, excited: Elizabeth's truck was there. I joined him at 7:45, with coffee. I was weary. So was Jacob. The long days and nights were taking a toll. While Jacob watched from his car, I went to see the desk clerk. I showed her the photos I had of Elizabeth. The young Pakistani woman tried to help me, but she admitted she hadn't seen Elizabeth. I pointed to the Ford in the parking lot.

"We share the lot with the Days Inn, next door," she said. "Perhaps the lady is staying there."

I walked over to the Days Inn. The clerk was an older Pakistani man. His name tag read Mr. Patel, the ubiquitous common name for motel owners in the south. I showed him the photographs. "No," he said after he studied the photos. "No, I have not seen this woman." I asked about the truck and pointed to it.

"Maybe she's staying at the Comfort Inn next door."

"Okay, I'll check," I said and thanked him. I left him one of my cards just in case he saw her. I knew leaving my contact information might damage my surveillance; he could easily tell her I was looking for her, but I doubted that would happen. If she showed up to rent a room, he wouldn't want to scare her off. In the meantime, Jacob continued documenting people and license plates. He would cross-reference them to see if any of these, other than Elizabeth's truck, had been parked at the motel the night before.

We suspended the surveillance at midnight. There had been no sign of Elizabeth.

Thursday, February 24

At 6 a.m. the client reported his wife had not returned home.

Jacob established surveillance at the motels at 7 a.m. Elizabeth's truck was still parked in the same spot. He had put a small pebble at the base of the driver's side rear tire the evening before. He had photographed the pebble when he placed it, and again that morning. The pebble was still in place. Her truck had not moved.

I arrived at the parking lot half an hour later with coffee from the Waffle House down the street. Jacob and I decided that since this was ground zero for whatever Elizabeth was doing, we should rent a room and set up a stationary video camera to watch the parking lot. We would take turns changing the tapes. Chad agreed to this plan. Even with the cost of the room, this was much less expensive than keeping investigators on the clock. I suspected Jacob would spend the night there rather than go back and forth from his apartment to the motel to change tapes. He didn't want to risk any gaps in the recordings.

We chose a third-floor room at the Days Inn, overlooking the parking lot. We set up the camera on a tripod and trained it on her truck, with an angle wide enough to see who dropped her off. Jacob stayed while I went to Wal-Mart to buy extra video tapes, junk food, and water. When I got back to the room, Jacob reported nothing had happened, and he left to go to his classes.

I stayed in the room for a while. I made notes, and made a couple of phone calls, but mostly I sat in the warm room and watched the parking lot. This was the most comfortable surveillance I'd ever conducted. At 11:46 a.m. I inserted a new tape into the video recorder, hung the Do Not Disturb sign on the doorknob, and headed toward my car.

As I reached the parking lot, I noticed a blue Dodge Ram truck, pulling a trailer with a matching blue motorcycle, enter the parking lot. I got into my car and closed the door, just as it passed me. There were two occupants in the truck. The driver was a muscular man with a shaved head, in his early 40's. The passenger was a woman with long dark hair.

Instinct told me this was Elizabeth Sandhill and her boyfriend. I grabbed my camera and began shooting photos. I used the zoom to bring up the information on the motorcycle and the trailer's license plates. Illinois. Land of Lincoln. I couldn't see the tag numbers clearly

My Final Divorce Case, Part Two

on the truck, but the plate was the same color as the other two. The Dodge Ram stopped behind Elizabeth's truck.

I rarely got this lucky, and I briefly panicked. We were all in the same parking lot. How could I record this without being caught? I smiled as I looked up at the motel room and silently thanked whatever had planted this idea in my head.

They sat in the cab of the Dodge Ram for a few minutes. Feeling conspicuous, I circled the lot slowly to retrieve the truck's tag number. Locked in an embrace, they were oblivious to my drive-by.

There was a military base sticker on the windshield of his truck. Hmm. I couldn't tell which base it was assigned to, but it looked like the type of sticker issued to active-duty military personnel. Military contractors, like my husband, used a different type of decal.

Exiting the lot, I turned toward Federal Highway and pulled into the parking lot of the convenience store. They would pass the store when they left the motel. Minutes later, Elizabeth drove up to the light and put her left turn signal on. I took a photo. She was headed north, toward Wetumpka. He drove past and turned right, toward Gunter Annex. I followed him.

He drove south until he reached the main gate for the base. He made a left turn onto the base and stopped at the security kiosk. I continued south on Federal until I could make a U-turn. Since 9/11, I'm unable to get onto military installations without Peter, or someone else attached to the military. I now knew the boyfriend was at the base, either on temporary duty or stationed there.

I called the client as I drove back to Wetumpka.

"Chad, I found her, and I've got some information," I said.

"Really? Where did you find her?"

I told Chad what had happened at the hotel. "We've got it on the video!" I crowed, hoping this was true. I'd been at this long enough to have things happen to evidence, mostly in the form of film damaged during the developing process. The stationary video camera used 8mm tapes. I would return at 3:30 to change out the tapes, and I asked Chad if he wanted to keep the room another night or two, to see what happened.

He agreed. I said Jacob would manage the shifts after 7:30 this evening through the next morning. Chad promised to call Jacob directly if she came home earlier, so Jacob would not have to keep changing tapes.

I returned to my office to run down the tags for the motorcycle and trailer. I asked Jacob to take a drive through Gunter Annex to see if he could get the truck's tag as well as the information from the sticker on its windshield. He called later to tell me he found the truck and trailer with motorcycle parked near the Air Force Inn. The sticker came from Warner Robbins AFB near Macon, Georgia.

Friday, February 25

The Illinois private investigator I'd contacted sent me an email. He had run the license plate numbers for me, and sent the registration information for the trailer, truck, and motorcycle. Back in the days before we had access to nationwide databases, private investigators were old school and resourceful, often reaching out to detectives in other states for help in gathering information. We rarely charged one another.

All three vehicles belonged to a Kevin Lee and Karen S. Hall, from a small town in St. Clair County, Illinois. I ran his name through the military locator and produced a current posting at Warner-Robbins AFB. He was a Master Sergeant, a non-commissioned officer, in the Security Forces. He had been in the military for twenty years; he had risen through the ranks of enlisted personnel and neared the time he could retire with full benefits.

Jacob nosed around and learned Hall was attending training at Gunter Annex. He'd been there for a month. Jacob got a copy of his duty papers. I didn't ask how. Hall and his wife lived on base housing in Georgia, and they had been married for about the same length of time as his military tenure. He was 41 years old and had one child.

My Final Divorce Case, Part Two

Chad exploded with anger when I relayed this information. He vowed to cause a tsunami of trouble for Kevin and Karen Hall. Chad threatened to call the base commander at Warner Robbins, and Hall's wife, and let the shit roll downhill from there.

"They need to know what he's doing!" he threatened. "I'll get that son of a bitch kicked out of the military!" My heart sank to my stomach. I didn't realize he'd lose his mind when given proof of his wife's infidelity. We had barely cracked the case, and he threatened to blow it.

He didn't express any anger toward Elizabeth. I managed to make Chad promise to sit tight and do nothing but allow us to build the case.

He promised, but I wasn't reassured. I realized I shouldn't have given him the information. His anger was a huge red flag. We'd been talking extensively since I signed on to the case, sometimes three or four times a day, which wasn't unusual with these cases. Sworn to secrecy, most clients need someone to talk to during the emotionally exhaustive investigative process, and mostly, I'd rather them talk to me than anyone else. I often joked I was part investigator, part therapist.

Like most clients, Chad was a conflicting mix of emotions. He cried. He was angry, hurt, and bitter. He was smart and we had worked together to build this case. He was normally level-headed, but confirmation of this affair had unmoored him, making him volatile and unstable. Warning bells were ringing in my head again, the second time in this case. I was anxious. My palms were sweaty. We talked until he was calm and rational. I methodically laid out our next steps.

For good measure, I called the attorney and gave him a rundown. I asked him to keep a close watch on Chad, and to reiterate what I had said about being patient and remaining quiet until the divorce could be filed.

"Revenge is a dish best served cold," I often told my clients, but I understood all too well the fury that accompanies the proof of betrayal.

Days passed with no activity. We cancelled the motel room and moved the equipment out. There had not been any other encounters. We'd been lucky. It seemed the day we caught them had been the last time they'd been together. Elizabeth stayed close to home through the weekend. During this time, Chad found a black and white photograph of three men posing together in the woods. I immediately recognized the bald man as Kevin Hall, Elizabeth's boyfriend.

While the next week was a quiet one, too, Chad had the sense she was planning to meet up with Hall. We remained vigilant.

Friday, March 4

Early in the morning, as the children left for school, Elizabeth told Chad she was going to New Orleans to pick up passports for two of their kids. Elizabeth and the junior high children were going on a school trip to Europe within ten days. She said she had not yet received the children's passports, even though she had applied for them a month earlier. She decided she would take the children's documentation to the U.S. passport office in New Orleans, to expedite the process. Chad suggested they take a few days off and go to New Orleans together. She stammered about other plans, work, *some things*. Chad kept his mouth shut and let her dig a deeper hole.

The passports had arrived earlier in the week. He had seen them hidden inside her jewelry box. He watched as she packed an overnight bag.

Jacob and I went on standby mode. I stayed close to her office and watched her. I was not going the distance to New Orleans, but I was going to follow her as best I could.

Jacob joined me, and when Elizabeth left her office, in her truck, we were both able to follow her. Rather than driving south to I-65 toward New Orleans, she drove north on U.S. Highway 231 toward the little town of Titus on Lake Jordan. She drove straight to a house on the lake. We had to be discreet as the roads around the lake tended to have little traffic. Jacob followed at a distance, and I held back, waiting for Jacob to tell me where she was.

My Final Divorce Case, Part Two

He called from the walkie-talkie and gave me an address. He said there was a blue Ford Mustang next to her truck, pulled up close to the house. It was daylight, and he was worried he would be caught if he tried to get the license plate information. We hoped to get it later. He had passed by the house and continued down the road a bit before doubling back, shooting some photos. He met up with me and we looked for a good place to wait to see if they would leave, either together or separately.

We decided one of us could go undetected in the area, but not two people in two different cars. I pulled my car out of the neighborhood and headed back to the convenience store on U.S. Highway 231. I got a much better cell signal there and called Chad to say I'd found her. I was afraid he'd confront them, so I was vague on details.

"Don't go looking for them," I said, ending the conversation.

Jacob and I stayed near the lake house throughout the day, then the weekend, taking turns for bathroom breaks, junk food, and coffee runs. When darkness fell, Jacob walked down the driveway to get the Mustang's registration. He was clearly trespassing, but we needed the tag number. He shot a couple of photos and memorized the number. Georgia plate, and no surprise here, the information later came back to Kevin and Karen Hall, of Warner Robbins, Georgia. *Bingo.* Same guy, different vehicle. The lake house belonged to Jerry and his parents.

Early Sunday morning, they left the lake house, and he drove north on Highway 14, toward Tallassee and then Georgia. Elizabeth went south toward I-65. Jacob followed her for two hours, to Evergreen, where she pulled off for gas. This is where Chad, Jacob and I determined he could turn around and go home. Chad speculated she was going to either Mobile, or on a mad dash to New Orleans, to bring back souvenirs for the kids; to prove she was there.

Late that evening I returned to the lake house and was pleased to see the garbage can had been pulled out to the curb. I used the video camera to film as I pawed through the contents of the can. There were food containers, with leftovers inside, and a cash receipt from Captain

D's fast-food restaurant on Highway 280 in Alexander City. There were half a dozen empty Diet Coke cans, and used paper towels, but nothing pointed directly to Elizabeth and Kevin staying at the house for the weekend.

Chad reported she came home "very late" Sunday evening and brought tacky gifts for the kids from New Orleans.

Things were quiet for the next week or so. She went to work and came home at dinnertime. She seemed withdrawn, almost sad, and reluctant to interact with Chad. She had little interest in the kids.

During this time, Chad had been busy gathering information for us to use. He got access to her cellphone records and gave me the phone number she'd been calling the most. I tracked down the number; it was Kevin's cell. He checked their credit card statements but found no out-of-the-ordinary expenses. His digging did uncover two withdrawals, totaling $400, from a joint savings account used to pay annual real estate taxes.

"Make a copy of the statement," I told him. "Give it to Phillip." We had wondered how she was financing her extracurricular activities.

One day, Chad "borrowed" Elizabeth's truck to pick up some fencing material for their yard. When he returned home, he told her the brakes felt mushy, and he offered to take her truck to have the brakes checked.

The next morning, Chad drove her truck to Prattville where he had a tracking device installed. He also had the brake pads replaced.

I had a car tracker that was given to me by a client who bought it when he thought his wife was cheating. She was. The tracker was about the size of a deck of cards, clunky to work with, and simply a pain in the ass. With a large magnet on the back, it could be mounted either under a bumper or in a wheel well. The main issue were the batteries that powered the tracker—it took four AA batteries—and had to be retrieved every 24 hours so the tracking data could be extracted before the batteries died. There was no backup storage system. I worried about using the tracker as a long-term device because it would be easy to spot, thus killing a case. But it worked perfectly if you wanted to know where your teenagers had really been the night before.

The tracker Chad had installed on Elizabeth's truck was mounted in the engine compartment and directly connected to the battery. He and I could watch her movements, in real-time, via a website. This was a phenomenal device. It meant I didn't need to follow her or figure out where she was. He gave me the access code, but he monitored her activities and pulled the report logs. For a few days she did exactly what she said she was doing.

We assumed her boyfriend had returned to Georgia, to his wife and family.

Thursday, March 10

Chad and I met at his attorney's office. He handed me a keycard that looked like it opened a hotel room door. It was unmarked. There were no identifying hotel logos. I went back to the motels and showed the clerks the key. Neither recognized it.

I showed the key to Jacob. He took the key to the Air Force Inn motel on Gunter Annex, where the clerk verified it as one of their room keys. Jacob asked if Kevin Hall had been registered at the motel for the particular dates, but the clerk refused to give him any information. She suggested Jacob go to the Security Forces offices, but as this was Kevin Hall's unit, we decided that was not a good idea.

Later, after taking my mother to the doctor for a routine physical, I stopped at the post office to check my box. I expected payments from some recent process services. I opened the box and pulled out several envelopes. I glanced through them.

"What a pretty dress," a voice said, close to me.

I turned around. I came face to face with Elizabeth. I froze. She smiled. She was more beautiful in person than in photographs.

"Oh, you startled me," I said, easing slowly away from the postal box. Did she recognize me? She moved in and inserted a key in a box, pulled out some mail. I glanced at the box. I couldn't see the number, I counted over and down, fixing the position of her box in my head.

"I'm sorry, but I love your dress," she said as she extracted an envelope from a pile and opened it with her fingernail.

"Thank you," I said.

She stood in front of the postal boxes, reading a handwritten letter. I went to the counter and bought a book of stamps. I made small talk with the clerk and waited for Elizabeth to get into her truck and leave. I walked back and retrieved the post office box number. I suspected the letter was from Kevin. It occurred to me she had another credit card, separate from the ones Chad knew, and the bills came to her post office box.

Chad was surprised to learn about the post office box.

That night he discovered a deposit slip for a credit union in Wetumpka, a bank different from where they had their joint accounts. He also found a paystub from her most recent earnings. The amount was higher than what she had deposited into their joint checking account. He suspected she'd been siphoning off her paycheck and putting money into the credit union account.

This new information could provide an additional prong for our investigation. If we could prove she was spending marital assets on her boyfriend, this could give Chad an advantage in keeping his assets, and perhaps his children, in the divorce.

Tuesday, March 15

In the meantime, Chad's lawyer prepared the divorce papers. I picked them up and took them to the courthouse to be filed. Elizabeth was flying to London early the next morning with the two children, on the school trip. Chad and Phillip wanted the divorce petition served to her that evening.

My Final Divorce Case, Part Two

"I want her to think about this while she's in London and how she's fucked up our family once and for all," he said. "And I want her to worry about what I may or may not know." The petition simply stated the marriage had been irretrievably broken. She had twenty days to respond. There was no mention of her marital indiscretions or of any of the evidence we had gathered, that would come later, during the "discovery" phase of the divorce proceedings.

Phillip had all the evidence we'd gathered, including our field notes and my final case report, videotapes and photographs. Chad knew she had misappropriated marital assets by not depositing the full amount of her checks. She'd also made two more substantial withdrawals from their savings account. He had examined the cell phone records and discovered she'd been carrying on the affair with Kevin Hall for the previous six months.

Chad stated in the petition she had "neglected" the children, a broad term with no specifics. He would later dare her to contest this. We knew Elizabeth had spent fewer than five complete weekends with them over a six-month period. Using the cell phone logs, Chad had put together a timeline of the evenings he had spent as a sole caregiver to their children. This included nights she didn't come home from work, dating back to the beginning of the phone calls between Elizabeth and Kevin. He made a graph showing the money that had disappeared from their accounts. He had located her actual pay statements and compared them with the deposits she had made into their joint checking account.

Chad asked to be given the house. He planned to refinance the mortgage within one year and split the equity with her.

He would continue to pay college expenses for her eldest son even though he was not Chad's biological child. "I raised him from the age of two; he's my son," Chad said. He planned to continue health insurance coverage for the four children. She would need to obtain her own health insurance, which was available through her employer. Chad also prepared a plan to pay off their joint debt load, but he requested she satisfy her own credit card debts.

Laid out in front of us on the conference table was a beautifully crafted divorce case. Based upon the evidence we had gathered, we felt confident Chad would prevail and be granted what he asked for. Phillip was pleased.

One thing was certain: Elizabeth had abandoned the marriage.

Although their flight was early the next morning, Elizabeth told Chad she had an appointment to show some land in Selma to a prospective buyer that afternoon. She promised she'd be home by early evening. He didn't want me to serve the papers in front of the kids. We needed a plan. He obsessively watched the tracker all day. She had gone to Selma. She was on Highway 80, headed east toward Montgomery. She called to say she needed to stop at the office to finish some paperwork.

I was ready to leave the house. It took ten minutes to drive downtown. Chad was to tell me when she turned onto U.S. Highway 231, toward Wetumpka. Once I knew she was on the highway, I would drive over to the office parking lot and serve her there. I grabbed an umbrella. It had been raining steadily for several hours.

Michelle was at our house. She had dinner with us and was doing multiple loads of laundry. She was in her first year of college and we never spent much time together.

Chad called. "She's in Montgomery," he said. "On I-85; she'll get off on 231."

As I was about to walk out of the house, I asked Michelle if she'd come with me. I said I'd pay her as my assistant and handed her the video camera. Her job was to record me serving the papers to Elizabeth. "One hour, tops," I promised.

"Okay, but for only an hour," explaining she had plans with her roommates.

My Final Divorce Case, Part Two

I handed her the keys and, as she drove toward downtown Wetumpka, I set up the video camera on a small tripod and plugged it into the lighter socket.

I signed and dated the service copy. I would only need to fill in the time. I was exhausted with this case and looked forward to a much-needed break. The phone rang.

"Change of plans, Susan," Chad said. "She's driving north on I-85. She's left Montgomery. She's not coming to Wetumpka."

"Do you think she could be taking the long way home through Tallassee?"

"Why would she take that route? You need to find her."

Oh, brother. This was not what I wanted to do, not at all. I sighed. "All right. Keep the tracker on, and I'll get onto 85 North. I'm in Wetumpka, so I'll pick up I-85 on the other side of Tallassee."

"I can't believe she's doing this," he said. "She goes out of the country in a couple of hours and doesn't even come home to help the kids get ready, much less pack her own bags."

I disconnected. *Shit.*

"All right, Michelle, we're going for a ride." I had her pull over, and I got into the driver's seat. "Call Peter, let him know what's happened."

She was a good sport about it, especially when I agreed to pay her at Jacob's rate, even though this sudden change would no doubt impact her plans. I drove up Highway 14 through the small town of Tallassee. It was a cold, wet night with few cars on the road. I hit 85 North, and when I got a phone signal again, I called Chad.

"Do you have her?"

"Yes. She stopped at 85 and 280. Opelika."

"280? Okay, there are motels there. That's the way to Phenix City and Columbus." I thought for a moment. "Opelika's halfway to Warner Robbins! She's meeting Kevin?" I said we'd get there as soon as we could. Chad promised updates should Elizabeth decide to go for a drive.

"We're going to Opelika?" Michelle asked.

"Yep. Sorry."

"How long do you think we'll be there?"

"No telling. You know how these things go. Please call Peter, let him know where we're headed."

Opelika is about an hour north of Montgomery. I didn't have far to drive from the Tallassee area, and I exceeded the posted speed limit, but not by much. The roads were sloppy with rain. As we neared the 280 exit, I asked her to get Chad on the phone. I needed to see where she was.

"She's parked," Michelle said, the phone still to her ear. "He said it looks like she may be at the Motel 6 there, to the right off of 85."

This was going to be interesting. "Michelle, turn on the video camera and get familiar with it. You'll have only one shot at this."

"I know how to use it, Mom," she said, with that familiar tone of teenage annoyance. She turned the camera on and opened its screen. I slowed down a bit. The road was drenched with water. The rain was heavy and the wind picked up speed.

I slowed for the Highway 280 exit and turned right toward Phenix City and Columbus, Georgia. I made another quick right into the Motel 6 entrance and slowly drove through the lot and past the office. This was a standard motor court motel—two stories, shaped like a U, with the office at the head of the building. The rooms all opened onto the parking lots, so people could park in front of their rooms. There were no interior hallways.

My Final Divorce Case, Part Two

I scanned the lot for and located the blue Mustang with the Georgia plates and the Ford F-350 with the tag that read Liza.

"Holy crap, there're the vehicles, Michelle." I pointed to the cars. "Get some footage."

She was already shooting video. I stopped behind them so she could film the plates, the vehicles, and the motel rooms behind them. Once she'd finished, I pulled around to the front and went into the office.

I greeted the clerk, another middle-aged Pakistani or Indian man, also named Patel, and handed him one of my business cards. I also showed him my driver's license and a photo of Elizabeth. She had rented the room. He hadn't seen a man. He showed me the registration form where Elizabeth had signed her name. He made me a copy of the form along with a copy of her credit card receipt. She had paid for the room.

But he would not give me her room number.

I showed him the divorce papers I needed to serve. He refused to tell me the number. He was polite, but he didn't want any trouble. I thanked him and went back to the car. I stowed the copies of the credit card receipt and registration form in the glove box.

Now that we'd found her, Michelle was antsy to get the service done so we could get back to Wetumpka. We noted the rooms that were occupied, versus the ones where the lights were out and the curtains open. We then selected four rooms we thought might be where Elizabeth and Kevin were—the ones closest to their vehicles. I showed her a photo of Kevin. She knew Elizabeth by sight. Michelle would serve the papers while I videotaped the service. I worried Elizabeth would recognize her.

"No, I don't think so," she had pulled the hood of her windbreaker over her head and tightened it. She had taken out her contact lenses and wore her glasses.

"Okay," I said. "It's a plan." I handed her the folder with the service copy of the divorce papers and a pen. She handed me the video camera. "Try upstairs first," I said.

She tucked the folder with the papers inside the windbreaker and got out of the car into the rain.

I began taping. She disappeared into the stairwell and then appeared on the second floor. She knocked on the first door, and a woman opened it. I saw Michelle speaking, then she turned and flashed a smile at me, shaking her head as the woman closed the door. She stepped to the next room. Michelle knocked and then waited a few moments. She knocked again. I could not hear her, but she said something through the door. Then she turned around and marched back to the car.

"The man yelled at me to leave them alone," she said. "He then said he was calling the office."

"I'll bet that's them," I said, and smiled at my daughter. "Good job."

"I think you're right," she said. "And thanks."

"Let's look like we're leaving," I put the car in gear and drove next door to a Subway sandwich shop. I parked in a spot where we could watch the motel room doors and keep an eye on their vehicles.

"Hungry?" I handed her my debit card. "Go get something if you want."

"I'm thirsty. Do you want a drink?"

"Coffee, please, if they've got it."

I kept both eyes locked on the motel rooms and watched the minutes tick slowly by. The storm had picked up again. We arrived after 8:15 p.m. I sipped coffee, and Michelle ate a sandwich. We talked about her classes. 9:30 came and went, and then 10, and then it was nearly 11. She had made some calls, first rescheduling, then canceling her plans.

"How late do you think we'll be, Mom?" She was tired. She carried a full load at school and worked a full-time job. She lived in a house

My Final Divorce Case, Part Two

with two other girls, and I knew they got by on little sleep. We were a solid sixty miles from home after we finished the service. I knew she was thinking of her laundry at my house and going to bed.

"I don't know, but probably not much later," I said. "She's got an early flight out of Montgomery. I doubt she's ready, and she's taking two of their kids." I assured her Peter would finish the laundry before he went to bed. "It's late. You don't have to drive back to your house," I said. "You can always sleep in your room at home."

At exactly 11 p.m., a door opened. It was the room where the man yelled at Michelle. We grinned at each other. Out walked Elizabeth, her clothing and hair disheveled, followed by Kevin.

"Game on," I grabbed the papers and got out of the car. She climbed into the driver's seat. Michelle had grown up in the PI business and knew the rules: someone always had to be behind the wheel in case a situation arose.

Kevin and Elizabeth were making out by the bumper of the Mustang, oblivious to the rain drenching them and to my approach.

"Elizabeth," I said, as I neared the couple, startling them out of their reverie. Heads alerted; two sets of eyes fixed on me. Shock, fear, puzzlement. They separated. They were still close, but no longer touched. I saw his jaw tense. I thought he might hit me.

"I have divorce papers for you." I pulled the folder out of my raincoat, flipped the papers to the Return of Service, and inked in the time. 11:03 pm. I closed the folder and handed it to her. I thought she'd turn away, refuse to take the papers, but Elizabeth reached out with shaking hands and grasped the folder.

"You have twenty days to respond from now, including weekends," I told them both, looking them in the eyes, "Have a good night." A shitty thing to say, I know. She wouldn't have a good night, and neither would he. She looked at me with a hint of recognition.

"You?" she asked.

I nodded, then jogged to the car.

Michelle had the engine running, the car facing the exit. I turned and looked at the couple, one final time. They were embracing. I got into the passenger side, and Michelle took off toward I-85 for Montgomery before I could latch my seat belt.

"Did you get it?"

"Yep," she smiled as she drove carefully over the slick roadway. I watched the footage and then called the client.

"Okay, Chad, she's served. We've got video of them, and she was standing right next to the boyfriend when I served the papers. It doesn't get any better than this."

"Wow. I didn't expect she'd see him tonight," he said. "I'm glad I put the tracker on her truck."

"Me too." I sighed. We were both quiet for a beat or two. The mood was somber and serious. "Hey Chad, I'm sorry this turned out the way it did," I said. "but we certainly built a perfect case."

He agreed, then said he would call me back. She was calling in.

"She's gonna be pissed," I said.

A few minutes later, he returned the call. "She said she had to run out to Wal-Mart in Montgomery to pick up things for the trip. She said it took her longer at the office than she anticipated."

"Really? She didn't say she got served divorce papers at the Motel 6 in Opelika?"

"Not a word," he sounded tired and sad. I tried to be upbeat and supportive.

"Hey, listen, Chad, good work. I know this had to be miserable for you. I'm finished with my end, and it's time for Phillip to take over, okay?"

My Final Divorce Case, Part Two

"Yes, I know."

"Chad, these next few weeks are going to be tough on you. Don't be surprised if she comes back from Europe and suggests a reconciliation. Don't take her back, Chad. Please don't let her undermine all the work we've done here."

"Susan, I promise I will never take her back."

Elizabeth flew to Europe the next morning without saying a word to Chad about the divorce papers.

Within a few days I completed the paperwork and billing on the Chad and Elizabeth Sandhill case. The attorney now had all the discovery, including the footage of the Motel 6 service. I had a copy of all the evidence as well. Chad was not keeping any discovery at his house. We didn't want Elizabeth to see what we had, not yet.

Phillip was thrilled with the quality of the work.

"Now we need to make sure he goes through with the divorce," I said. "That's your job."

Phillip smiled. "Yes, we've discussed this. This isn't the first time he's come to me to prepare for a divorce. You know, Chad's one of my closest friends. For years, I encouraged him to try to make things work out with Elizabeth, for the sake of the kids. But she's not a nice person. She's a liar, she's a narcissist, and she doesn't care who she hurts. She manipulates Chad. She strings him along until she finds another boyfriend." He sighed. "But this is it. We're going to get him divorced. No more reconciliations. I'm done with him if he takes her back."

I didn't hear from Chad for about six weeks, except for a final check mailed to my post office box. There was no note with the check. I was disappointed. We went from multiple calls a day to nothing in six weeks. The silence made me uneasy.

As the days ticked by, I suspected the Sandhill divorce was off.

And then, out of the blue, he called.

"Listen, Susan, I know you said you wouldn't work for me again if I took her back. But I'm begging you. Would you please help me put together another case?"

At least he didn't bother with excuses or explanations. I was tired. My mother was dying. My Army son was headed to Iraq. I was burned out with exhaustion, weary of people and their problems.

My cover was blown. Elizabeth knew who I was: the woman in the pretty dress at the post office was the same woman who served her divorce papers at the Opelika Motel 6 in the pouring rain.

Who knew what he had confessed to her during their reconciliation?

"Sorry," I said. "I'm out of the divorce business."

Several months later I ran into Phillip in the grocery store. I inquired about Chad.

"Oh, didn't you hear?" he said. "Elizabeth divorced him. She got the kids, the house, and child support. I didn't represent him. Chad moved to Birmingham, got a lawyer there."

Several days later, I drove by the Sandhill home in downtown Wetumpka. Her truck was parked in front, alongside Kevin's blue Mustang and the Dodge Ram truck. The Georgia and Illinois plates were gone, replaced by Alabama license tags.

And then I knew exactly how this situation had played out. She reconciled with Chad, promising to never cheat on him again. He took her back, and all the evidence we'd gathered was no longer usable. Just as I had warned. Once the dust had settled, Elizabeth filed for divorce.

She got everything she wanted: the house, the kids, half of Chad's 401k, and the boyfriend, who became her husband.

I shook my head at Chad's stupidity.

That was my final divorce case.

II

Lies, Alibies, and Homicides

2005 to 2023

The Phoenix

The years flew by. What had begun as research for a mystery novel had morphed into a profession. I served papers all over Alabama and into Florida, Georgia, and Tennessee, making connections with attorneys and their secretaries. I worked custody and divorce cases, found missing people, gathered records for lawsuits, and even cracked a corporate embezzlement case. The thief who bankrupted the company was the woman with the cats. The evidence was in her garbage—along with the kitty litter.

By the summer of 2005, I was exhausted. I had completed a divorce case and swore I would never work another. My clients were well-heeled enough to hire me, on top of paying attorney fees, but that did not make them likable. They were privileged, annoying, and often lied to me. Many refused to bear responsibility for at least some of their problems. There was that adage: there's his side of the story, there's her side of the story, and the truth lies somewhere in the middle.

My mother died that July from complications of dementia. After settling her most immediate affairs, Peter took me to Vermont and Montreal for a long vacation. We spent time with friends, and I grieved, oblivious to much of the beauty that surrounded me. I evaluated my work and realized I was exhausted by the people who retained me and their problems.

Midway through the trip, while taking a long bath in a beautiful downtown Montreal hotel, I decided to close the agency. I had created a business from an idea—one process service, one attorney, one client at a time. I was proud of what I had accomplished, but I was simply burned out.

Southern Lies and Homicides

The next day, I received a phone call from a paralegal at a large corporate firm in Birmingham. There was a group of attorneys working on a project, and they needed an investigator to gather records in Montgomery, would I be interested? One last shot of work would be okay, and we arranged a date for me to meet with the team.

That phone call changed my life.

The assembled attorneys were from Palo Alto, California, Washington, DC, and the offices of Bradley, Arant, Boult Cummings, a large national corporate firm with their main offices in Birmingham. They were working on behalf of Melvin Davis, a Black man from Montgomery who sat on death row, convicted of committing a double murder in 1996. The pro bono team examined and investigated every aspect of the murder case brought against Davis, and testimony presented at his original trial in 1998. The goal was to obtain a new trial for Davis, or new sentencing, to remove the death penalty. I was fascinated by these lawyers, who provided services to a man who had been failed by his court-appointed attorneys.

Melvin and his brother Princeton had been selling marijuana to help support their family, from their mother's home in Gibbs Village, a housing project in the roughest area of Montgomery. An informant, Charlie Boswell, Jr., reported the criminal activity to the Montgomery Police Department, and conducted planned drug buys: one from Melvin, and three purchases from Princeton. The Davis brothers were arrested and charged with multiple counts of drug possession, sales, and intent to sell marijuana. This was Melvin's first arrest. He learned the identity of the informant, and three weeks prior to Thanksgiving, Melvin met with three of his associates, Marcus Dunn, Derrick Singleton, and Antonio Jointer, to discuss ways to silence Boswell. According to testimony, it was decided they would kill him.

On Thanksgiving night, November 29, 1996, Melvin, Singleton, and Jointer went to the Topflight Disco, a private club in downtown Montgomery. They met up with girlfriends. When the club closed at 2 am, Melvin, and the two other men drove to an address where they thought informant Boswell Jr. lived. Charlie Boswell Sr., the informant's father answered their knock, and assumed they were there to see his friend Eugene, who was sleeping in a back room. He allowed the three men to enter. Melvin was armed with a .45 caliber pistol, and Singleton carried a .35 caliber pistol. Jointer was unarmed. They realized they had the wrong address.

According to the trial transcript, "for no reason, except they were in the path of the defendants as they fled," resident Timothy Ray, 27, was shot seven times, execution-style, and John Bradley, 67, was shot three times at point-blank range. Both men lay dead as a third man, Eugene Smith, was seriously wounded by a gunshot to his head, Smith recovered and testified at the 1998 trial, identifying Melvin and Derrick Singleton as the shooters.

Afterward, the men met up with their girlfriends at a Waffle House restaurant for breakfast. Jointer sat at a different table.

The murders went unsolved for over a year until Marcus Dunn was arrested on drug charges. To secure a plea deal, he gave investigators information about the homicides. Melvin was convicted of the capital murders of Bradley and Ray, the attempted murder of Eugene Smith, and conspiracy to kill Charlie Boswell, Jr. Singleton was also convicted but received a life sentence with the possibility of parole. As of this date, no parole hearing has been set for Singleton.

While the post-conviction legal team dissected the transcripts of the trial and examined the work of Davis's court-appointed trial attorneys, I was asked to gather information. They already had a mitigation specialist on the team, but the attorneys were concerned by her lack of progress.

They gave me a list of records, and I went to work. Most, like Melvin's school and medical records, were easy to obtain, and as I knocked out the tasks, I was assigned more duties. Records lead to interviews, and soon, I was working with Melvin's mother, his brothers, extended family members, former girlfriends, ministers, and associates, to learn about Melvin's life, to learn how he became a drug dealer and convicted murderer. I became well-versed in his family's history, his environment, education, community, and his lifestyle.

Teamed with several of Melvin's attorneys, and with two social workers trained in death penalty mitigation, I learned that telling a client's history to a judge and jury is vital to preventing a death sentence. Most people we interviewed during these few months were lay witnesses, the people who knew Melvin and would have been willing to tell the court why his life should be spared during the sentencing phase of his trial. He was described as a good brother, a good mentor to other boys in the community, and supportive of his family, and his child.

With my eldest son Jacob, who pieced together the daily crime statistics from microfilm from the timeframe of the murders, we discovered the Montgomery police department had been manipulating neighborhood crime statistics: the agency periodically renumbered districts to show that segments of the city had become safer through diligent policing, while others had become more unstable, and thus, needed more federal assistance to combat a rising crime rate.

Under scrutiny we realized there was only one area that was consistently crime and drug-riddled, and coincidentally, it was the Gibbs Village neighborhood, where Melvin lived with his family. The sector, renumbered repeatedly, remained the most dangerous in Montgomery. No amount of federal money changed the situation. The Davis family lived in a crime-blighted, impoverished area, and Melvin and his brothers had adapted to their surroundings. I was stonewalled from gathering information from the MPD, but armed with a subpoena, the records were eventually turned over to our attorneys. Yet the practice continued. Federal money flowed into the MPD crime-fighting coffers, while the consistently renumbered area, comprised of federally subsidized housing, remained dangerous.

Psychology and social work experts, family, and friends testified at Melvin's hearing in January 2006, to convince the judge that errors had been made by his original trial attorneys. Despite the diligent work and compelling arguments, Melvin remains on death row. The attorneys and the social workers found my skills useful and recommended me to the post-conviction teams working for Jimmy Davis and Domineque Ray, two other Alabama men convicted of capital murders.

I was hooked by this work. I chased stories, conducted interviews, and gathered information that could, potentially, change the outcome of a conviction. Death penalty mitigation work allowed me to use the skills I had honed as a daily news reporter at the beginning of my professional career.

5W + 1H. Who, what, when, where, why, and how. The reporter's formula worked for mitigation investigators as well.

From August 2005 through February 2023, I worked on thirty-seven capital murder cases. Half of my clients faced trials with the possibility of a death sentence, and the others awaited a death warrant. My clients and their families were not entitled or affluent; they were the poorest of the poor, people from the margins of society, saddled with every imaginable cultural affliction, including generational poverty, sexual abuse, drug and alcohol addiction, untreated familial mental illness, and a lack of education and work skills.

These are people who struggle with daily life.

My clients were poor historians: they rarely understood how their lives differed from most mainstream Americans. Most people cannot imagine walking a mile in the shoes my clients wore.

I learned, through this work, that any problems I face can be easily overcome.

The Redhead in the Blue Rambler

An event or situation can shape our lives, subconsciously influencing our passions, our belief systems, and our professions. What inspires people to become artists or scientists or policy makers? I know a boy whose dream is to become a garbageman. He can't explain why. What fuels desire? Why am I fascinated by crimes and mysteries? What inspired me to become a journalist and investigator?

All families have secrets. I've spent decades collaborating with clients and their loved ones, to gain their trust, to learn their stories, the details of their truths and traumas. But what of the riddles of my own family? Recently I began to inspect the contents of the closets that belonged to my family of origin.

Born in the second decade of the 20th century, my parents were Depression-era children raised with rigid work and social ethics. People did not "air their dirty laundry in public," as my mother would warn when I overheard an adult conversation not meant for my ears. Religion, politics, and sex were forbidden conversational topics in polite society, and were only marginally discussed with me. I was raised to be "seen but not heard," to smile, be unfailingly polite, and to mind my own business.

I am mostly polite.

One day in April 1986, I helped my widowed mother sort my father's paperwork while my small children napped in my old bedroom in our Miami home. I found a checkbook with a register for an account solely in my father's name. There were notations of $25 checks sent monthly to a woman, the most recent written in my father's jittery hand just weeks prior to his death. The name was unfamiliar, and I was hesitant to ask questions, as my father had enjoyed occasional dalliances during their long marriage. Could this be one of his lady friends? Was he paying her hush money? Was there a lovechild in the mix?

The questions itched like blisters of poison ivy, and I showed my mother the transaction record. She remained quiet, her blue eyes brimmed with tears—but she refused even one droplet to spill onto her face. She took the checkbook from my hand, and placed it into a box, without a glance.

"Did your father ever tell you about the gas station robbery?"

No, he had not, although there'd been clues: bits of overheard conversations: the night watchman, robbery, death row. I knew he had owned a Shell automotive station in an emerging area that eventually became very valuable commercial property. There were photos of me as a young child, three-, four- and five-years-old, posing with my father in front of the office, standing with a clown during a promotion, eating an ice cream cone by a gas pump. By 1966, my father no longer owned the station. The pink house they'd purchased with the GI bill was sold, and we moved to a new home three miles to the southwest. Once, when I was a teen in the mid-1970s, my sister said she wished we still owned the property at 67th and Bird Road. The station had been razed. A McDonald's restaurant anchored the intersection.

"Your father sent money to his family for years," my mother said. "He felt guilty about what happened to the night watchman."

And then she got up from the kitchen table and went to her bedroom, closed the door, and ended this conversation.

Decades passed in a whirl. By the mid-1990s, my mother was diagnosed with dementia. Her memories and motor skills were obliterated by small transient ischemic strokes. I can only rely on the few stories she shared about her life. My sister Kathy, 15 years older than me, tells me about her childhood. She wants me to know her recollections about our parents, and our aunts, uncles, cousins, grandparents, from the years before I was born, because even though we were raised by the same parents, our situations were quite different.

She knew them when they were young and vibrant. I knew them as older and diminished.

Curious about the events surrounding the checkbook I'd found; I asked her about the gas station robbery.

She was a teenager when it happened. I thought she'd have the details.

"I don't remember anything about it," she said. "I was furious I had to share a room with you."

Impressed by her ability to carry a grudge for six decades, but still eager to learn some details about the robbery, or get a glimpse of my father, I consulted the *Miami Herald* archives. I hoped to find a small article that would satisfy my need to know. I quickly found dozens of news stories about a murderous rampage from one week in 1960, when I was not yet two years old. Eerily, all the components of this story—mysteries, murders, a likable killer, a witness interview, and a death sentence—were elements that formed my work as a criminal defense investigator.

The articles weren't hard to find. They spanned years, the most recent appearing in 2005, written in a journalistic style I grew up reading in the *Miami Herald,* a style I call blue or lurid or, at the very least, breathlessly excited. Here are the details:

Rambler Found: May Be Killer's

Murder and mayhem struck Miami one week in 1960 when a young man, variously referred to in newspaper accounts as a bandit and a madman, killed two men and seriously injured a third during a series of gas station robberies. The injured man was shot four times but managed to drag himself from a service bay into the station office to call the police. Later, in the emergency room at Doctor's Hospital, he described his assailant:

"He had red hair," Jack Lincoln Beecher, 28, told the police. "He drove a blue Nash sedan." Beecher lapsed into unconsciousness, but the police had enough information to launch a 300-person manhunt for the killer, also referred to as a *berserker* and *a mad-dog*. Before he was apprehended, he would murder yet another person, a 62-year-old woman abducted from a parking lot. The red-headed killer surrendered shortly afterward.

The wounded man, Jack Lincoln Beecher, was the night watchman at my father's station.

The redhead in the blue Nash sedan was Dennis Whitney, a 17-year-old runaway from California who was tied to multiple gas station robberies and murders as he crossed the country to Miami. In those days before credit cards, gas station registers were filled with cash at the end of the day. How much money was stolen from my father's station? I knew from my sister, who did remember some things, that my father tucked a bag thick with cash into his shirt when he came home for dinner each evening. There was money in the gas station register at 3 a.m.—payments from those who filled up their tanks late at night, or who came in to buy a candy bar or a pack of cigarettes—as Whitney did that fateful night.

The stories were so vibrant I could not resist including much of the *Miami Herald* reporter's words. Rose Allegato laid out the "Gold Coast Murder Timetable"[4] for her rapt audience:

10 p.m. Sunday, February 29, 1960

Ken Mezzarano, 21, stood in front of the cash register at Frank and Ken's Service station and counted the day's receipts.

"Killer stalks in soundlessly, fells young Mezzarano with a single .22 slug in the back of the head. He never saw the bandit."

3:15 a.m. Monday, March 1

Five hours after Mezzarano was shot, the killer struck again.

"This time, death came instantly to the victim—Arthur Keeler, 53, nightman at the Tom and Sam's Atlantic Station."

His body was discovered at 3:15 a.m. by an airman from Homestead Air Force Base who had stopped in to make a phone call and saw Keeler's feet sticking out of a washroom, dead from two bullets in the left side of his head, his broken glasses lying next to his face.

Frantic police officers began a manhunt through the area near the two service stations, armed with few clues and no suspects.

The killer next targeted my father's gas station.

3 a.m. Thursday March 4

The assailant, dubbed the killer-bandit by reporters, struck again, the third time in four days.

"This time, the berserk bandit fires four bullets into Jack Lincoln Beecher, 28, at Waller's Shell Oil Station, Bird Road and SW 67th Avenue.

"Riddled with .22 caliber slugs, Beecher dragged himself to a phone to sound the alarm to police. The third shooting makes the manhunt for the killer-bandit one of the largest in Dade County history.

"More than 300 men are mobilized."

3:30 a.m.

"The wounded night watchman provided the first break in the baffling four-day terror spree.

"He had red hair,' Beecher said before he lapsed into unconsciousness. For the first time, police have a description of the kill-crazy bandit, and the car he used, a blue Nash Rambler."

Later that morning, Ken Mezzarano died at Doctor's Hospital, where Jack Lincoln Beecher continued to fight for his life.

After this third robbery, my father, and other station owners, were urged by law enforcement and the president of the Allied Gasoline Retailer's Association to close their stations nightly before 9 p.m. But night attendants armed themselves against a potential attacker, despite pleas from officials warning innocent people could be harmed by this practice.

Indeed, this happened:

Friday, March 4

A jittery gas station attendant began to change a customer's tire when a "nickel-plated derringer dropped from his pocket. The gun goes off. The bullet strikes the customer in the abdomen." The customer was identified by name and home address, but there are no additional details. I don't know if he lived or died.

8:45 p.m.

In North Miami, miles from the gas stations, a 62-year-old woman, Elizabeth Selby, left a Sears store when the "notorious red-haired bandit" forced his way into her car, by pistol-whipping the woman and shoving her onto the passenger side. Her husband, Major Selby, was not initially concerned when she didn't return home after the stores closed. He said her car was sometimes unreliable, and thought she may have had trouble, or got into a conversation with a friend. When Elizabeth failed to return home by 8:45 p.m., he drove to the parking lot to find her. Her car was not there. By 2 a.m., she had not returned home. Distraught, Selby called the police, who "have no hint yet the mad-dog killer has struck again."[5]

2 a.m. Saturday, March 5

"The killer slays Mrs. Selby in a heavily wooded area near U.S. 1 and the Atlantic Ocean at Jupiter.

"He fired two bullets into her after she tries to batter him with a hammer. The crazed killer drags the woman's body to the beach, can't start her car, then walks two blocks to a nearby house. Boldly, he breaks in, stays 20 minutes while Bonnie Boales, only 16, lying quietly, terror-stricken in her bed, watches him with wide eyes."

2:15 a.m.

"The bandit, now discernible as a youth, goes into the bathroom of the Boales home, washes the blood of his latest victim, presumably, Mrs. Selby. He pours peroxide on his hands, applies adhesive bandages.

"Calmly, he returns to the kitchen, makes and drinks a cup of coffee, eats a dish of ice cream."

2:30 a.m.

"The bandit finally leaves. Shivering from fright, Bonnie jumps from bed, calls the police."

3 a.m.

Mrs. Selby's body is found near a beach in the small town of Jupiter, nearly 100 miles from the gas station shootings. A manhunt began.

11:45 a.m.

The killer was captured, less than two miles from Mrs. Selby's body. He identified himself as Dennis Whitney, 17 years old, from California. "He confesses to Palm Beach Investigator H.L. Conyers that he is Miami's dreaded gas station bandit. He admits he killed Mrs. Selby."[6]

The Aftermath

"It's a wonderful feeling to know he is in custody," said Jack Waller, operator of the station where night watchman Jack Lincoln Beecher was shot multiple times."[7] My father had armed himself, and along with a Metro-Dade detective, had kept his station open after the shooting, despite pleas from the authorities to close early. I'd like to believe my father, a decorated WWII POW, stood guard at his station, hoping the *mad-dog berserker* would return so he could exact revenge on the red-headed killer for casually taking three lives and severely wounding his employee.

"I think we ought to have an old-fashioned Western hanging," said Bob Newbold, another Miami station owner, after Whitney was arrested.

Miami Herald reporters had immediate access to Dennis Whitney. Rose Allegato, an assistant news editor, wrote a series of articles based on a lengthy interview she held with him in the Palm Beach County jail the day after he was apprehended.

To my surprise, Ms. Allegato provided much mitigating evidence to explain why the young Whitney had turned to a life of murder and mayhem. He had been one of ten children, loved his mother, but had been physically abused and frequently beaten by his father. His sole sister and one of his brothers traveled to Miami after his arrest. They said Dennis Whitney believed his father killed their mother, although she died from cancer when Dennis was 11 years old. Within a year of her death, he was arrested for theft, and the crimes continued from there. A psychiatrist at a juvenile facility noted his IQ at 125, which meant he was able to comprehend new information and apply it to situations effectively. An IQ of 100 is indicative of average intelligence. Only 5% of the population has an IQ greater than 125. Whitney also had an aptitude for drawing, the only class he passed prior to dropping out of school. In the interview, Whitney confessed to killing seven people.

"This is the boy, only 17, who robbed and killed one day—and picked cotton the next to make money to eat. A killer who took seven lives as casually as you'd brush a fly off your arm."[8]

Whitney's cross-country murder spree took just three weeks. By the summer of 1960, just months after the gas station shootings, Whitney was convicted of killing 53-year-old Arthur Keeler and sentenced to death. He was also convicted of murdering Elizabeth Selby and received a life sentence for her death. By today's standards, there was information that might have prevented Whitney from a death sentence. But mitigation—an unimaginable concept not required in capital cases for another 35 years—was not part of the judicial process in the 1960s on those defendants awaiting trial.

The interviews with Dennis Whitney continued in the lead-up to the summer trial. In fact, Jack Lincoln Beecher, wounded at my father's station, was so concerned about the attention Whitney received from the press, he gave his own interview.

Beecher was interviewed ten days after the shooting, while he recuperated in Doctor's Hospital. A photo shows him reclined in a hospital bed, a cigarette dangled from his mouth, while he held a large photo of his assailant, Dennis Whitney. It's clear Beecher led a sad and daunting life from a very young age.

Southern Lies and Homicides

The piece began:

"And what about the 'traumatic childhood' of the guy in front of the gun?

Jack Beecher's childhood, stacked up against the turbulent forces that apparently turned a boy into a bandit, make Dennis Whitney's childhood look like a Sunday School picnic." [9]

Beecher's parents divorced when he was a young boy. His father took him, and his mother kept his little sister, Mary Frances. His sister, a toddler, fell into a tub of scalding water and died. There is no further mention of his mother. His father boarded him around, and then he died when the boy was seven years old. Beecher went to live with an aunt and uncle in Miami and grew up with their two sons, Walter and Olin, who were like his big brothers. When he was a teen, Walter was killed when his truck collided with a train. Olin and his young wife were asphyxiated by a gas leak.

He dropped out of school because he had been held back often during his elementary years, and simply felt awkward about being in a classroom with younger students.

Beecher considered himself lucky that he had aunts and uncles. He went into the Army and served during the Korean conflict, but he had unspecified underlying health issues that required two surgeries in Japan, and then another five in Miami.

He liked his work at my father's station, he said in the interview with reporter Joy Reese Shaw. He gave details about the robbery and shooting.

"I was scared, real scared," he admitted. "I knew I was dead—and sure wanted to live."

Whitney held Beecher at gunpoint and demanded the night watchman find some plastic-covered cable to bind his hands. He showed the reporter how he crossed his hands behind him and waited to be tied up. He thought, charitably, that the first time Whitney's gun discharged was accidental, as he tried to tie Beecher's hands.

"Anyway, I guess he decided to finish the job."

Beecher said the floor in the service bay was greasy as he had sprinkled it with a powered cleaner just prior to the robbery and shooting. He pulled himself across the floor to the telephone.

"It was a wall phone, and I grabbed hold of the phone book and tried to pull myself up. I thought sure it was going to give way under my weight." With great effort, he was able to grab the phone.

"I fumbled in my pocket and came up with a half dollar and had to go back for a dime. Finally, I found one and dialed the operator."

"I told her to get the police—that I'd been shot and was bleeding like a stuck hog."

"The operator wanted me to hang on," he recalled. "But I couldn't. I was too weak."

He tried to memorize details about the killer but had not realized Whitney was six feet tall. Beecher expressed no anger and did not seek retribution. He believed the courts would administer the proper punishment.

"There sure are a lot of good people in the world, "he said. "I've been lucky all my life."

In 1963, just two days before Whitney's scheduled execution, defense lawyers won a stay, which kept his case active in the appellate courts. On June 29th, 1972, the U.S. Supreme Court declared capital punishment unconstitutional in the landmark case, Furman v. Georgia. Whitney's sentence was commuted to life, and the inmate numbering system was reconfigured by the department of corrections. Whitney became Florida inmate 000001, with headlines labeling him Florida's Prisoner Number 1. He focused on drawing and painting and remained incarcerated at Raiford Prison until his death in 2005.

On August 1, 1972, a little more than a month after the death penalty was abolished and Whitney re-sentenced, Jack Lincoln Beecher, my father's nightwatchman, died alone in his trailer in the Everglades. He was 40 years old. For 12 years, he lived with a bullet from the shooting lodged behind his left ear. His aunt reported his death. She said he suffered from severe headaches from the bullet. Beecher was a veteran and received a small monthly military pension and spent his days hunting and fishing. I believe his aunt was the woman my father sent money to, even long after Beecher's death.

I hope he knew my father never forgot him.

Lunch with Frankie

"Wow, look at this story on NPR," my husband said as he handed me his Apple iPad.

> *Alabama Sheriff Legally Took $750,000 Meant to
> Feed Inmates, Bought Beach House*[10]

Reading the article, I recalled the day I met with a young inmate during lunchtime at a county jail. He ate a sandwich on white bread so stale the crusts fell away when he lifted it to his mouth. We delicately pried apart the slices to find a measly smear of peanut butter. The news piece explored why my client, and thousands of other prisoners throughout the state, were fed food that should have been thrown away.

The article, written by a *Birmingham News* reporter, cited reports of county sheriffs who received state funds earmarked for feeding prisoners, but through a legal loophole, they were allowed to spend this money however they wished. And spend they did. Some sheriffs bought vacation homes, and others funded businesses. This annual windfall was akin to winning the lottery, only better: this income was tax-free.

According to Alabama law, sheriffs are responsible for feeding all prisoners under their control in the county jails. In early 2018, the state provided approximately $2 per inmate per day for three meals. What funds the sheriff did not spend on food, was money he (or she) could legally pocket—an unusual sort of salary bonus. Forty-nine Alabama sheriffs faced a federal lawsuit for failing to produce records of the food purchased for their inmates. The suit was filed in January 2018 by the Southern Center for Human Rights and the Alabama Appleseed Center for Law and Justice.[11] This funding system turned feeding prisoners at the Alabama county level into a for-profit industry. Frugal spending meant greater windfalls.

It is possible to eat a relatively balanced diet on $2 per day (in 2011 dollars),[12] although this is considered to be "extreme poverty" by the World Bank and is an amount much lower than the official poverty rate of $8.30 per person, per day, as established by the United States.[13]

There are annual charity challenges in which people deliberately set a food budget of $2 per day for five days and strive to live within the guidelines. They cannot supplement the food allowance with any pantry or refrigerator items they have on hand. The most notable of these challenges is Live Below the Line, a program that offers personal stories and shopping tips. One woman shared her food purchases for the five-day experiment, purchased with coupons:[14]

Pasta	$0.49	Bagels, qty 6 (near expiry date)	$0.99
Pasta sauce	$1.79	Cream cheese	$1.79
Instant Ramen noodles, qty 2	$0.50	Yogurt (near expiry date)	$0.99
Tinned vegetable chili	$1.79	Carrots, 1.4 lb	$0.99
Frozen vegetables	$0.67	Bananas, 1.6lb	$0.08
		Total (oops, 8 cents over)	**$10.08**

This is certainly no-frills, basic eating, yet I could not find any experimenters who described eating stale white bread with paper-thin smears of peanut butter like Frankie Bradford ate that day at the Chambers County Jail in Lafayette, Alabama.

Some will argue an accused killer doesn't deserve to be fed decent food,[15] but this line of reasoning disregards basic human rights. What does it say about a system that rewards those who keep inmates in a constant state of food deprivation? Many of those incarcerated, like Frankie, do not realize they are malnourished. For them, extreme poverty and food insecurity is normal, a part of everyday life.

On or about May 30, 2008, five young Black men got into a car in Camp Hill, Alabama, headed to the Walmart in Opelika. They rolled down the windows as the air conditioning didn't work. They had spent the night playing video games and planned to spend the day hanging out with girls. Four of the boys brought their guns. But the fifth, Timothy Heard, felt vulnerable without his piece. He asked the driver to take him by his grandmother's home so he could get it.

The four others said no. They didn't want to make the detour to rural Loachapoka.

None of their weapons had been legally obtained. They'd been stolen from homes and cars in their communities. On streets across America, and especially in poor towns like Camp Hill, guns are currency and traded for drugs, but are also used to pay rent, settle gambling debts, and purchase food. Typically, young adults sell drugs because they can't do anything else—for them, handguns are a standard issue. These five teenagers lacked the education and the skills needed to place them on a path to lead them out of Camp Hill—a trajectory that could sidestep violence and crime.

The car overheated near rural Waverly. The driver, Jonathan Askew, 19, pulled to the side of the road. Frankie Bradford, 18, sat in the passenger seat. He co-owned the car with Askew, and they made weekly payments to the man who sold it to them. Both got out of the car and met at the trunk, to retrieve the bottles of water they carried to refill the cracked radiator. They waited for the radiator to cool before they emptied the water bottles into the reservoir.

Two of the young men got out of the back seat and stretched in the mid-day sunshine. Timothy Heard, 20 years old, remained in the car, complaining he didn't have his gun. Tempers flared.

Somebody said, "Shut the fuck up. We ain't going to your granny's."

Somebody shouted, "Shoot him! Shoot him!"

With no warning, gunshots broke the stillness—scattering birds in a frenzy of flight and feathers. Timothy Heard was hit multiple times, bleeding out in the back seat, until he lay dead. By firing into the car, with the intent to kill the young man, the shooter became eligible for a death sentence. Because they were together, in the car with the victim—and not one of them took out a cell phone and called 911—they were all culpable in the murder. Instantly, all four of these young men became eligible for murder charges even if they didn't actively fire the rounds that killed Timothy Heard.[16]

The two young men who had been sitting in the backseat, one a seventeen-year-old juvenile, were told to pull Heard's body from the car and drag it into the woods near the side of the rural road. The four wiped down the inside of the car as best they could, then drove back to Camp Hill and cleaned the car a second time before splitting up and returning to their homes. A week later, the juvenile confessed to his uncle about the killing. He handed his uncle the murder weapon, who turned it over to law enforcement.

Tim Heard's body was found by two hunters shortly thereafter.

The story unraveled as each of the four young men was arrested and charged with murder.

They each named Frankie Bradford as the shooter.

The motive? Backseat participant Dexter Martin told the District Attorney Frankie killed Heard because it was rumored Heard snitched to the police about an earlier shooting near Camp Hill. The older brothers of both Frankie and Jonathan Askew had been suspected as the assailants. It was believed Heard was killed to prevent him from testifying against the elder Askew and Bradford brothers.

As the killing of Tim Heard was a potential capital case, none of the defendants were bond-eligible and remained in jail pending trial. Three of the young men, including the juvenile, were confined in the Chambers County Jail, in Lafayette. For his protection, Frankie was housed at the Randolph County Jail, miles away from his co-defendants. Once the three were sentenced and moved to separate prisons, Frankie would be transferred to Chambers County to await trial.

Jonathan Askew, described by every person I interviewed as the ringleader of their group, received the lightest sentence, and was temporarily paroled in 2013.[17] The other two defendants, including the juvenile who confessed his involvement, pled guilty to murder and received life sentences with the possibility of parole. In exchange, all three agreed to testify Frankie Bradford had been the lone shooter of Timothy Heard.

Twenty months after the killing, Frankie Bradford was charged with capital murder. In March 2010, I was court-appointed to his case as a mitigation specialist.

I found Frankie to be a young twenty-one-year-old. He had been locked up since June 1, 2008. Rail thin, he stood at six feet, seven inches, and towered a foot over me. His hair, bushy and kinky, needed to be cut and tamed. He had not shaved in months. He didn't have any soap, shampoo, toothpaste, deodorant, or a razor. Family members occasionally put a few dollars into his jail account so he could buy hygiene supplies, but these deposits were so small and infrequent, he shyly confessed he bought soft drinks and candy bars, true luxury items, rather than necessities. He was, he said, 'in solitary confinement,' with little contact with others, and didn't think about how he looked or smelled. He'd had no family visitors in months.

The jail in tiny Wedowee, where I first met Frankie, was an hour's drive from Camp Hill. Transportation for his family was tricky—a lack of gas money, reliable cars, and time off from work during visitation hours made seeing Frankie difficult. Visits from his two court-appointed lawyers were sporadic. Frankie hoped when he was moved to the Chambers County jail, in Lafayette, people, especially his brother, would be able to see him more frequently. Lafayette was a shorter, twenty-minute drive from Camp Hill.

Frankie tried to give me answers as I walked him through the mitigation questionnaire, but it was evident he had no clear understanding of who his family was or the people he came from. He hadn't seen his mother in years and did not know where she was living. *Somewhere in Florida?* he thought. His grandmother had recently died. He said his father had died, but he couldn't recall spending time with him, not even as a child. And, as we spoke, he indicated that perhaps the man he called his father wasn't his father, and his grandmother may not have been a blood relation. He became confused, trying to parse the facts of his family relationships. There was a story to be told, but he wasn't clear about the details. Frankie gave me his older brother's phone number. He said they were close. Frankie had lived with the women he called his grandmother, aunts, and cousins in a doublewide mobile home in Camp Hill until his arrest. He gave me an address and phone number for them.

I asked him about the legal charges. Did he understand he was charged with capital murder? Did he understand he could receive the death penalty? Tears replaced his bright smile. He understood the gravity of the situation. He admitted he was afraid. I explained how I would help him.

I set out to learn Frankie's story.

The word guileless comes to mind when describing Frankie Bradford. He was the most childlike of any client I'd worked with. He smiled continuously, he wanted to please me, and he didn't appear to be anxious to leave the jail, unlike many clients who either want to walk through the doors as free men or go on to prison to serve their sentences. He seemed comfortable and I wondered why. As I investigated, I became convinced he'd somehow been coerced into the killing by his co-defendant, Jonathan Askew. Askew, the most criminally savvy of the four, was the first to strike a plea deal with the prosecution and was rewarded with the lightest sentence of all four co-defendants. The two other young men received life sentences.

Who is guilty of murder? The Nuremberg trials struggled with the issue of culpability, much as I did as I worked this case. Who is more at fault when a crime is committed? The person who gives the orders, or the person who follows them?

Frankie's attorneys liked him, as did his teachers and high school guidance counselor. I liked him. We were sickened to consider the possibility of Frankie receiving a death sentence. Those who knew him had a great deal of empathy for Frankie Bradford. I interviewed his juvenile probation officer, who declined to speak specifically about

Frankie on the record with me but wrote a sentencing statement on Frankie's behalf to present to the court. This officer genuinely worried about a good outcome for Frankie. We planned to subpoena him as a mitigation witness during the sentencing phase of Frankie's trial so he could tell the judge and jury why Frankie's life should be spared.

Those who knew Frankie described him as "slow," "gentle," and "kind." He was labeled a follower, not a leader. Mitch Joiner, a high school history teacher and basketball coach who had taught all the young defendants, and their siblings, at the Camp Hill School, said he didn't believe Frankie was capable of original thought, much less able to plan and execute a murder without external influence.

"If you said to Frankie, let's get pizza, he'd say 'okay.' If you said to Frankie, go stand outside in the rain and wait for it to stop, he'd say 'okay' and go stand in the rain and wait for it to stop. If you said go shoot this guy, he'd probably say, 'okay.' That's Frankie. He wouldn't talk back or ask questions; he would do what you told him."

"A good soldier?" I asked.

"Yes," Joiner said. "Frankie was a good soldier."

During my interviews with Frankie's friends and family members, Jonathan Askew consistently emerged as the leader of the four young men who were charged with Timothy Heard's death. They self-identified as a gang.[18] Those who knew him said it was easy to direct Frankie's actions, and you only had to tell him to do something. Intent is an essential element of capital murder, and, by all accounts, Frankie lacked the ability to pre-meditate. When the defense attorneys for Frankie's co-defendants blocked me from questioning them, even after they were sentenced, we concluded Jonathan Askew ordered Frankie Bradford to shoot Timothy Heard.

There was no doubt Frankie was the shooter. He admitted as much when he spoke with his presumptive grandmother, Dorothy Roberts, in a phone call from the Randolph County jail in Wedowee.

"Son, did you shoot that boy?" she asked. "Tell the truth." He could not lie to his grandmother. He admitted he had, much to the dismay of his defense team. Despite numerous warnings, Frankie forgot all personal phone calls were recorded. Fortunately for Frankie's defense, Ms. Roberts died before she could authenticate the recording and testify to the confession.

I learned, through cousins and aunts, that Ms. Roberts, the woman who raised him, whom he called "grandma," had no blood relationship with Frankie. The man he called his father was Ms. Robert's son, a mentally and physically disabled man. Ms. Roberts and her son told the courts he was Frankie's father, so Ms. Roberts would receive a monthly Supplemental Security Income (SSI) check for Frankie. Both Ms. Roberts and her son died before I was able to question them about this arrangement.[19]

Frankie's aunts, who also had no blood relation to him, told me his mother, Shirley Ware, had willingly surrendered custody of baby Frankie and his brother because of her alcohol and drug problems. Ms. Roberts agreed to take them in as foster children, and she raised the boys with her daughters and grandchildren in a large double-wide trailer in a neatly maintained residential area of the small town.

Frankie had grown up in Camp Hill, Alabama, an isolated and rural backwater community, a town that was slowly dying. Camp Hill has grown smaller with the passing of each year: in 2010, the U.S. Census noted a population of 1,014, which was 159 fewer people than ten years earlier. By 2020, the population was 923, and 35% of its population lived below the poverty line.[20] With few reliable transportation options and a lone gas station, residents had a challenging time earning a living. Public transportation to other communities was nonexistent. In 2015, Edward Bell School, the sole remaining public school in Camp Hill, was closed. All students are now bussed to nearby Dadeville.

Getting to and from work is a conundrum for impoverished rural families—if you don't have a reliable vehicle or access to a transit system, how can you get to work? And if you can't get to work, how can you maintain reliable transportation? Living and working in

Alabama revealed a cruel truth hidden by the bucolic beauty of rolling hills of farmland and forest—public transportation infrastructure in the South is rarely robust enough to handle the needs of a community, even when it does exist. A car is required because jobs are rarely located within rural communities. When my family and I lived in the Montgomery area, we watched as the bus routes were slashed, providing fewer services to communities, typically the ones with the most need. What transport remained was more expensive, and less convenient. This was painfully ironic—Montgomery is known for the bus boycott that launched the Civil Rights movement yet public transportation is now a fractured system at best.

When the economy of Camp Hill boasted cotton gins and a brickyard, the railroad went through town, but those businesses are long gone. As is the railroad. There is an operational gas station and convenience store in Camp Hill, but little else. I watched people buy groceries at this store with their food stamps—chips, lunchmeat, processed cheese slices, cereal, and milk, all costing much more than food at a real grocery store. Could you find a head of lettuce or a tomato at the Camp Hill convenience store? No. An actual grocery was miles away. This town was a true food desert.

There is a private school in Camp Hill, the Southern Preparatory Academy which was formally known as the Lyman Ward Military Academy. It was originally founded in 1898 by Unitarian minister Dr. Lyman Ward to provide education and vocational training to rural and impoverished White Alabama boys. Since the early 1970s, it has been transformed into a military academy for grades 6-12. Tuition and uniform fees range from $21,000 per year. The school once intended to instruct impoverished local White boys is now a boarding school for elite White boys. Lyman Ward is the primary employer in Camp Hill—providing janitorial, maintenance, groundskeeping, and cafeteria jobs to the residents. Frankie's grandmother, his aunts, and cousins have worked there, as maids and cooks.

Teenagers in many towns and suburban areas find after-school and summer jobs in fast-food restaurants, car washes, or grocery stores to pick up spending money for food and clothes, or to help supplement family earnings. There were no jobs in Camp Hill for teens like Frankie and the four other boys, in the car with him that March day.

Frankie had gone to both the elementary and junior high schools in Dadeville, a larger town in Tallapoosa County, and briefly attended the Edward Bell High School in Camp Hill. I retrieved his school records. Frankie had struggled academically from an early age. He quit school when he was told he needed to continue with Special Education classes in high school. His IQ was exceptionally low, and it was suspected he was borderline for Intellectual Disabilities, which is currently the accepted term for those who were once labeled Mentally Retarded. I needed to find concrete evidence of prior IQ testing, as the results would be used to build a defense against a death sentence. In 2002, in Atkins v. Virginia, the Supreme Court determined that executing a mentally retarded person was a cruel and unusual punishment and was, therefore, a violation of the 8th Amendment of the U.S. Constitution. I requested his Special Education records from the Tallapoosa County Board of Education, hoping to obtain a baseline IQ test. A score of sixty-five or below would give Frankie a fighting chance of getting out from under the death penalty.

I gathered every scrap of information I could find about Frankie. I spent several hours with a sympathetic guidance counselor who wept during our interviews because she had tried to help each one of the four defendants, hoping to keep them from dropping out of school in the years before the killing. She had not known the victim as he had lived in a different school district. She and Frankie's "grandma" had begged him to stay in the Special Education classes so he could graduate from high school, but his shame at being labeled *special* overwhelmed him.

She said, "Some of the other students called him retarded."

The counselor was heartbroken at what had happened between the five young men that day near Waverly. She offered to testify for Frankie at his sentencing and provided a concise and heartfelt sworn statement on his behalf. He, like every child who passed through her school, was important to her.

Lunch with Frankie

I found his mother, Shirley, in an Orlando nursing home and visited her. She had been chronically ill for years and multiple strokes left her wheelchair bound. She allowed me to gather hundreds of pages of her medical and psychiatric records. These accounts painted a sad portrait of chronic alcoholism, drug addiction, and prostitution, beginning at the age of thirteen. She admitted to drinking alcohol and smoking crack throughout her pregnancy with Frankie. When she professed to want to help her son and communicate with him, I brought her paper, envelopes, pens, and postage stamps before I returned to Alabama. When I learned she never responded to Frankie's letters, I realized some distances cannot be bridged.

I found his biological father. He lived rent-free in the back room of Camp Hill's convenience store in exchange for janitorial and general maintenance services. He also guarded the store at night. He was married to a schizophrenic White woman, who was only marginally improved by sporadic doses of high-priced medication. Unable to work, she received a small monthly SSI check, which supplied them with cigarettes and an occasional beer. They had no car. They were generous of spirit and wanted to help Frankie but there was little they could do, short of calling me, often collect, to hear the latest news. They began writing to Frankie and sent him an infrequent money order so he could buy a few incidentals.

As we neared the trial date, some good news: his IQ was exceptionally low. Our court-appointed psychologist reviewed all his records and conducted testing on Frankie. The psychologist for the prosecution concurred. We now had the documentation to support the removal of the death penalty. Plea discussions began. I continued to give him updates and relay family news. On one such visit, due to a late start on my part, I found myself at the Chambers County Jail right at lunchtime.

I thought I'd need to wait around town while the inmates ate their lunches. I apologized to the duty sergeant for my timing but asked if I could see Frankie. He disappeared. Minutes later, he unlocked the gated door and brought me into the meeting room.

"I'm going to bring Frankie in here with his lunch tray if it's okay with you?"

"Yes, of course," I said.

"Would you like a tray?" he asked.

"Of lunch?" I was surprised. He nodded. "Oh, no, I'm okay. But thank you." I was genuinely touched by his politeness. He offered sweet tea, but I declined. Although I've lived in the southern U.S. for most of my life, I've never developed a taste for sweet tea. My mother, a transplanted Midwesterner, always said Southerners put so much sugar in their tea a spoon could stand upright in the glass. My teeth ache when I think of drinking the stuff.

As the officer went to find Frankie, I looked around the small area used as a library and meeting room for attorney visits. Plain, handmade wooden shelves held a collection of used books for the inmates who could read. I scanned the spines—the reading material was Christian-based, with King James Bibles and annotated collections of children's Bible stories and hymnals. There were quite a few romance novels, their covers tattered and worn. I smiled at these. During one visit Frankie had asked me for books, "like the kind my grandma reads," but he couldn't explain what he meant. One Saturday, my husband and I spent a morning at a used bookstore in Montgomery, buying a boxful of books for Frankie. We carefully selected ones we thought he'd enjoy, ones our kids had read when they were in the fourth and fifth grades, like *White Fang* and *Island of the Blue Dolphins.*

Silly us, I thought as I thumbed the spine of one of the books we had given him. Frankie had thanked me for the books but couldn't hide his disappointment. I later learned Frankie didn't want classics, he wanted romance novels because of the steamy sex scenes. He just didn't know what that genre was called.

Within minutes, Frankie shuffled into the meeting room, his hands cuffed, and legs shackled. He smiled broadly at me. There were two white plastic folding tables in the room. I chose a table away from the heavily barred steel door and pulled out a rickety wooden chair. The guard placed the food tray on the table and again offered me lunch. I shook my head, no, and thanked him. He left the room, locking us in.

Frankie sat down in front of his tray. He waited, unsure about eating in front of me. "Please, go ahead, eat," I said. As Frankie began, I looked over the dirt-encrusted lunch tray. He had been given two sandwiches. They were made from white bread so stale the crusts had separated and were dangling off the sides. I couldn't tell if there was anything between the slices of bread.

"Frankie, is there something on the bread? What's on the bread?"

He gently pulled the bread slices apart, and we examined the sandwich. There was a translucent layer of smooth peanut butter spread across the bread, the layer as thin as a piece of paper. I marveled at the skill it must have taken to spread such a paltry amount of peanut butter on this stale bread. A dollop of applesauce plopped onto the filthy tray accompanied the sandwiches. A tooth-marked plastic spoon was provided for the applesauce. A grimy plastic cup, with a faded University of Alabama Crimson Tide logo, was partially filled with tepid water. The cup offered a small irony—we were amid rival Auburn University territory.

"Frankie, is this what you usually eat?"

"Yes, ma'am," he smiled, "but sometimes we get jelly, too."

The tray was typical of the ones used in school cafeterias, made from thick, heavy plastic with molded indentations to hold plates, bowls, and cups. It was grubby from years of improper and haphazard washing. I wanted to pick it all up and drop it in the trash. I resisted the urge to track down the warden, the sheriff, or anyone in charge, and demand an explanation as to why Frankie was being fed food that was garbage.

Frankie didn't understand why I was upset. He smiled and I suddenly realized this was his normal. He had eaten food like this for much of his life. He was grateful for the meal, for any meal he'd ever received.

People with little compassion or empathy have said Frankie was lucky to be alive and fed. I've said to them, "When a person is in jail, it's because he's awaiting trial. We're supposed to be innocent until proven guilty. These people—who are at the mercy of the sheriffs to feed and house them, have every right to be treated with dignity."

In response, I often receive dumbfounded stares and angry retorts.

What, I ask, is so puzzling about simple human kindness?

In March 2012, Frankie was sentenced to life with the possibility of parole. I had moved out of the state a month earlier and was unable to attend the hearing and say my goodbyes. Shortly after his sentencing, I received a handwritten letter from Frankie.

"Hey, Miss Susan," it began.

> *Just something to brighten your day. But I hope you are fine + all is well. As of myself I'm aight just coolin like always + praying God bless me through this situation. Thank you for the card + the words of encouragement that let's me know you care so I truly appreciate it real talk. Oh + can't forget to thank you for getting the death penalty off da table but I don't think I would of got it because I'm not a bad person + anybody who knows me know that. I know it's just a procedure they have to go by, but hopefully, I make it out of this perdicament (sic) so I can repay you for all you've done for me. But I'm about to end this letter I just wanted to drop you a few lines to thank you for everything so you take care + keep in touch.*
>
> *Sincerely Yours, Frankie* [21]

He is eligible for parole in 2029.

Lunch with Frankie

I wish Frankie well. He has been housed at a minimum-security work prison for the past few years. I hope when he returns to Camp Hill, he will have some skills, find employment and be able to feed himself adequately.

Since the news of an Alabama sheriff's appropriation of three-quarters of a million dollars of meal money broke in early 2018, Governor Kay Ivey pledged to change this funding practice. In April 2019, the Alabama Legislature, flush with generosity, passed new legislation, increasing the daily inmate food budget an additional 25¢ to $2.25, and forcing all sheriffs to allocate, spend, and properly account for this public money. Food is to be purchased with this money, not beach houses.

$2.25 a day. Try eating on that budget every day.

Lost Time

My office phone rang. It was 7:30 in the morning on Monday, May 8, 2006. I ignored it as I swept through the office, preparing to leave. My schedule was tight with little time to waste. The ringing stopped. I grabbed my purse, keys, notepad, and a plastic sandwich bag filled with quarters off the breakfast table.

My cell phone chirped a Latin marimba beat. *Figures.* I fished it out of my purse and took off my dark glasses to read the caller's ID. Michelle. She never calls this early. I had to answer.

"Hi, sweetie. Is everything okay?" I stepped out of the house into the garage. Opening the passenger door, setting my purse, the notebook, and the sack of quarters on the seat.

"Where are you?"

"I'm at home, but I'm leaving. Why?"

"Mom, tuition is due today, and I need you to pay it now."

I sighed. "Michelle, I need to be at the prison by 9:45. I must leave now. I'll be home around two, two-thirty. I'll pay it then."

"No, I need you to do it now, otherwise you'll forget, and I'll lose my classes."

"When I get home." I pressed the button to open the garage door. "You were here last night. Why didn't you say anything then?"

In all honesty, I'd thought about her tuition—both kids' tuition—the night before but didn't want to pay it then either.

"Mom, please. Mom. Just do it now. I need these classes to graduate on time."

Her voice cracked. *Crap*. She was going to cry. I grabbed my wallet out of the handbag. Michelle knew how to manipulate me.

"Fine," my voice thick with irritation. "Hang on." Back through the house to my office, I sat down at the computer, turned it on.

"What are you doing? Are you on the site yet?"

"No, I had to turn on the computer.... It's taking a minute."

"Well, you'd better hurry because I have to be at work soon," she said.

"Uh-huh," I rolled my eyes. "I understand."

The computer took forever to boot up. Finally, I logged into the university's website and viewed my daughter's account.

"Alright, I'm there. Let me find your bill." I found her class schedule and saw the bottom line.

"Ugh. You're taking fourteen hours during the summer semester?"

"Yes. I want to graduate on time."

"Honey, you're a sophomore. You're not close to graduating. You're just getting into your major courses."

"It's all good, Mom. My advisor said I should take these classes over the summer. And they fit into my work schedule."

"Oh, Michelle, these classes, on top of your job, will be a struggle this summer. These don't look like easy courses."

"It's okay, Mom, I know what I'm doing."

Lost Time

"Listen, my credit card is going to take a serious hit right now, so you'd better do well this summer. If you're in over your head, figure it out right away. Don't wait too long to drop the classes so I can get a credit. I don't want to lose money. I'll be seriously pissed."

"Oh, thanks, Mom!" Michelle sang the words. I entered the credit card information.

"Hang on," I said. "Let me get a receipt. I'll email it to you."

"Have you heard from Jacob?" she asked, as I received the payment confirmation. I checked it to make sure it was the correct amount. It was. I printed the receipt.

"No, I haven't spoken with your brother in a couple of days, but we'll see him tomorrow, for his birthday." I glanced at the receipt and turned off the printer. "Why?"

"Because his tuition is due today, too. You might as well pay it now while you're on the site."

"Oh shit!' I dragged the word out to two syllables. She was right, so I logged into my eldest son's university account.

"Are you going to pay his tuition now?"

"Yes, Michelle. I'm doing that now." I glanced at my watch with growing anxiety. I had to enter the credit card number twice.

"Okay, I'll tell him if I see him around school today. Thanks, Mom. Love you!"

And she hung up before I could respond. I rolled my eyes again. The transactions were finished, and I had added nearly $5,000 to my credit card. Poof. Forget the Mexican resort vacation this fall. Forget the kitchen renovation. Not for the first time, I pondered the math of raising children and multiplied the financial cost by their sense of entitlement. And, not for the first time, I was thankful their brother Danny, my middle child, would have the GI bill.

7:45. The timing was too tight for comfort. Fifteen minutes late, and my appointment would be canceled.

I backed out of the garage, turned the car around, and coasted down the hill before inhaling. My heart was racing. I wiped sweaty palms on a napkin. I slowed my breathing, with long inhalations and exhalations on the way to the highway.

As I merged onto 231 South, I considered the options. At this time, morning traffic would be heavy, especially close to downtown Montgomery, but it would thin out the farther south I drove. Today, the scenic route through horse farms was my choice. I cranked the music, *Girl with Faraway Eyes*. Rolling Stones. Perfect. I settled in with Mike Marrone's Wake-Up sets on The Loft for the drive.

The drive was smooth and I chewed up the highway. Holman Prison was exactly 136 miles from my house, and I had made great time. It would take

fifteen minutes to process into the maximum-security prison—I was scheduled to see my death row client, Domineque Ray, at ten. I was allowed two hours to work with him, and I needed every minute of it.

I pulled off the highway one exit before the prison. I needed to use the ladies' room and fill up the car for the drive back. I refused to use the prison facilities after seeing a rat scurry behind the toilet the first time I'd come to Holman. The prison was old, and the visitors' bathroom was run-down and, while not filthy, it certainly could have used a daily dose of bleach. The black toilet seat was sketchy. The room screamed for a coat of white paint. The smell of mold, mildew, and dirty mop water lingered in my nose long after each visit. Without a doubt, these institutional-grade fixtures were original to the prison, which was built in 1969. Each time I visited Holman, I was taken into this bathroom by a gloved female guard. She'd pat me down to make sure I wasn't smuggling contraband into the prison. Some guards were more enthusiastic than others.

"Slip off your shoes," she'd say.

Lost Time

She would pick up each shoe and shake it to ensure there were no drugs or weapons.

"Spread your legs," and she'd swiftly but thoroughly swipe her hands around my hips and down my legs if I was wearing slacks.

The commands were always the same: I had to spread my legs, pull my bra away from my breasts, and shake my hair loose. Thankfully, I could keep my clothes on.

When I reached the gas station, I parked next to the diesel pump and reached into my purse for my wallet. I didn't feel it. I pulled my purse onto my lap and opened it. It wasn't there. I panicked, searched under my notepad, and through my purse again. Nothing. I got out of the car and fumbled under the passenger seat, on the sides of the seats, and in the backseat, everywhere. I didn't have my wallet.

I sat back in the seat and closed my eyes, to retrace my steps. I pictured the wallet. I'd left it on my desk after I'd finished paying the tuition bills.

Well, *she-ee-it*. With three syllables.

I had driven two hours for an attorney-scheduled appointment, and I didn't have my driver's license, which I was required to surrender, along with my car key, when I entered the prison. This was my job, and I clearly needed the billable hours, which I couldn't bill if I didn't get into the prison.

Oh goddammit. Six hours of billable time down the drain, not including writing the interview notes and briefing the attorneys. I thought for a minute. Perhaps I could convince the Warden's secretary, Paulette Godwin, to let me in. Ms. Godwin was the *de facto* manager of Holman. No one got into the prison without her approval, but I'd been visiting clients at Holman so she definitely knew who I was.

It couldn't hurt to ask.

I went into the gas station and used the ladies' room. Fortunately, there was half a tank of diesel, and this would easily get me home. I got back onto the highway and drove to the next exit.

Holman Correctional Facility is surrounded by rolling hills and farm country. Cows dot the countryside. A peaceful two-lane road runs through a heavily forested piece of land past the maximum-security prison, one of two prisons that house death row inmates in Alabama. A short drive down the road brings you to an expansive, clear-cut area on which the fenced facility has been positioned in a north/south orientation. The prison's serene appearance is offset by seven tall guard towers—like ominous beasts standing watch over both the prisoners and one hundred yards of open space—the buffer between the prison's fences and the encroaching tree line. Sharp loops of concertina razor wire wrap the top of the fence.

I pulled into the parking lot at 9:54. I had cut this one too close. The lot was always full, and I sometimes had to park off the pavement on the side of the road and hike up to the entrance. This day, a little luck was with me, and I found an open spot. This buoyed my confidence.

My purse locked in the trunk, I walked toward the guard tower closest to the entrance, carrying the legal pad, pen, the baggie of quarters, and my car key.

"Hey!" I yelled and waved. A guard waved back with his shotgun, in a friendly manner. I walked up a couple of steps to the first set of secured, enclosed gates. A buzzer sounded, and the gate unlatched. I pulled it open and entered the enclosed passageway. The gate slammed shut and locked behind me. I walked through the passageway to the other side, and the next gate buzzed and unlocked. I pushed through it, and it slammed shut and locked behind me. I walked up the steps to the front door of the prison and pressed a button. The door unlocked, and I pulled it open. I was now a prisoner myself, locked inside Holman Prison.

A young female guard greeted me, a familiar face. "You're here to see Domineque Ray, right?" she asked. "He's already waiting."

Looking beyond the guard, into the glassed visitation area, I saw my client. Domineque waved to me. I smiled and nodded my head to him.

"Sign in and give me your license and keys."

Sighing as I picked up the pen next to the visitor's log. "Look, I don't have my license. I left my wallet at home in Wetumpka and realized it when I got to Atmore."

"I can't let you in without your license, honey."

"I know you can't. But do you think I can speak with Ms. Godwin?"

"Sure, hang on." The young Black woman entered the warden's office. Momentarily, she returned with Ms. Godwin.

"Now, Susan, you know I can't let you in to see Domineque without your license," Ms. Godwin said. "You know the rules."

In her late 50s with steel gray hair and a deep southern growl, Ms. Godwin was a woman revered and feared by everyone who came to Holman. I knew a mitigation specialist who once gave Ms. Godwin the shoes off her feet during one visit simply because Ms. Godwin admired them. It turned out the women wore the same size shoe. I wished I had an extra pair of cute shoes with me.

"Please, Ms. Godwin. I was here last week." Frustrated, I needed to salvage this trip.

"Come on in here, and let's talk," she said, beckoning me into her office. "You drove all the way from Wetumpka, right?"

She walked behind a desk and sat down and motioned to a chair nearby. "Sit down, honey."

I sat. I smiled. I settled into the vaguely uncomfortable folding chair. "I just realized I'd left my wallet on my desk this morning. I was in the car, ready to leave, when my daughter called."

"Is everything okay? How old is your daughter?"

"Everything is fine. She's twenty. She called to make sure I paid her tuition this morning, online. I wanted to wait until this afternoon when I got back, but she was insistent."

"Where is she in school? Auburn?"

"Yes, my son, too, so I paid his tuition as well. It took what seemed like forever, and I got distracted."

"So, you took your wallet out of your pocketbook and used a credit card and then left your wallet and drove all the way down here?"

"Yes, ma'am. I realized I'd left it when I stopped at the gas station, at the first Atmore exit. I was hoping I could still get in today."

"Well, Susan, I'm sorry, but I can't do that. You know the rules. We have to secure your driver's license, and if you don't have a license, I can't let you inside. Do you have your passport?"

"Uh, yeah, no, I generally don't carry my passport to prisons."

"Well, perhaps you should reconsider this policy," Ms. Godwin said with a grin. I had to smile as well.

"As you know," Ms. Godwin continued. "We have to be able to identify everyone here, in case there's trouble, like a riot, or a fire, or a tornado, or a *hurrycane*. You'll have to call Mr. Racher and tell him to fax me a letter so you can come back tomorrow."

"Well, I don't want to admit to the attorney I messed up," I laughed, embarrassed. "Just this once, please? You know who I am."

She reached down below her desk and pulled out her purse. She pulled two ten-dollar bills from her wallet and handed them to me.

"Here, take this, for gas and lunch. You can pay me back tomorrow."

I was touched by her generosity. "Oh, no, I'm okay, really. But thank you." I held up my bag of quarters.

Lost Time

"Five dollars isn't going to get you home to Wetumpka," she said, and then eyed the bag more closely. "Do you have more than five dollars in there?"

"Maybe." I winked. "I have half a tank of gas, so I'll be fine getting home, but I really appreciate your offer."

Ms. Godwin stood. "I'm going out to my patio for a smoke. Want to join me?"

A side door led into a small courtyard with two benches. There was a clear Plexiglas roof and a partition wall to provide privacy from the parking lot. A glimpse of deep blue sky was visible. The floor was concrete. A large metal ashtray sat on one bench, and a paperback book lay next to it. "This is my break room," she said. "I've been growing flowers here for years, trying to make it feel like a place other than a prison." She had multiple pots of old-growth, blooming roses and gardenias. The fragrance was intoxicating.

She opened a leather case and pulled out a cigarette and a lighter. "Want one?" She handed me a cigarette. Ms. Godwin smoked generic menthols, not my favorites, but I smoked with her, enjoying a rare moment of warmth in this maximum-security prison.

"You've been here to see Domineque quite a bit lately," she said. "Is his Rule 32 hearing coming up soon?"

"Yes, this fall. We have a lot to do. I was supposed to work with him today about some interviews I've had." I momentarily thought of Domineque's co-defendant, whom I'd seen recently at St. Clair prison. He declined my offer of soda or chips. Surprisingly, there was a cigarette machine in the visitation room. It held three types of cigarettes, all generic brands: menthol, non-menthol, and unfiltered. On my two occasions with him, we stood together at the machine while he selected the ones he wanted to smoke. He made his decision deliberately, thoughtfully. The visits and the packs of cigarettes were a rare treat for this man. He worked through my difficult questions about his friendship with Domineque, and his confession to law enforcement about the murder of a 15-year-old girl, all the while gently holding the pack of smokes with the patience of Buddha.

"Well, you can talk with him tomorrow. I know he'll be happy to see you—he doesn't get any visitors, and he's been here for what, about ten years?"

"Since '99, almost seven years."

"I don't think his mama's been here, all this time." She stubbed out her cigarette.

"Gladys J. Ray," I smiled. "No, she can't get here to see him. She doesn't have a car, she doesn't have transportation, but she writes to him. I'm constantly buying stamps for her."

"She doesn't miss a day with those letters," Ms. Godwin said. "She doesn't say much of anythin.' Jus' that she misses him and wants him to come home."

"Yeah, like he's a big boy at sleep-away camp, right? You read the mail, don't you?" Ms. Godwin nodded. I put out my cigarette, regretting I had smoked it. Now I smelled like a dirty ashtray.

"She's something," I said. "She loves it when I work in Selma. She insists we go to Captain D's, and then she acts like she's a celebrity."

"Captain D's, huh?"

"She loves the combo fish platter with hush puppies and a large sweet tea."

"Well, now, I s'pose Ms. Ray is a bit of a celebrity in Selma. Being the mama of a boy on death row probably sets her apart from the other mothers."

"Yeah. Not a distinction I'd like to have," I said. "Gladys always chooses the table in the middle of the restaurant, the most prominent one. She faces the door and greets everyone who enters… she waves and smiles. 'Focus, Gladys, focus,' I tell her. 'We've got to save your son's life.' And she waves, eats, and has a good time. I call her the' Queen for the Day,' after the old tv show. She loves that. She smiles and giggles."

Lost Time

Ms. Godwin and I laughed like two old friends swapping gossip.

Gladys was always delighted when I took her out. The truth was she didn't invite any of us on the legal team into her home, not even the lawyers. We'd have to put her in our cars and drive her somewhere that served food if we needed to talk with her. One time she convinced me to take her to Walmart. I spent $200 on items she 'needed.' Whenever Gladys knew I was coming to Selma to work on her son's case, she'd dress up and wait outside for me to pull my car behind her tiny Section 8, government-subsidized duplex. She didn't use her front door, and if it had been raining, she'd direct me to park in a specific spot on the side of her house. The septic tank flooded when it rained, and she didn't want me to drive through the sewage field. She didn't want to walk through it either.

"She calls here from time to time, wantin' to make sure her son is safe," Ms. Godwin confided. "She gets upset when we get bad weather, you know, she's worried about tornadoes and bad weather. I tell her we always take good care of her son, keep him safe." She shook her head, squared her shoulders, her demeanor somber.

"She doesn't understand he's like to die here, does she?"

"No." I shook my head.

"Well then," she sighed. "Bless her heart."

"Yeah, bless her heart," I sighed. "Gladys doesn't understand the death sentence or what's happening legally for Domineque. She hasn't seen him in all these years, not since the trial. She refuses to admit her son has been convicted of murdering a teenaged girl and could be put to death." I looked up. The tiny patch of blue sky above Ms. Godwin's garden had clouded over. "She worries about him, but she doesn't have anyone to spend time with, or anything to do with her days."

"Is he her only child?"

"She has another son. He lives in Indiana. She has family in Selma, but they're distant from her. She misses Domineque."

"She doesn't keep any money on his books," Ms. Godwin said. "That's how I knew she didn't have the ability. Before the attorneys took his appeals, he couldn't buy deodorant, soap, or toothpaste, let alone the luxuries like candy bars or soda pop."

Life without hygiene products. I had once assumed jails and prisons provided essentials to the inmates, but I quickly learned little is given to them, other than a uniform, a cot and three meals a day. Everything else, from deodorant to toothpaste is considered non-essential and must be purchased by the prisoner. Since death row inmates are not allowed to have jobs inside the prison, they rely on others to help them.

"No, Gladys gets a small S.S.I. check, but her sister is her conservator and pays her bills, so she doesn't have anything but a few dollars to get her through the month. I'm glad the lawyers help Domineque."

"They do, and they got him a Christmas box last year. It was the first time he'd had one in a long time. You can always tell who has people on the outside who can help, and those who don't. There are so many here who have no folks. It's hard on them, 'specially at Christmas."

I considered the consequences of having no money, not just temporarily like today, but always. Since beginning to work on these cases, I pondered poverty as a way of daily life and the limited options it brings to the decisions we make about food, transportation, shelter, clothing, education, and medical care. The comforts that I, and many of us, take for granted, are not reliable in the homes and communities my clients came from. I'd had some tough times, but there were always people I could count on for help if needed. Gladys had no one, not really. She was destitute and mentally ill. Her son was on death row for murder. Whatever my problems were, they paled in comparison to those of Gladys J. Ray.

As I sat with Ms. Godwin, I realized the anxiety to produce billable hours that day was gone. I was inconvenienced, nothing more. In a few minutes, I would walk out through those gates and get into a beautiful car and drive home, as free as a bird. I'd pay off the tuition charges at the next billing cycle. There is much to be thankful for in my reality.

"I know you don't think so, but it's funny you forgot your wallet after payin' all that college tuition this morning. Here you showed up with a sack full of quarters so you can buy treats for Domineque. To give him a little sunshine." Ms. Godwin drew out another cigarette and offered the pack to me. I shook my head no. She lit it, inhaled deeply. "And Domineque's mama would probably love to come see him but can't because she doesn't have the money to pay someone to bring her here."

I nodded. The irony was not lost on me, although I wasn't sure if she was being accusatory because I didn't bring Gladys to see her son. In her view, I could do this, but for me, and for the legal team, it was a matter of keeping my relationship with her professional, and our costs in line. Again, the economics of a situation. Arrangements would be made for Gladys and her son to spend time together during the hearing in Selma.

"Do your children know how lucky they are?" She looked at me directly.

Tears filled my eyes. I gave her question some thought. "No, I doubt they realize how lucky they are, but I'll give you their numbers. You can call and tell them," I joked, but my voice broke with emotion.

She stood up, crushed her cigarette, and pulled open the door to the prison. "Tell Mr. Racher to fax me a letter today so you can come back tomorrow, and bring only five dollars with you, a'right? Rules are rules. I can't be breakin' them for you."

I shook the bag of quarters. "Now, Ms. Godwin, I need to bring more than five dollars. I buy Domineque a sack of chicken wings he cooks in the microwave, and those cost four bucks, then he needs at least two sodas and a candy bar. And I need caffeine too. I never get out of here for under ten bucks."

She smiled knowingly. "See you tomorrow." She disappeared into her office. "Drive safely, and don't forget your driver's license."[22]

A Trail of Breadcrumbs

It began as a perfect day: the weather was clear and sunny, cool for May. I drove northwest on Highway 111 in my pretty BMW X5 sedan, a recent upgrade from the VW Jetta. I wore a new skirt and blazer, leather shoes with kitten heels, my hair styled, a dash of mascara and lipstick. A spritz of Shalimar. I had a case interview scheduled that morning and planned to meet a friend in Birmingham after a round of records retrieval.

Lost in music, I blew past a Sheriff's deputy driving toward Wetumpka. I glanced into the rear-view mirror and saw him decelerate, then make a U-turn into my lane, lights flashing. I lifted my foot from the accelerator to slow the engine, then lightly braked and slid into the breakdown lane as he pulled behind me, effecting a traffic stop.

The deputy, a middle-aged Black man, asked if I knew why he pulled me over. I nodded. He said he clocked me at 74 in a 55 zone. I apologized. He ran my driver's license and car tag, and a check for outstanding warrants.

"This sure is a nice vehicle," he said. I thanked him.

"I'll bet you can fly in this beauty."

How to answer? If I said yes, I would admit to intentional speeding. If I said no, he would know I was lying.

"I'm going to let you off with a warning today, Miss Susan," he said, as he handed me the license and registration. "Just use that cruise control to stay out of trouble," he winked. I smiled, relieved.

Just because I have trouble with rules, I set the cruise control for 58. The deputy made another U-turn and continued his drive back to Wetumpka. I tried to call my husband, but that 31-mile stretch of road, from Wetumpka to Clanton and I-65, was a dead zone for cell service.

I called Peter once on I-65 North. His colleague Keith spoke in the background.

"Keith wants to know where you're going today," Peter said.

"Tell Keith I'm going to Hueytown to do an interview, then request some records in Bessemer, and meet Paula for a late lunch at the Galleria."

"Hueytown, Keith, she's going to Hueytown."

"Oh, hell no!" Keith grabbed the phone from Peter's hand. "Are you by yourself?"

"Yes, Keith."

"Oh no," he said. "No, ma'am. It's not safe for you to go to Hueytown by yourself.

"You wait until Peter can go with you."

Keith was excitable by nature, so I laughed, dismissive of his worries. I promised to call when I left Hueytown. This would be a routine workday. There was nothing to worry about.

Or so I thought.

In early 2006, I was retained to assist in a death row client's post-conviction appeals for an upcoming evidentiary hearing, to try to have his sentence commuted to life without parole. Alan Miller received legal assistance from attorneys from the Chicago-based international corporate firm Sidley-Austin. Initially I was assigned to work with one of the team attorneys, Maria, a third-year associate, who tasked me

A Trail of Breadcrumbs

with interviews of the client's extended family members, which included a paternal uncle and cousins.

"I've met extensively with his mother, his brother, and his niece," she said. "I've got all their information."

"I don't think you need to see them," she said.

She was wrong, but I said nothing. I'd do those interviews, too.

I chose a day to work on this case and called the uncle, Perry, to arrange a meeting. Maria had said he was disabled and couldn't work. I suspected he collected Social Security benefits, so I brought duplicate release forms and planned to go to the Jefferson County agency in Bessemer to request his records after the meeting.

In those days, our cell phones weren't smart, and the navigation device I used was a TomTom, purchased from Amazon and powered by the car's cigarette lighter. There were no Bluetooth systems yet, at least those the average consumer could use. So, before I left my home that morning, I put the uncle's address into the MapPoint program on my computer, printed a set of directions, and read them. They seemed accurate.

I followed the directions and came to the turn-off for Perry's home. The name on the road sign didn't match the one on the printed directions, but sometimes this happened. It was not unusual to find streets with multiple names, especially in small towns. Online directions sometimes only took me so far; often, I had to smell my way to a destination, like a bloodhound. Seriously, I would roll down the car windows as if breathing the air would help me locate an address, much in the way folks turn down the radio to see better. I picked up the phone to call the uncle for verification. No signal. Of course.

The neighborhood was more solidly middle-class than I had anticipated: the well-kept houses were less than a decade old, lawns mown, with flower beds blooming and weeded. I spotted the house number and slowed to a crawl, and pulled onto the driveway, where a trim middle-aged man, dressed in khakis and a pressed shirt, stood near a Jeep.

He waved as I parked. I got out of the car.

"Perry? I'm Susan Lehmann." I extended my hand.

"Who are you?" he asked. "Who are you looking for?"

"Perry Miller, I spoke with you last night. We have an appointment to talk about your nephew." Suddenly I was uncertain, something was off here. I held the printed directions in my hand, with my notepad, a business card, and an email from the attorney. I glanced over the papers.

"Let me see those." I handed him the printouts.

He read the directions.

"I don't know where this is. How did you end up here?"

After a brief explanation, he introduced himself as an agent with the Alabama Bureau of Investigations. He asked me to wait a moment, then went inside his house with my paperwork. Minutes later, he came out, shaking his head.

"The address is to a trailer park. It's not far from here, but I think I should go with you."

"Why?"

"It's not safe for you to go alone."

An intense feeling of dread silenced me. Ted Bundy's face flashed in my mind, the way he looked as he dined at a table with my friends and me at a Tallahassee restaurant, the night before the brutal Chi Omega murders in 1978. He employed pseudonyms and false professions when meeting young women. That winter evening Bundy introduced himself to my friends and I as Vance Irack, and said he was training as a paramedic to support himself through the FSU law program.

A Trail of Breadcrumbs

He didn't mention he was a serial killer wanted in multiple states who had escaped from a Colorado jail.

Now, years later, in rural Alabama, I stood in front of a brick house, inexplicably thinking about the psychopath who had impacted my life in more ways than most folks could imagine.

Who was this guy, and why had I found him?

"So, I'll follow you?" I asked. He shrugged into a sports coat to hide a shoulder harness and gun.

"No, I'm going to ride with you," he said.

I struggled to make sense of this situation. I sought to remain in control.

"No, you take your car, so I won't have to bring you back here," I said. "I have a full day of work ahead of me."

"Another officer will meet me there. He'll give me a ride home," he said. "Let's go."

"Wait a minute. You need to explain what's happening."

He nodded. "I'll tell you as we drive."

Don't let him in the car. Call someone, anyone.

But there was no phone signal. I had to do the interview, but I had no idea where the uncle lived, the directions brought me here, to this man who waited for me to unlock the passenger door.

"Nice car," he said as he latched the seat belt. "I didn't realize defense work paid this well."

"This is more a result of my husband's work than mine," I said. "He's a contractor for the Air Force."

"How's he feel about you working for the bad guys?"

"You'd have to ask him." I was so frightened, so vulnerable, so confused, I could barely breathe.

He gave me directions, and I followed them. His demeanor was serious and quiet. I tried to formulate a plan to let someone know I had an armed stranger beside me. I glanced at the gas level, hoping for an excuse to stop, but the car was three-quarters full. I decided to stop for fuel anyway, to be recorded on a security camera, talk with a clerk, someone who might remember me later, if needed.

After a quarter mile or so, I spotted a two-pump station with a small convenience store and pulled into the lot.

"I need some gas, and to use the restroom," I said. He nodded. I chose the pay inside option on the pump, filled up and then went into the store.

"See my car," I said to the clerk, a young woman, who looked out the front window. "There's a passenger inside who says he's a cop, but I don't know him, and I'm a little worried." She raised her eyebrows in alarm. I handed the woman a credit card to pay for the gas, and a business card. "If someone comes looking for me, I want you to remember I was here, that we talked."

She nodded and placed my business card next to the register as she ran the credit card. A half-smoked cigarette burned in an ashtray next to her. I wanted to bum one, to smoke and talk, to tell her this story, to find a bit of humor, but I had a stranger in my car and places to go.

"Hey, hon?" she called as I pushed through the door. "How'd you say your name?" she asked. "Leeman?"

"That'll work."

Back in the car, I turned the ignition on but remained parked.

"Okay," I looked at the guy. "Tell me what's going on here."

A Trail of Breadcrumbs

"When you said the name Perry Miller, and showed me that address, something rang a bell," he said. We were on a county highway interspersed with small shotgun houses and trailers.

"You'll want to begin slowing, the turn is coming up on the left, in a quarter mile."

"I called my office and had a sergeant run the name and address on your papers," he continued. "Watch now, here's the turn."

The sign on the trailer park said Shady Lane, with a posted speed limit of 15 mph. I slowed to make the sharp turn. The road was shaded by old-growth oak trees and bright azalea bushes. The foliage was overgrown, untamed, and partially hid the older model trailers lined up and down the neighborhood. Driveways were a mix of broken asphalt and weeds. Some lots were untended, yet others had small gardens bursting with flowers.

"And I was right," he said, picking up the dangling thread of the conversation. "He has several outstanding arrest warrants."

"For what?"

"Failure to report to his probation officer, for starters," he said.

"Okay," I shrugged. Failure to report was a standard reason to terminate parole, but not one that would motivate an arrest. Like a broken taillight or an expired tag, failure to report to a parole officer is a secondary offense. He must be a violent offender. A scary thought. But this guy could be lying.

"What are the charges?" I asked.

The man cleared his throat. "Turn right at the next street. I'll hop out. The trailer is on your left, third one down."

"Where are you going?"

"There are two other officers set up near the trailer. I'll cut through the woods behind his trailer and stay behind it, out of sight."

"Wait. What am I supposed to do?" I made the turn and stopped, as he took hold of the door handle.

"Take care of what you need to. Get his signature, talk with the guy. Try to stay outside of the trailer, where we can see you. He has a porch by the front door. Ask to stay outside."

"Okay."

"Here's my card. Call if you need help." He placed a business card in the console cup holder. "How long will you need with him?"

I glanced at his card and wondered how I would call him, standing outside this trailer, if I didn't have a phone signal. Maybe if I yelled over Perry's shoulder loud enough?

My interviews were usually as comprehensive and time-consuming as the person would tolerate. I had planned to spend an hour with this interview. I try to get as much information during the first meeting as possible, especially from extended family members. Unless they had extraordinary information about the client and his upbringing, one meeting was all I needed until we got close to a court date and prepared the witness to testify. But I was spooked by this situation. Now, I just wanted it to be over.

"I can get by with some signatures on release forms," I said. "Maybe 15 minutes?"

"All right," he opened the car door and stepped out. "I'll see you then." He disappeared behind a cluster of pines overgrown with kudzu. I drove slowly, until I saw the mailbox with the name Miller and a number. I pulled into the driveway and parked behind a faded red Chevy pickup truck. The rear back tire was flat, the front windshield a spider web of cracked glass. I made my way to the front of the trailer and gingerly climbed the rotted wood plank stairs. There was a covered gazebo adjacent to the stairs, with two tattered chairs and a table.

My hand trembled as I knocked on the exterior screen door. A small dog yapped wildly, and a pair of feet lumbered toward me. The front door opened and there stood Perry behind the screen, an overweight man in his 60s, clad in a dirty tee-shirt and tattered white underwear. He pushed the screen door open for me to enter. He was unshaven, his graying hair greasy and yellowed and uncombed. He smiled, showing ragged teeth stained by a lifetime of tobacco and poor hygiene. His toy poodle nipped at my leg. I looked at her matted fur and her own yellow teeth and wondered how she ended up here. She growled and nipped at my foot again. I confess I wanted to kick her.

Overwhelmed by fear and revulsion, I struggled to maintain a level of professional courtesy, balanced with confidence and an aura of *don't fuck with me*.

"How about we sit outside, it's so nice today?" I nodded toward the deck.

"Nah, come on in," he said. "I found some family pictures you might want to see. They're in the living room."

Although I needed to remain on the porch, I had limited time to get those papers signed. If I didn't, I couldn't bill for the day. Rather than argue, I negotiated.

"I'll come inside if you put some pants on," I said. He nodded, then pushed open the screen door. As I entered, he bent his knee and bowed. To my horror, he grabbed my hand with an elaborate flourish and pulled it to his mouth, as if to kiss it. This unexpected movement unbalanced me, and my pen and notepad fell to the ground. Startled, angered, I jumped away from him, tensed my body, poised to attack if he touched me again.

He closed and locked the door behind me. I looked for the back door and assumed it was in the kitchen. Not far away. I could reach it.

"Don't touch me again," I warned. "Unlock the door and leave it open."

To my surprise, he opened the solid door, which gave me a glimmer of relief, but didn't allow for much illumination.

"I'm sorry," he said. "I didn't mean to upset you."

The interior of the trailer was dark and stuffy, lit by ornate table lamps with red and gold velvet shades. The windows were covered by dark brocade curtains, which blocked all light and any possibility of airflow. The smell of decay, of old furniture, soiled laundry, an unwashed body, a filthy bathroom, and ancient cooking odors, created a rancid mélange, a stench that prompted me to retch once. I urged myself to breathe through my mouth. He offered a soda, then sweet tea. I declined, stating I had to cut the meeting short this time, another unexpected meeting came up, and just needed him to sign the papers. I promised to come back, and I knew I would, but not alone.

"I want to show you some *pitchers*," he said, "I stayed up last night looking for them, for you."

"What kind of pictures?"

"Me and my brother, with our dad, when we were kids."

Family photos go a long way toward understanding cultural backgrounds, and our legal team needed all the insight I could gather. Our client, Alan Miller, had specifically targeted, hunted, and shot co-workers to death one random summer day while reciting Bible verses about a prophesied apocalypse, signaling the end of days. After killing three men at two different job sites, he intended to go home to kill his mother but was stopped by car trouble.

An extensive interview with his uncle Perry, in the right context, could yield valuable information about the paternal family belief systems, giving us some insight into why Alan went on a killing spree one fateful Friday morning.

"Okay, I'll look at them, but you have to put some pants on before I do."

His shoulders sagged with disappointment. "I want you to see me, to look at me, to see that I don't have that mark." His voice trailed off in a whimper.

A Trail of Breadcrumbs

My skin crawled. "What mark?"

"The mark of the beast," he said. "I am a man of God, not a disciple of Satan."

Holy mother of God, I could have passed out right there. I choked on a scream, pressed my hands into fists. "Okay, I believe you, but please put some pants on, okay?"

He agreed and went to the back of the trailer. I pulled out three different forms: a HIPAA-compliant[23] medical release, a blanket release of information, and a Social Security Administration form for the release of records. I had the pen ready. My hands shook. I trembled with fright. To distract myself, I studied the living room: there were four framed prints on the walls, each depicting dark scenes from what I gathered was the Book of Revelations, with rivers of blood, writhing bodies with mouths twisted by screams, people fleeing from fires, smoke-filled skies, certain death. The End of Days leading to the Rapture? He had two swords mounted on a wall, and a Bible open on a coffee table.

The dog watched me from his perch on the couch and emitted low growls each time I moved.

Perry came out of his bedroom. He had combed his hair. He wore a pair of pants and a dress shirt, and a heavy dose of aftershave.

"Let's sign these papers," I said, and I walked him through the releases. He moved a little too close to me, and I inched away. He dutifully filled in his Social Security number and date of birth on the forms.

How much time had passed? Were there other agents outside the trailer, or was the armed stranger perpetrating a hoax?

Perry showed me some photos. There was one of him and his brother Ivan, my client's father, holding a rattlesnake when they were teenagers. Their father stood to the side, smiling, proud. Perry said their mother had also been a preacher, and a skilled snake handler.

"She had the touch, they both did," Perry said, his voice laden with deep pride and awe for both his mother and his brother. There was another photo of my client Alan and his brother, aged 4 and 5, terrified as their father Ivan placed a rattler on their outstretched arms. I asked if I could take the photos, to have copies made. This pleased Perry.

"Ain't never seen anything quite as beautiful as the way Ivan calmed them serpents. It was a wonder. He'd whisper God's words to them, and they'd go right to sleep. He had the gift."

"Did you preach? Handle snakes?" I asked.

"Oh, sure. Got bit too, all us boys handled 'em. Had a cousin die from snake bite. Wasn't a believer."

"Did you speak in tongues?"

"Yes, ma'am. Still do when the Holy Spirit passes through me."

"Where's your mother? I don't see her in any of these photos."

"She ran off one day and never came back," he scratched his chest. "People said she was touched by evil, and they saw her dancing at midnight with the goat man."

The Goat Man. A fixture of storytelling by charismatic Pentecostals in the South. It was more likely the woman had been murdered by her husband. I'd heard many stories of women who just simply up and left their homes and their children, never to be seen again. They simply vanished.

Or did they?

Just then, there was a knock on the screen door. I looked out to see my companion, the armed stranger.

"Mr. Miller, I need to speak with you," he said. "You," he pointed at me, "leave now."

I grabbed the releases and the photos, then moved to the door and pushed through, past the officer, and into my car. There were two other men, guns drawn, standing on either side of the trailer lot. I got into my car and drove away.

Later that evening, I logged onto the Alabama court system and researched Perry Miller, something I should have done before driving to his trailer by myself. He had been convicted of beating and raping a woman at knifepoint and received a 14-year sentence.

He was paroled after serving less than six years. Prior to my visit, he had been charged with false imprisonment and the attempted rape of a young female neighbor. He was out on bond and had failed to show up for a court appearance. A separate charge of indecent exposure had been filed against him. There were two outstanding warrants issued for his arrest.

How had I found the driveway of an Alabama Bureau of Investigation officer that day? I puzzled over the events, those printed directions. I stashed those papers in the client's box of records. I had watched as the armed stranger place a business card in my car's cup holder, yet I never again found it.

I obtained a roster with photographs of ABI officers and combed through it, trying to find the guy who had accompanied me. I got copies of Perry's arrest and apprehension reports, but there were no names of arresting agents. A year later, before taking an attorney to see Perry, I ran the directions again. I put in my home address as the starting point and Perry's trailer as the endpoint.

This time, the directions put me on a different route, one that led directly to the trailer, with no detours to a residential area where a man stood on the driveway as I pulled in. Who was he? I guess I'll never know. But I'm still here to tell the story.

Perry Miller died in 2019. Alan Eugene Miller was executed on September 26th, 2024, at Holman Prison in Atmore, Alabama. He was 59 years old.

The Persecution

Amanda[24] recalled the evening her daily life shifted from pleasantly ordinary into an existential nightmare that lasted a decade.

"I remember thinking, 'I'm sleeping. I'm dreaming. I'll wake up soon.'" She shook her head, her hair partially covering her face, while tears filled her eyes. "Please help me."

She extended her right arm toward me, then stretched her fingers as far as she could. I reached over and grasped her manacled hand. I knew I shouldn't take her case, but I couldn't say no.

"Tell me your story," I said.

Shortly after 5 p.m. on September 23, 2003, Amanda left her job at a medical supply store to pick up her daughter Carrie from daycare. The little girl was typically happy and excited to see her mama, but on this evening, Carrie was cranky and listless. The owner of the daycare, Debbie Rodgers, was out of town, attending an event with members of the Sheriff's Department. Ms. Rodgers had left the nursery in the hands of her daughter and a friend, both teenagers. The high-school girls handed off the babies and toddlers to their parents. Noticing Carrie was out of sorts, Amanda asked them if she'd napped that day. They assured her Carrie had slept.

"She played and tried to walk a little," one said. "Then she had a long nap."

The other girl said Carrie had fallen near some stairs while trying to walk. Amanda pushed that aside and made no comment: at sixteen months, the baby was not yet walking. "She scooted on her butt,"

Amanda said. I flashed on an image of my own daughter, the youngest of three, who didn't walk until she was 14 months old; she simply liked being carried by adults and dragged around by her brothers. I made a note to get Carrie's pediatric records.

"Carrie was clumsy and chubby, heavy for her age," Amanda said. "She had no muscle tone, and she couldn't balance herself." Her lack of body strength left her vulnerable to the jostling and pushing of the other toddlers in her daycare group. Her little body was often a map of black, blue, purple, and green bruises from her tumbles and collisions with walls and furniture. Weeks earlier, after a conversation between Amanda and Ms. Rodgers, Carrie was moved from the toddler room to the baby room, where it seemed Carrie would be safer from the more dexterous and assertive toddlers.

It was a difficult decision. Carrie's safety was the primary concern for the move, but Amanda worried the little girl would not get the stimulation she needed to develop her motor skills if she was not around children her age. She had discussed Carrie's lack of physical progress with the family pediatrician, who urged them to wait until after Carrie's second birthday, to see if she had caught up with some of the growth and developmental markers, before performing tests for any underlying health issues. Amanda suspected the teens running the daycare had put Carrie in with the toddlers that day, but she was too tired to press the issue.

Carrie's biological mother had been forced to surrender custody of the baby earlier in the year. The woman was bedridden with Hydrocephalus and Spina Bifida and unable to care for Carrie. She could not lift her or bathe her. Carrie entered the foster care system. Her caregivers were neighbors of Amanda and her husband Scott, who instantly fell in love with the little girl with golden blond hair and big blue eyes.

"She was a little doll, a gift from God," Amanda said. "She was meant to be part of our family."

Amanda and Scott had been trying for a year to have a baby. With a twist of irony, Amanda learned she was eight weeks pregnant the day they adopted Carrie, May 12, 2003, just nine days shy of her first birthday.

Leaving the nursery that day in September, Amanda placed the child in her car seat and drove to the home of her in-laws, to pick up her five-year old son, John, who stayed with his paternal grandmother each day after kindergarten. Weary herself, she lifted Carrie out of the car and brought her inside to visit for a few minutes. Both Scott's mother and his sister commented on Carrie's disposition. She didn't want a cookie. She was tired and withdrawn, not her typically alert and happy self. Her forehead was warm. They suspected the little girl was cutting a tooth.

Amanda brought the children home and fixed them a quick dinner of microwave lasagna with cheddar cheese. Carrie was lethargic and not interested in eating, yet another indication something was wrong.

"She loved to eat," Amanda said. "She always cleaned her plate."

Amanda gave her a dose of Children's Tylenol, hoping to manage the fever and help the baby feel better.

"I bathed Carrie. She was tired and clingy, sleepy, not acting like herself." Amanda put Carrie down in her crib. It was close to 7 pm.

She bathed John, and the two of them lay down in the master bedroom and watched television for an hour. This was their normal weekday evening routine.

Scott worked until dark on construction sites and often did not return home until after the children were fed and asleep. Exhausted from her pregnancy and long days spent on her feet, Amanda dozed off during the television show.

At 8 p.m., she put John to bed in the room he shared with Carrie. Amanda checked on the little girl, then returned to her bedroom. A brief time later she looked in on John, to make certain he was sleeping and not playing with toys. He was sound asleep. She checked on Carrie.

"She and I had a game we'd play. I would say to her, 'say ma-ma,' and she'd always respond, even when she was asleep. But that night, I had an odd feeling. Carrie didn't respond to my voice. I picked her up. She didn't respond to me at all. It was dark in the room, so I took her to the bathroom. I saw she had pink, frothy foam coming out of her mouth. She was breathing, but she didn't respond to my voice, or my touch."

"I took a washrag and kept talking to her as I cleaned her mouth. There was some of this foam on her tee shirt. I took off the shirt, and Scott walked in. He saw that she was breathing, but non-responsive. He took Carrie to the kitchen and flipped the light on. Scott took her to the couch, and I called 911. The dispatcher wanted to talk with Scott, so I gave him the phone."

Within minutes there were three groups of firefighters and paramedics from area stations. Initially there were no police officers present, but Amanda recalled a woman asked to see the baby's crib. The responders left and took Carrie with them. No one told either Amanda or Scott what they thought was wrong with the baby.

"No one would talk to me or let me touch her. The paramedics put Carrie on a gurney and took her away and wouldn't tell us anything." Neither parent was allowed to ride to the hospital with their little girl.[25]

Amanda and Scott put John in Scott's truck and followed the ambulance to the local hospital. Scott called his parents, and Amanda's, and they all rushed to the emergency room. After an initial examination by the ER staff, Carrie, without her mama or daddy to hold her hand, was airlifted to Children's Hospital[26] with a grim diagnosis: severe head trauma.

Carrie was placed on life support while a multitude of tests were performed. Six days later, on September 29, 2003, it was determined the brain injury she suffered was so profound she would never regain consciousness. Specialists said there was no brain activity. The little girl with golden blond curls was removed from life support and pronounced dead.

She was 16 months old.

The Persecution

The official cause of death was blunt force trauma to her head. The autopsy was completed the next day. Numerous tests were conducted, including drug and toxicology panels before her body was released to a funeral home, to be prepared for burial.

Several months later, Amanda and Scott, and their extended family members welcomed a baby girl, who did much to soothe their broken hearts.

But the question of how Carrie had been injured plagued everyone, especially Amanda. She had fallen many times, and a month before her death, she'd cracked her head on the coffee table at Scott's parent's home—a blow so loud and painful sounding that those who witnessed the fall were sickened. But the baby caught her breath and kept playing.

After the little girl died, both of Amanda's children were removed by social workers for the Department of Human Resources, taken into protective custody, and briefly placed into foster homes. The authorities didn't trust Amanda as a caregiver. Eventually, the children were placed with Amanda's parents, and later, they were returned to Scott.

The results of the lab tests conducted on Carrie's body were not released until December 22, 2004, more than fifteen months after her death.

The following month, in early January 2005, Amanda was arrested and charged with first-degree murder. The judge set a cash bond of $100,000, a huge sum, which was raised within 24 hours by members of their large and supportive Baptist church. She was bonded, released, and allowed to remain at home with her husband, and to be with her children until her next scheduled court appearance. The families pooled their funds and refinanced their homes to pay an additional $100,000 to hire a criminal attorney, Rich McClellen, to defend Amanda.

Amanda appeared in court to be arraigned on murder charges on March 29, 2004, her extended family and church members surrounding her. She planned to enter a not-guilty plea. But the prosecutors ambushed her and her attorney. Amanda was charged with capital murder rather than first-degree murder, because the victim was a child under 12 years of age. Amanda's bond was immediately revoked.[27] Stunned, surprised, shocked, she was pulled away from her family and taken to the county jail, where she would remain.

For a very long time.

The capital murder indictment began a sojourn through the Alabama legal system Amanda was completely unprepared to take.

As this was a capital case, it was necessary, according to the American Bar Association, for Attorney McClellen to bring in a second defense lawyer. He tapped Jim Thompson, who specialized in real estate transactions, wills, and divorces. He had been partnered with his father in a law practice for twenty years. Jim had never worked on a criminal case.

Nearly 14 months later, on May 17th, 2005, during her formal arraignment on the capital murder charges, Amanda, wearing an orange jail jumpsuit and manacled, pled not guilty in open court. She was returned to the jail cell, where she continued to wait for the wheels of justice to turn.

But her case lingered for another six years, until September 2011, when a trial date was suddenly set for October 24th. Subpoenas were issued for the prosecution witnesses. The defense now knew exactly who would be testifying against Amanda. In a *pro forma* move, the Judge authorized funds to hire a mitigation specialist. This funding should have been offered by the judge, and a specialist hired, when Amanda was charged with capital murder in 2005.

The $100,000 retainer the family paid to Rich McClellen had been spent over the years, with little to show for the money. Her family members had no additional funds for lawyers. Amanda and her attorneys had to petition for indigent defense status, meaning the State of Alabama would pay her legal fees, at a much lower hourly rate than either McClellen or Thompson routinely charged their clients.

The Persecution

Baby Carrie, golden-haired and blue-eyed, had been dead for eight years. Amanda's daughter, an infant at her first arrest, was in elementary school. Elder son John, in kindergarten when Carrie died, was now in junior high. The children had grown, daily life had continued, while Amanda sat in jail, awaiting trial. Her husband Scott and their extended family members remained steadfast, unwavering in their support for Amanda.

Jim Thompson called while I was vacationing with my husband at a resort in Cancun, Mexico. I was on the beach, deep into a novel and a margarita, likely not my first of the day. Jim had been given my contact information by an attorney from the Equal Justice Initiative (EJI), a non-profit agency housed in Montgomery. EJI provides legal representation to poor defendants, and many of their clients are on Alabama's death row.

Jim told me Amanda's story. I was intrigued and asked many questions, but I explained I couldn't take Amanda's case. Peter's job was relocating him to Ogden, Utah. We would leave Alabama in several months.

I asked if Amanda had undergone a competency evaluation. She had not. These are routine tests, primarily administered by a psychologist to determine if defendants understand the charges they face and to discover low IQ or diminished mental capacity. In Alabama, an IQ of 79 or below was viewed as possible mental retardation, a term now referred to as intellectual disability or intellectual developmental disorder. Jim said he would file a motion with the court, requesting a competency evaluation. We knew that request would postpone the trial, a delay that would allow for some mitigation work to be done.

"Even if I could work for her, there's no way I can have the mitigation completed within a month. I like to have at least a year, more time would be great," I said. I had thirteen open cases, in various stages of development, and only one was likely to resolve prior to my move. I would commute monthly for several years to complete the cases, an expensive and exhausting commitment. I could not, in good conscience, take on another client.

Jim asked if I could recommend another mitigation specialist. I knew several, but none were doing pre-trial work in Alabama simply because we would not be paid by the state indigent defense fund until cases were resolved. It could be years before payment and expense reimbursement.

Maybe it was his persuasive skills, or the tequila, but he wore down my resolve during the 35-minute phone call. I agreed to travel the following week, to meet with him, attorney Rich McClellen and Amanda House, but only to consult for a few hours.

On September 22, 2011, eight years to the day after Carrie was fatally injured, I made the 115-mile drive from my home to Jim's office. I agreed to talk with the lawyers, and then meet with Amanda at the jail, to brainstorm ideas to help with her defense. I was determined I would not sign on as an investigator.

But the timeline of the case puzzled me. Why had the prosecutors taken so long to bring Amanda's case to court? If they had enough evidence to seek a death sentence, why had they waited so long to bring the case to trial?

Jim and I met at his office. We sat at a conference table, which contained stacks of files, reports, police, and witness statements, accompanied by multiple legal pads filled with notes for Amanda's case. He'd spent years trying to strategize her defense. I was impressed by his dedication to freeing Amanda, whom he believed was innocent of killing her baby. Jim is a humble man, with a keen sense of humor, a counterpoint to the aloof and arrogant lawyers I often encountered. We made small talk about the case, waiting for attorney McClellen to show up, who eventually called to say he was running late. Jim and I went on to the courthouse, where we were to meet Amanda. While there was a legal visitation area at the jail, Jim feared word of my presence would tip off the prosecution that the defense had retained an investigator. This community was small and insular: many of the witnesses subpoenaed to testify against Amanda had connections to law enforcement officers, and my efforts could be obstructed.

The Persecution

Also concerning were jailhouse snitches. Amanda was warned repeatedly never to discuss any aspect of her case with anyone in the jail, particularly other inmates. It was feared an inmate would attempt to trade a better sentence by giving information about Amanda to prosecutors. Most cases I've worked have had at least one snitch who claimed the defendant "confessed guilt" to them. They try to trade this often-false information to a prosecutor willing to cut the snitch a plea deal. This scenario terrified the young woman.

We chose a table at the back of an empty courtroom. The lights were dim, and two guards escorted Amanda. She was handcuffed, her arms pulled tight behind her, her ankles bound by a chain and lock. She shuffled across the floor. At my instruction, the cuffs were unlocked, with her wrists reattached in front of her, so she could sign release forms.

Her light brown hair was long and unkempt. Her skin was blotchy, from a starchy diet, poor hygiene, and little sunlight. Amanda's glasses were old, the lenses scratched and cloudy, the prescription outdated. Even so, she was an attractive young woman, and, at 36 years old, should have been in the prime of her life. But Amanda had been rendered wild by the harsh conditions of jail. She had few, if any luxuries: no shopping trips or manicures, no lazy Saturdays watching cartoons with her kids, no holiday celebrations or fresh fruit, and little kindness. Her jail-issued jumpsuit was dingy and wrinkled. I knew she was self-conscious about her appearance, and a spark of anger surrounded her, like an aura. She was proud. She stood tall, fists clenched, shoulders squared, daring someone to confront her.

And once the guards retreated, she gave me a glorious smile.

"Thank you for coming to see me."

After she told the story of Carrie's brief life, we launched into the mitigation questions. I learned her parents' names, their phone numbers, their occupations. Amanda was unlike any of my other clients: she had a loving and nurturing upbringing; she was close to her parents. Her sister was her best friend. She'd attended school at a private Christian academy, from kindergarten through graduation.

She'd had no academic difficulties but was sanctioned several times for unruly behavior: once for chewing gum, and twice for talking and laughing in class. Spanking was the school punishment for all infractions, but afterward staff members would pray with the 'wayward' student and assure her she was loved by all, especially Jesus. Amanda's mother was a volunteer at the school. Amanda's father was an auto mechanic. Amanda grew up in a supervised and controlled environment. She had no criminal history; she was the antithesis of all my other clients, who were exposed to chaotic environments of substance abuse, generational poverty, trauma, violence, severe and often untreated mental health disorders, and, quite often, missing parents.

Midway through our meeting, Amanda needed to use the restroom. She asked the guard, who was lounging in the Judge's chair, playing on his phone, if he would please take her to a women's room.

He stood up from the chair. "If I have to take you, I'm not bringing you back here," he yelled across the courtroom. "Meeting's over," he announced.

"Wait a minute," I yelled, looking at my watch. "We're scheduled for three hours, and we have at least 90 minutes left."

He explained that if Amanda had to use the bathroom, he would have to call for a second guard to assist in escorting her back to the jail. Then he had to find a female officer to take her into a restroom and stay with her.

"She'll need to be searched for contraband," he said, an insinuation that either Jim or I had slipped her some forbidden object, like a cell phone or a weapon. "Then we'd have to bring her back here, and I don't have time for that."

Amanda was mortified and ashamed by this exchange. I suggested that I accompany them to a restroom in the courthouse, to make short work of this issue.

"Ma'am, with all due respect, I don't know who you are," he said. "And I'm sorry, but I don't trust you, and I'm not going to break

The Persecution

protocol for a prisoner, especially her," he nodded at Amanda. "She's a…"

Baby killer. He didn't say the words, but I bet he wanted to. I mentally dared him to say those words. At that specific moment, I realized how unsafe Amanda was in that jail. The adage about prisoners went through my mind:

Cop killers are worshiped; baby killers are beaten to death.

Furious, I bit my tongue and chose my words carefully, as I approached the guard. He dropped his hand to his sidearm. Mindful of this movement, I realized he viewed Jim and I as threats to his safety. I stopped in my tracks, a dozen yards away from him.

"Ms. House needs to use a restroom. Her lead attorney is not here yet. We are in the middle of an important meeting, one that I cannot reschedule. Please get a second guard and escort her to the jail. Then bring her back here. We'll wait."

"That will take about 30 minutes," he said. I nodded. He radioed for another guard.

In that moment, Amanda became my client. We had to get her out of that jail.

Over the next year, I gathered her records, interviewed family members and friends, teachers, and church members, often over the phone, which is not ideal for noticing body language, gauging emotions, or determining who would make a good sentencing witness. Jim and I brainstormed, and occasionally, we'd meet in his office when I traveled to Alabama for other clients.[28]

Amanda's safety was a pressing concern. We discussed filing a request to move her from the semi-rural county jail to another facility. At the time I was working a post-conviction case out of Fort Payne, a town near the northern Georgia border, and was impressed with the small DeKalb County Jail. The personnel were kind and professional.

The facility was new and kept clean by the prisoners, and not one of them knew Amanda was charged with capital murder in the death of her baby.

Her family was resistant to the move. She would be housed 60 miles away from her husband, her children, and their extended family members. Amanda was accustomed to frequent visits, and her family members worried the increased distance would be a hardship both in time and expense.

With little hesitation, Amanda chose to transfer to DeKalb County, and this proved a godsend to the young woman. I visited her several times while working in Fort Payne, and the difference in her demeanor was remarkable. She was free to move within the facility. She performed some administrative tasks, and she taught other inmates to read. The jail personnel liked her, as did the other inmates. She was still a prisoner, but she glowed: someone had cut her hair, her jumpsuits were clean, she was busy, active, and no longer terrified of the other inmates or the officers.

At my urging, Jim discussed Amanda's case with an attorney from the Southern Center for Human Rights, an Atlanta-based nonprofit organization that provides legal services to incarcerated people. The attorney was intrigued by Amanda's case and provided invaluable assistance to Jim through frequent phone calls, emails, and visits. Primary attorney Rich McClellen had gone AWOL. I suspected that earning a capped payment from the state didn't hold his interest.

The trial was set for August 27, 2012.

Jim issued subpoenas for our mitigation witnesses, which included Amanda and Scott's parents, Amanda's sister, and the family minister. There were two medical doctors, specialists who had reviewed Carrie's extensive records, who planned to testify to the possibility of underlying health issues, and the scenarios that may have surrounded the fatal injury.

The Persecution

Jim also issued a subpoena for Debbie Rodgers, the owner of the daycare Carrie attended. Jim's secretary had found a photo of the woman traveling to an event the morning of Carrie's final day. She was a prosecution witness, and we expected her to testify that Carrie had not suffered an accident sufficient to fatally crack her skull at the daycare.

This newspaper photograph would be enough evidence to dispute her testimony. She'd left the center in the hands of a teenaged daughter and her friend. We discussed interviewing the two young women who'd handed a listless Carrie to Amanda that day. They were adults now, and I argued for meetings, but Jim urged patience.

In the lead-up to the trial, Jim and I conducted two crucial interviews. The first was with the director of the funeral home that managed Carrie's burial. Her little body had been embalmed. Unfortunately, the embalmer had recently died. The director had Carrie's file and discussed a curious detail: the embalmer had found Carrie's skull bones were so brittle and inflexible he couldn't work with them—a strange occurrence in a toddler.

According to his notes, the technician soaked the skullcap in a formalin solution for several days to soften the bones enough to mold her head back together for the viewing and funeral. In his report, he likened the toddler's skull bones to the ossified bones of an 85-year-old woman. Could that hardening be indicative of an undiagnosed health issue? Her biological mother had Encephalitis and Spina Bifida—could the baby have craniosynostosis, a condition that causes the bones to fuse and harden too quickly, often resulting in deformity and seizures?

Jim got a copy of the embalmer's report and consulted the medical specialists.

The second interview was with a woman who had worked at the first daycare Carrie had attended. She was a prosecution witness. She had noticed bruising on Carrie's body, and fearing for the child's safety, reported this to child protective services. During our conversation, the woman admitted to having suffered several mental breakdowns, and was hospitalized shortly after making the report. She willingly gave us the names of her doctors and the facilities where she had received treatment. She signed HIPAA-compliant medical release forms so I could obtain her extensive treatment records. As much as Jim detested the thought of forcing this woman to discuss her personal struggles in an open court, he had the ammunition to question her perception of child abuse. We needed everything we could find to impeach, or at least discredit, what this woman, and other witnesses, would say.

It didn't take long for prosecutors to learn we were questioning their witnesses. We braced for their response.

Suddenly, two weeks prior to the August 2012 trial, the court date was rescheduled to January 28, 2013. Jim re-issued subpoenas on December 20th.

Then, the progression of the case took a sudden turn.

Over the course of 2013, the prosecution negotiated an agreement with Amanda and her attorneys: they would drop the capital murder charges if she pled guilty to variations of murder, first-degree, or second-degree negligent homicide or manslaughter. Amanda was torn; she wanted to maintain her innocence in the death of her child, but she also wanted to go home.

On January 21, 2014, Amanda entered an Alford plea, also called a 'best-interest' plea in which a defendant does not admit guilt to a specified crime, but states it is in her best interest to plead guilty. By agreeing to this plea, in this case, manslaughter, Amanda admitted the evidence produced by the prosecution would have likely persuaded a judge or jury to find her guilty beyond a reasonable doubt. Prosecutors declared a victory, but so did we.

After being incarcerated for 9 years and 18 days, Amanda was finally free to go home. She would serve two years of unsupervised probation, but she was out of jail. I waited all morning at my home in Utah for news, and finally, Jim's call came.

"Someone wants to talk with you," he said and handed the phone to Amanda. Emotionally overwhelmed, Amanda thanked me for my support, my work, and my friendship. Tears soaked my smiling face. It was a good day, a rare day when you do this work.

The Predator

Michael Reid[29] was lonely. He was 27 years old, working menial jobs, living with his parents, had never been in love. He spent his evenings online, scanning dating sites, posting in chatrooms. One evening, he received a message from a woman named Shelly.

"Hi," she began. "I saw your profile and wanted to say hello."

Surprised to have a woman show interest, Mike responded, and they began an online conversation that continued for weeks. They talked about themselves, their hobbies, families, friends, and their insecurities, but very quickly the dialogue became sexual. Both admitted they were virgins.

Shelly, who initially said she was 25 years old, dropped her age to 21.

That was okay with Mike. He believed he'd found a girlfriend. Their enthusiasm for one another grew. She lived in Autauga County, about an hour's drive away.

Evenings passed. She said she was 19.

A conversation later, she confessed to being 17.

Something about this age shift, and the fact she was a minor, bothered Mike. He shrugged off his doubts.

Then she said she was 16.

Then 15.

Mike expressed concerns about her age but enjoyed their 'conversations,' which were conducted completely through instant messaging.

Shelly urged him to meet with her, and they agreed they wouldn't have sex because she was so young. The night before their first date, Shelly said she was 14 years old. Despite this, Mike agreed to meet with her, as 'friends.'

On Thursday, March 30, 2006, Mike drove his van to a public park near Prattville, to meet Shelly.

As he pulled into the driveway, he saw a girl in pigtails, swaying on a wooden swing.

When he stepped from his van, he was swarmed by police officers and thrown to the ground. The girl on the swings was not Shelly but an employee of the Autauga County Sheriff's Department. Shelly, the young woman he had shared his innermost thoughts with, and had, by his admission, fallen in love with, didn't exist. Mike had corresponded with a 50-year-old male sergeant in the Prattville Police Department, who had participated in a sting operation to catch online sexual offenders.

Mike Reid was taken into custody and charged with felony solicitation of a child by computer, a violation of Alabama Statute 13A-006-110.

There was an avalanche of evidence against Mike: All the conversations between 'Shelly' and Mike were written. The lengthy transcripts from the computer chats were sexualized and raw. A family friend recommended an attorney, Alston Keith of Selma, because of their church association. Attorney Keith met with Mike and his parents. Once retained he spoke with the prosecuting attorneys and read the transcripts. Mr. Keith urged Mike to take the deal offered by the DA: plead guilty, and the judge could levy a reduced sentence.

Mike had no prior arrests. He had two speeding tickets on his record from his early driving years. He had dealt with them responsibly. Defense attorney Keith thought it likely Mike would receive a light sentence, perhaps probation and community service. He doubted Mike would be incarcerated, although he could be ordered to register as a sex offender, a term Mike found offensive and wildly inaccurate.

On October 11, 2006, with his attorney's assistance, Mike pled guilty to the solicitation of a child by computer. His sentencing was scheduled for December 5.

"I should have known I was being set up," Mike said during our first meeting, prior to his sentencing. "When women saw my photo, they'd scroll right by and keep searching." Mike Reid believed women found him unattractive.

But during the month they communicated, "Shelly" not only made conversation with him, she and Mike engaged in heartfelt conversations with promises to be each other's first sexual encounter.

"I should have known this was a hoax," Mike said, his voice choked with emotion.

At the urging of attorney Keith, I was retained on November 21, 2006, to help prepare a formal statement for Mike to present at his sentencing. Prior to our initial meeting, I read the arrest report and the legal documents, including the transcripts of the chats. The conversations were sexual and mutually promiscuous; the words lewd and lascivious come to mind.

In this sting operation, adult male police officers trolled chat rooms to find men to engage in sexual conversations, then encouraged the banter. Alston Keith, who routinely dealt with legal matters such as wills, divorces, and real estate, also provided some criminal defense representation; indeed, I'd worked on several cases with him. Mr. Keith viewed this arrest as entrapment, but prosecutors called it a felony sex crime against a child.

But where was the child?

By the time of this arrest, catching sexual predators had become something of a national spectator sport. In November 2004, NBC aired a Dateline episode called *To Catch a Predator*. It was a success. Dateline producers collaborated with members of an online watch group, Perverted Justice, also known as PeeJ, to develop additional episodes of the show.

Show host Mike Hansen, with an NBC camera team, established computer operations to lure men to houses, in different geographic locations across the country, with the promise of sex with underage youth. PeeJ members posed as minors, aged 10 to 15, on chat sites and waited for adults to approach them.

These decoys obtained personal information from the adults seeking encounters with children and teens, including their names, ages, hometowns, professions, and contact numbers. Meetings would be arranged over the phone, and members of PeeJ contacted law enforcement agencies to alert them in advance of the sting operations.

Wildly popular, Dateline aired twelve episodes of *To Catch a Predator* through 2008. The tactics employed by Hansen, his team, and PeeJ, were controversial, and their methods of trolling chat groups, then enticing men to homes with the promise of sex with children, were seen as harassment and entrapment by defense attorneys. PeeJ and host Hansen insisted the decoys didn't initiate conversations about sexual encounters but waited for the men to begin the dialogues.

Members of some communities objected to men being lured to their neighborhoods for illicit sex. One law enforcement agency refused to prosecute twenty-three men caught up in the sting operation. In 2008, the show was cancelled after a man committed suicide in front of a camera crew while law enforcement served a search warrant for his computer. After his death, pornography was found on his hard drive, and members of the crew and PeeJ felt their tactics were exonerated by exposing the man to public scrutiny. The victim's sister sued NBC, *Dateline*, and Hansen, and an out-of-court settlement was reached. The show was canceled, although episodes are in continuous worldwide reruns.

The Predator

Taking a cue from the Dateline shows, by early 2006, at least two Alabama law enforcement agencies, one in Prattville and one in Demopolis, had set up similar operations to catch pedophiles and sex offenders.

Mike Reid had the bad luck to chat his way into the Prattville Police Department sting operation.

Mike had pled guilty, so there was no point in disputing his guilt in the sentencing statement. We met just prior to Thanksgiving. I urged him to make immediate lifestyle changes to demonstrate to Judge John Bush he was making better choices and no longer spending hours on the computer, seeking companionship.

Mike took my advice to heart. He volunteered at a soup kitchen and homeless shelter, serving meals to those in need on Thanksgiving, and beyond. He joined a church group. He attended therapy sessions. He worked in his family's business, relieving some burdens from his ailing father. He became physically active. His demeanor brightened.

"I feel happy again," he said during our second meeting.

We learned that regardless of his sentence, Mike would have to register as a sex offender. My son, an apprentice investigator, physically measured the distance between the Reid home and the nearby elementary school, just to ensure he lived outside the 500-foot distance requirement. If the house was within that distance, he would not be allowed to serve out his sentence at home. Fortunately, the home was well outside the distance.

As a registered sex offender, Mike would be branded and stigmatized. His name and face would appear on databases, and he would never be able to work around children, but he could live in a household with minor children if they weren't his victims.

We found this ironic: how could the victim in this case live in his household?

Unless Mike was the victim.

If Mike was the victim, who, then, was the predator? Was it the police officer who trolled the chatrooms, hoping to entrap men for soliciting sex with minors?

Judges are required to consider several factors when imposing a sentence. In felony cases, a presentencing report is developed, usually by a probation officer, to make recommendations to the court, suggesting either incarceration or house arrest. This account is submitted to the judge, the prosecution, and the defense and examines the defendant's criminal background, including any juvenile charges.

The harm caused to the victim, and to the victim's loved ones, is assessed. Was the victim a parent, a breadwinner, a valued member of the community? How has the victim, or the victim's family, been affected by the crime?

Preliminary sentencing reports typically consider other issues, including:

Was the defendant remorseful?

Was a weapon used during the commission of the crime?

Does the defendant have a corrective action plan?

Keeping this in mind, after interviews with Mike, I wrote a lengthy sentencing statement for him to read to Judge John Bush, who had been a circuit court judge for two decades, elected every four years on a platform of 'tough on crime.' I stressed to Mike the importance of an apology—to the Judge, the community, and the members of law enforcement—for his role in this situation.

Mike was genuinely remorseful about his actions that led to the arrest. He had not used a weapon, although the prosecution viewed the computer as such. Mike had an action plan: community work and therapy. He would take on more responsibility in his family's business, as his father was ailing. Mike promised to use a computer solely for work. His own computer had been seized by police officers; legal expenses had drained his accounts, and that of his parents. In any event, there was no money to buy a new computer.

We anticipated the hearing would be perfunctory, and attorney Keith requested leniency in sentencing, encouraging house arrest, but asked that if Mike had to serve any time at a prison, it would be at an honor farm, a minimum-security facility for first-time offenders.

I arrived at the courtroom expecting a solemn procedure. Rather, the room was filled with spectators. I had to take a seat near the back, sandwiched between people I didn't know. The arresting officers, members of the sex crime task force, and most of the employees of the local law enforcement offices were present, gathered to witness Judge Bush sentence Mike Reid.

"He's a child molester," the woman to my right told me. "And God said he needs to be punished. Lock him up and throw away the key." She smiled, smug in her beliefs.

This was a festive, celebratory atmosphere. Filled with dread, I worried about how the tone of Mike's statement would sound to this hostile crowd. It was written for Judge Bush, not for these bystanders.

Someone had rallied the faithful. This audience wanted blood. *Atonement.*

Mike stood with attorney Keith in front of the judge, surrounded by the people who had prosecuted him, his back to the audience, and bravely read his statement, remorseful, crying. My anxiety mounted; the statement was too long. Judge Bush was bored, people in the courtroom talked and laughed.

I was humiliated for Mike.

With little hesitation, Judge Bush sentenced Mike to 15 years in prison. The courtroom erupted in catcalls, applause, cheers. Members of law enforcement hugged and smiled; high fives flew. It was as if a notorious serial killer had been sentenced to die.

Stunned, shocked, Mike was rapidly taken into custody. I never saw him again. As he vanished into a holding cell behind the judge, I overheard a comment:

"He won't be a virgin for long."

People laughed.

Mike served six years, seven months in prison, primarily in protective custody in an honor and faith dormitory at the maximum-security Limestone Correctional facility in Harvest, Alabama.

He retained an attorney to develop a Rule 32 appeal, citing Ineffective Assistance of Trial Counsel, which was filed in 2010, but his petition was dismissed within months. When Mike was paroled, he duly registered as a sex offender. He found work in a restaurant. The Sex Offender Registry Notification Act (SORNA) requires registrants to check in with a probation officer monthly, and they must notify their POs if they lose, or change jobs, within 72 hours.

Mike developed an interest in photography and began taking classes. In 2014, Mike posted an ad on Craig's List, offering to photograph people for free. "I was working on improving my photo skills," he said. A woman in Mountain Brook, a well-heeled Birmingham suburb populated by doctors and lawyers, hired Mike to take some family photos. She learned Mike was a registered sex offender and reported him to law enforcement. Mike was arrested and charged with a violation of SORNA. He was also charged with the failure to notify his probation officer when he changed his restaurant employment.

He was convicted of both charges.

"And then, I realized my life was going to continue to be difficult," he said. He retained a Bessemer attorney to appeal his original felony conviction of Soliciting a Child by Computer. The attorney found a case eerily like Mike's. In August 2006, shortly after Mike was arrested, a Demopolis, Alabama, man named was convicted of Soliciting a Child by Computer in a similar sting operation. His case was successfully reversed by the Alabama Court of Criminal Appeals in

The Predator

2012, and the man was exonerated. Mike's attorney filed a similar appeal in January 2019. The issue was:

Can a person be convicted when an actual child was never solicited, even though that person believed he was soliciting an actual child?

On May 25, 2021, the appellate court ruled in favor of Mike by acknowledging the lack of a child victim in his case. The ruling read as follows:

This Court unanimously held "that the plain language… as it existed at the time of the relevant conduct, required that a defendant solicit an actual child and not an undercover officer whom he believed to be a child."[30]

Put differently, before May 22, 2009, using a computer to communicate with an adult who is posing as a child was not criminal conduct punishable under §13A-6-110, Ala. Code 1975.

Mike, now in his forties, is free to live his life. His convictions, including the SORNA violations, have been cleared in the court system. It will take a while for his name to drop off search engines. He asked me to change his name in this story.

He is reluctant to discuss this case, but he's angry and dismayed that he's lost so much of his life, blamed for a crime he did not commit.

"Who was the victim?" he asked, "and who was the predator?"

The Armory

The client sat across the table, his back to the door, vaguely answering my questions. His cuffed hands stretched behind his head; fingers flicked the door lock.

Latch, unlatch, latch.

Click, click, click.

He studied my face for a reaction.

There was a bank of windows behind me, easy to open, wide enough for someone as slight as Brandon to slip through to the ground. The conference room was on the second floor of the courthouse, one floor below the jail. An easy fall for a young man, even handcuffed. I knew he considered those windows a gateway to freedom. I often had to repeat my questions. He wasn't paying attention.

Brandon was a young man charged with brutally beating another man to death over a disagreement two years earlier. He was held without bond[31] as he faced a death sentence, or a lifetime in prison. He answered most of my questions in a sullen and dismissive manner, with a lot of *I don't know*. He seemed to be weighing his options, occasionally looking at me, eyes gleaming, daring. *Should I stay or should I go?*

Brandon turned in his chair and opened the door. "Hey," he yelled down the hall. "Guard."

There was no answer. The deputy who had escorted Brandon from the jail was not seated outside the conference room, as he had assured me. Brandon closed the door. Smiled. Turned to face me. I was anxious, scared, yet composed, trying to focus on the next question. He leaned his chair against the wall and stretched his cuffed arms back.

Latch, unlatch, latch.

Click, click, click.

On January 30th, 2006, Bruce Pigg was beaten to death with a garden hoe, allegedly by Brandon Jarrett and James Brannon, in what was described as an argument over drugs and money.

Brandon, 25 years old when we first met, was accused of murdering Pigg, 40, in Double Springs, Alabama, a small town in Winston County, near the borders of Mississippi and Tennessee. A co-defendant, James Brannon, was also charged with capital murder, but he agreed to testify against Jarrett in exchange for a more lenient sentence. Three other young men were arrested on charges of conspiracy to commit murder, and they sang like choir boys in exchange for plea deals.

The two assailants, Brandon and James, along with the three other young men, stashed Pigg's beaten and battered body into the back of his 1985 Chevy Blazer and drove to a nearby motel. The five checked into a room, paid with money from Pigg's wallet, and spent the night watching television, getting high and drunk, while the victim's body remained overnight in the SUV, barely covered by a tarp. The next day, they dumped Pigg's body in a pine thicket about 30 yards off a road, in a heavily wooded area of the Clear Creek Campground, on the southern border of Winston County. Pigg's Blazer was abandoned four miles away from his body.

Brandon and James were quickly arrested, based on a confidential tip. They were charged with capital murder, and the aggravating charges were robbery and kidnapping. The three others were charged with conspiracy to commit murder, as, according to the prosecutor, "they witnessed it (the murder) and apparently did nothing to stop it."

The Armory

Attorney Melvin Hastings of Cullman, Alabama, was court-appointed to represent Brandon. He had a general legal practice and handled primarily real estate, wills, and divorces. An attorney for only six years, he had had no previous death penalty training. At the urging of the non-profit group Equal Justice Initiative, Melvin had me court-appointed as a mitigation specialist for Brandon's case in early 2008, two years after his arrest. Melvin and I had our initial meeting in February, and Brandon's mother, Starlett, joined us.

As mothers will, Starlett blamed herself for her son's troubles and searched her soul to understand the causes of his issues. He had a lifetime of illegal substance use, she explained, suggesting they stemmed from the abuse he had suffered as a young boy from his stepfather. Starlett had given birth to Brandon in 1982, when she was 22 years old. She did not include the father's name on Brandon's birth certificate. She married Rodney Taylor two years later, and gave birth to Brandon's half-sister, Crystal, in 1985. Eight months later, in March 1986, Starlett filed for divorce from Rodney, and he was ordered to pay child support for both children, even though Brandon was not his biological child. Rodney had frequent visitation with Brandon and Crystal.

A year later, Starlett gave birth to another son, Jason Taylor. Rodney Taylor, Starlett's ex-husband, was Jason's father. Shortly after his birth, Starlett petitioned the court to halt Brandon's visitation, alleging Brandon was being beaten and harmed by her ex-husband. But Crystal and baby Jason continued to visit their father.

When he was just over two years old, Jason died from blunt force trauma while at his father's home. Rodney said his son "fell off a swing set." The autopsy listed the death as accidental. To Starlett, her baby's death was suspicious, even deliberate. Crystal's visits were halted.

Starlett cried as she spoke about the death of her baby, and worried about the beatings Brandon had suffered as a young child, at the hands of her first husband. Brandon had struggled in school and was placed in special education classes. He was often in trouble, both in and out of school. His behavior, she said, was at times 'out of control.' He dropped out of high school. She married again, to a man named Roger

Kelsoe, who, she claimed, loved Brandon, and tried to teach him to be a good man. Starlett was helpful in providing the names of doctors, schools, contact information for assorted relatives, and in signing releases so I could obtain many of her personal records.

After Starlett left, Melvin took me to lunch at his favorite bar-b-que restaurant, a staple in all southern towns. At his urging, we dined on fried chicken and biscuits and gravy, washed down with a gallon of sweet tea. I wondered how people could eat like this every day. We then drove to Double Springs, a 37-mile trip to see Brandon.

It is routine for a defense attorney to introduce me to his client. By the time I joined a case, the attorney had usually established a working relationship, based on trust, with his client, and we would all meet so the client would know I was working on his behalf. A court order was issued by presiding judges which instructed jails to allow me to have legal contact visits with the inmates as a member of the defense team.

Brandon was happy to see his attorney. He was respectful, articulate, and forthcoming. His standard-issue jail uniform was neat, and he was clean-shaven. He stood to greet me, executing an awkward handshake with his cuffed hands. *Smiling, friendly, engaged*, I wrote in my case notes.

He signed releases for his medical records, his school records, jail records, and so on. I had a tough time reconciling this friendly young man, thin and slight, with the image of him beating a man to death with a garden hoe.

But when I saw him again several months later, he was surly and smug, unshaven, and sour smelling, focused more on leaning his chair against the wall. Latching the door, click, unlatching it, click, and gazing out the window. A clear intimidation tactic.

Unlike most clients, he had no interest in the work I had been doing on his case. He did not care that I had met family members or friends or former teachers. He did not have much regard for me, or other women. He treated his mother rudely. School records indicated he did not respond well to women teachers. He had shown respect during our first visit, but that was because his attorney was present. Likely,

The Armory

Brandon viewed me as a nuisance, someone to be tolerated. He did not seem worried about a death sentence.

It was as if he had a plan.

Latch, unlatch, latch.

Click, click, click.

Late that August, I met Dr. Catherine Boyer, the clinical and forensic psychologist appointed to Brandon's case, at the Winston County Jail. She was to conduct a mental evaluation, IQ, and other testing on Brandon. Attorney Hastings had visited him the previous week, to prepare him for Catherine's visit. I provided her records and case reports as I gathered them. I made the introduction. They met in the conference room with the windows. He was unwashed and unshaven.

These evaluations typically take about 90 minutes. I had brought a book to read, and case files to update while she worked with Brandon. We were to meet with family members that afternoon. I waited outside the visitation room. Within twenty minutes, Catherine came out, harried and upset.

"I'm not going back in there," she said. "He's scaring me."

This was significant. Catherine worked primarily with criminals. Every Monday, she conducted competency evaluations in Columbus, Georgia, for prosecutors, and then she worked on defense teams in Alabama, primarily on death penalty cases. She was confident, calm, and professional. She was tough. A pro. But Brandon Jarrett unnerved her.

He had been locking and unlocking the door. Staring at the windows.

Latch, unlatch, latch.

Click, click, click.

I saw Brandon one final time, in December. When I arrived at the jail, I was told we could not meet in the conference room that day. It was being painted. That was good news. I had expressed my concerns about the lack of a secure meeting room to the warden after the visit with Catherine, and he had said he would find a better meeting room.

That day I was taken to the third floor, to the Sheriff's offices. I was led into a large room and shown to a table. I sat, got out my legal pad and pen, and reviewed my list of talking points for the visit. Within a few minutes, Brandon was brought into the room. He sat at the table, said hello. The guard left, closed the door. As Brandon slowly looked around the room, a smile spread across his face. I followed his gaze.

We were in the weapons room. The armory. The room was lined with glass-fronted cabinets, filled with shotguns, rifles, ammunition, tear gas containers, batons. Tactical gear. Brandon was mesmerized. His mouth hung open.

I was terrified.

Had we been deliberately placed in here, or was it merely an oversight? Unsure, I tried to focus on the tasks I needed to accomplish. But I couldn't work. I gathered up my belongings, excused myself and went to find a deputy.

The area was deserted, eerie. Somewhere a phone rang, unanswered. I began to panic, was this a set-up? I walked faster. Why did they put an accused killer in the weapons room? Did they want Brandon to try to escape? Did they want a bloody stand-off? A reason to kill the killer?

Maybe I was collateral damage. I was a defense investigator, and some law enforcement officers have suggested working defense is akin to working for the devil, the dark side.

I made my way to the central office. I found a deputy and explained the situation. He took off running toward the arsenal. I found the stairs and left the building. I never saw Brandon again.

The Armory

In early 2009, Brandon Jarrett pled guilty to the murder of Bruce Pigg in exchange for a sentence of Life with the possibility of parole. The date for his first parole hearing is October 1, 2026.

Murders in the Black Belt

A Selma lawyer, whom I will call Jimmy, called one Friday afternoon, in late October 2006. I knew him from a post-conviction case I had just completed. He had been one of the attorneys charged with Ineffective Assistance of Counsel (IOC) and I had worked on behalf of their client, who had received a death sentence ten years earlier, to demonstrate the legal errors committed during the trial. They had done little mitigation, for starters.

While our intents were at cross-purposes during that hearing, both defense attorneys had asked for my business card. I had already completed some defense work for the other attorney.

Jimmy spoke in a gravelly accent I associated with rural, southern Alabama. One syllable word stretched to two or three, uttered in a folksy, aw-shucks, manner.

"My client, Charlie Bennett, killed two men, in sort of a *Pulp Fiction* scenario," Jimmy said. On or about June 18, 2004, Charlie had been a passenger in the backseat of a car driving on a highway through rural Uniontown, Alabama. According to investigators, the two men in the front seat, Alvin Smith, and Kenneth Dixie, were each shot in the back of the head and died instantly. The car careened off the highway and came to rest in a soybean field, where a farmer found the car, and the bodies, the morning of June 19th.

"Charlie said he was fooling with the gun," Jimmy said, "The driver hit some bumps in the road, and Charlie said the gun 'just went off,' like in the movie. The bullet killed the driver, and then he said he shot the other to 'shut up his yelling.'"

Charlie should not have been in that car: just 18 months earlier, he had pled guilty to a federal charge of bank robbery, and a state charge of assault. He was sentenced to four years in state prison for the assault charge, and eight years in a federal prison for the bank robbery. The sentences would run concurrently. His court-appointed attorney said U.S. Marshalls escorted Charlie from jail to court hearings, and he assumed Charlie would remain in federal custody to serve the longer sentence for the bank robbery. But after the trial, Charlie was sent to state prison, to serve the sentence for the assault charge.

Due to the overcrowding of jails and prisons, many state sentences provide for early release dates in exchange for good behavior. But federal sentencing guidelines require full terms be served, with no credit for good behavior, and no early parole. In a stunning example of systemic failure, Charlie was released from an Alabama prison on May 1, 2004, after serving less than half of the state sentence for the assault conviction. Charlie should have been transferred by U.S. Marshalls to a federal penitentiary to serve the rest of his term, but they were not notified of the pending release date. The doors swung open, and Charlie walked through them, a free man. Charlie was not scheduled for release from federal custody until 2010.

Just 49 days into his unexpected freedom, Charlie was back in state custody, charged with the murder of the two men. Prosecutors sought the death penalty. Robbery was the ancillary crime, as a second offense was necessary to obtain a capital sentence. While he disputed the robbery charges, he never denied the murders.

Jimmy asked me to gather and prepare the mitigation for Charlie's upcoming trial and sentencing.

"What's the timeframe?" I asked, mentally reviewing my workload for the next year.

"We'll talk about that when we meet," he said. Jimmy mentioned he would be in Prattville, a nearby town, Sunday morning. I agreed to meet him there.

"I'll give you a file of information, and a copy of your funding order."

Murders in the Black Belt

We met in front of a chain motel. He stood to the side of the entrance as he waited for me. He looked like he had stepped out of a Truman Capote story of southern decadence, clad in a blue and white seersucker suit, a Panama hat, smoking a cigar, which he stubbed out when I approached. He handed me a slim folder, which contained a copy of a mitigation funding order for $3,000, and a page of handwritten notes.

"There's an aunt or a grandma, I think this is her," Jimmy said, pointing to a name and phone number written on the flap of the folder. "His father's serving life without in Leavenworth, Kansas."

"Where's mom?" I asked, wondering why my name wasn't on the court order for funding.

"Who knows? Last Charlie heard, she was in California. Druggie. Could be dead."

"What's the time frame of this case?" I asked. "Has the trial been scheduled?"

He shuffled his feet and cleared his throat. "Tuesday. We'll go to sentencing on Thursday."

"What? This Thursday?" He nodded. I was stunned. "Is this all you have for mitigation? I recalled the reason we had met in court: *Ah, yes,* he had failed one client and put him on death row.

"Why did you wait so long to hire a mitigation specialist?"

"We did have one. She even went to Kansas to meet Charlie's father." He pulled a tattered business card from his jacket pocket and handed it to me. "Just call her. She said she can't work on this case anymore, but she'll give you all the information she's gathered."

I looked at the card.

"Where is she?"

"I think she's in Wetumpka too." He walked toward his car. "Meet me at the Perry County jail tomorrow morning, just before ten. We'll see Charlie. Talk more then." He opened the door to an aged Lincoln Continental.

"Where's the jail?"

"It's in Marion, you can't miss it," he started his car. "See you tomorrow." He waved from the window.

Marion, Alabama. That was a new town for me. I got into my car and dialed the woman's number. The call went to voicemail. I grabbed a telephone book from the car trunk and looked up her name and address, hoping the listing was current. She lived in downtown Wetumpka. I would drop by. Fingers crossed, she was home. A thought danced through my head:

I should have never taken this case.

Sure enough, the woman, whom I will call Martina, was home, and she was none too happy to see me. Thin, with long jet-black hair, I pegged her for mid-40s.

"I can't believe he hired you," she said after she grudgingly held open the screen door to allow me inside. Her small shotgun house was filled with furniture, likely from a much larger house, perhaps inherited from deceased family members. Everything smelled old and decayed, of mildew, cigarettes, and death.

"Did he give you a check for me?"

"No, was he supposed to?" I was puzzled.

"I stopped doing work when he didn't pay me."

"Were you court-appointed?"

She nodded. "I have a funding order."

A light bulb went off. I opened the folder Jimmy had handed me and pulled out the copy of the court order, which suspiciously didn't have my name on it. I studied the date: February 23, 2005. Huh. I suspected this was a funding order generated for her, not for me. I handed it to her.

"Does it look like this?"

She examined the paper, then handed it back. "Yes, that's it. I got this about two years ago."

"Martina, it's my understanding we don't get paid by the state until the case is completed, does that sound correct?"

"Yes, but I had all these expenses from going to Kansas, you know, hotels and meals, airfare, and a rental car." She picked up a pack of cigarettes, shook one out, and lit it. "He promised to pay me, and now he's hired you."

"Wait a minute. Have you given your work to him? School records, interview notes…"

"No, I said he could have my work when he paid me." She sucked hard on the cigarette, clearly agitated. She pushed open a sliding glass door, to let fresh air inside.

"Was he supposed to pay you out of his pocket? Didn't he ask the court for extraordinary expenses to cover your travel?"

She lit another cigarette and stubbed the first one out in a crystal ashtray. She didn't care where the money came from. She wanted to be paid. She was upset. I quizzed her about the work she'd done.

"Did you get his school records?"

She shook her head.

"His medical records?"

"No," she said.

Those were the basic mitigation records, the documents that are the building blocks to begin to explain *how*, as in, how did this person end up charged with capital murder?

"What do you have?"

"I told you, I went to Kansas to see his father."

"And what did he say? Do you have some interview notes I can see?"

"I'll give them to you when I get paid."

I sighed. "The trial is this week, with sentencing on Thursday. Can you please help me out?"

"Why should I? You shouldn't do any work either."

This could be true, given the short fuse I was riding four days to sentencing. The attorney was not engaged. This woman baffled me. Everyone who did indigent defense work in Alabama knew we didn't get paid until the trial and sentencing were complete. That was the rule. Another thought rolled through:

At least I won't have to wait long for payment.

"Have you done any other cases?" I asked, still curious about her work and why I had never heard of her. Women defense investigators were rare in Alabama; mitigation specialists were rarer still.

"Are you a social worker, a PI?"

She shook her head.

"No."

"How did get hired for this case?"

She opened the door and ushered me out. I never saw her again.

As I drove home, I mulled over this encounter. Martina, by her admission, was neither a PI nor a mitigation specialist. She was not a Social Worker and clearly was not a clinical psychologist. Why would Jimmy have hired her? The court order specifically required a trained defense investigator. I could still back out. I didn't have to take the case.

But I'm always up for a challenge.

I briefed Peter, then pulled together my toolkit for the next day. The Perry County Courthouse was 89 miles from my house. I'd never been to this part of Alabama. MapPoint said it would take two hours, and Marion was north and west of Selma. *In the middle of effing nowhere*, I thought as I printed the directions, and assembled release forms for Charlie Bennett to sign. I slipped my notary seal and ink pad into my briefcase, in case there was no one to notarize the documents at the jail. I was ready to leave early the next morning. There was no time to waste.

It was a long drive with limited cell reception.

Jimmy's car was nowhere to be seen. I parked in front of the nondescript brick building, surrounded by concertina wire and weedy grass. A sheriff's deputy, a middle-aged, paunchy White man, approached me as I entered.

"Are you Missus Lehmann?" he asked, pronouncing my name as Leerman.

"Yes, I am," I said.

"Come with me. Mister Jimmy called a while ago, said he couldn't make it today, and you're just to go ahead and meet Charlie, so you can get started."

Somehow, this didn't surprise me. The deputy led me into a dingy attorney meeting room, where Charlie Bennett was handcuffed to a scuffed-up table. He was 23 years old, a young Black man, in a world of trouble. He was quiet, but gracious and seemed to take his lawyer's absence in stride. I explained why I was there, and he told me what he knew, while he signed the release forms. He had an elderly grandmother, whom he had lived with, on a small piece of farmland in Uniontown, a rural town in Perry County. His father was serving a life sentence for murder in Leavenworth, Kansas. He believed his mother was dead. She had disappeared when he was a little boy. Death was the only explanation that made sense to him. He could not believe she would just abandon him. He'd gone through the 11th grade in Thomaston, a rural community. He had no friends, no connections. He was alone. He suggested I talk with his teachers.

"Maybe they can help?" he suggested, a spark of optimism in his eyes, a tentative half smile.

I studied this young man, sitting by himself with a stranger, his own attorney AWOL. I thought of my own sons, one a year older than Charlie, one a year younger, both trying to navigate adulthood, albeit with a better map than Charlie held. Despite my worries about payment and having enough information to present at sentencing, I knew I would help him.

The woman who notarized paperwork was out that day. I was glad I brought my gear. His grandmother sat in the reception area of the jail. Jimmy had asked her to meet me. She was a woman of few words and offered little to the conversation. She planned to testify and had arranged for time off from work for the trial, which began the next day. We briefly talked through her testimony for his sentencing. She would explain his parents' disappearances, how raising him had fallen onto her shoulders, with no family support and little assistance from the government. She worked multiple jobs, all poorly paying, simply to keep a roof over their heads. She had been ill-equipped to raise a child, and she would tell this to a jury.

We knew Charlie would be convicted of capital murder. All we could do was try to avoid a death sentence. She understood.

Were there any others who could testify for Charlie?

She gave me the name and number of the family minister.

That was it. I thanked her and headed to Uniontown.

Charlie had little medical care from infancy through adolescence. He said he had been to a clinic a few times. The facility was a single-wide trailer parked in a commercial lot in downtown Uniontown. Most of the commerce had fled the area, but the clinic was open. It was the sole provider of medical care for the impoverished residents of the town and outlying rural areas.

There was a doctor, a nurse, and a receptionist staffing the clinic that day. There were no patients in the building. I explained I needed records for Charlie. The doctor and nurse came out to the waiting area to chat with me. They knew of Charlie, but he had not been treated medically there for years. The doctor said the poverty in the Black Belt of Alabama was "staggering" and cited Perry County as the poorest in the state. "The medical needs here are unimaginable," the nurse said.

The receptionist made copies of the general and medical releases Charlie had signed, then disappeared into another room. A few minutes later, I had his immunization forms, notes from a physical conducted when he was five years old, ordered by the Alabama Department of Health and Rehabilitation, and a sports physical for school. That was the sum of Charlie's medical care.

They wished me luck.

I did not have an address to drive by the house where Charlie had grown up. He had gone to school in Thomaston, a town in Marengo County, twenty miles from the clinic on Highway 25. It was a rural stretch of some small houses and farms, a stray dog or two, broken down cars raised onto blocks, collapsing barns, and churches. Lots of small churches, Baptist and African Methodist Episcopal (AME) congregations, common in the south. Thomaston was a fleabite town: I didn't see any businesses once I hit the welcome sign. The Amelia L. Johnson school housed grades pre-K through 12th. There was a small, crowded reception area and I explained to a curious secretary I was working for Charlie and needed to obtain his school records.

The principal heard our conversation and stepped away from her office to speak with me. She knew Charlie and was aware of his criminal trouble. She took the release forms and returned shortly with his file folder. She pointed me toward a copy machine just as school let out for the day. Children stared at me, a White woman, a stranger, as they passed, to catch their buses. She suggested I return the next day, to speak with his teachers. I finished photocopying the file, made note of his teacher's names, and the principal promised to let them know I'd be back the next morning. I took the records and left.

Jimmy called just as I was leaving the school. He was at the courthouse and wanted an update. They had finished jury selection. The trial would begin in the morning.

"Did Martina give you her notes, case reports, records?"

"No, to all of it," I said. I relayed what I knew and asked if her expenses were to come out of my funding order.

"No," he said. "You have a separate order."

He assured me I would be paid. I returned home for the evening. After a late dinner, I began writing the case report and generating an invoice. I logged 11 hours and 303 miles that first day and gained little information.

"Sometimes, mornings, I'd see him running down the highway, towards the school," the teacher said. "I'd toot my horn, and wave, to let him know I saw him."

The high school teacher, who coached football after school, wiped his brow, his bright smile faded into concern. He shook his head.

"He could surely run, yes, he could. He ran like the wind."

I could have asked why he didn't stop to give Charlie Bennett a ride to school those mornings. Instead, I let him tell me about Charlie. An innately talented athlete who could not play sports because there was no money for uniforms, no transportation for after-school activities. Other teachers told similar stories. They had all driven past Charlie as he ran multiple miles, to school in the early mornings when he had missed the bus, sometimes in heavy rain, sometimes in terrible heat, and in the cold. They praised his running ability, his determination to get to school on time, when other teens would simply give up and return home. Every one of the six teachers I interviewed smiled, hung their heads, shrugged. One wept.

"Wasn't there someone who could have driven him to school? Wasn't he old enough to drive?"

Charlie lived out in the country, with a relative, I was told. They were poor, *hardscrabble* poor, like many of the families of the children they taught. The items most of us take for granted were luxuries in that community. Maybe they had no working car; but if they did, they probably didn't have gas money, or if they had gas money, they needed the car to go to work.

His support system was fragile, ephemeral. Charlie had been on his own.

Several spoke of the pervasive, generational poverty that afflicted their community. More than half of the residents lived below the poverty line. These teachers, paid by a state with abysmally low property taxes, were likely among the best-educated and highest-paid people in the Black Belt, a swath of black dirt land that sprawled through 17 counties from Alabama into Mississippi. Teens could not get after-school jobs because there were no businesses to offer employment. A drive to a convenience store could be thirty miles round-trip.

Perhaps the places we are born and raised play a greater role in our future success than many other factors. We know that being born into abject poverty and abuse can be overcome when there are options, avenues which lead to opportunities for achievement, if someone gives you a compass. Charlie had raw talent and dedication, but he had no one to guide him to the roads that led away from the Black Belt, toward places that offered prospects for a better life. On his own, and out of desperation, Charlie made bad decisions and faced a death sentence.

As I drove back to the Marion Courthouse, to arrange subpoenas for the teachers who'd offered to testify at his sentencing, I visualized Charlie running along Highway 25, trying to get to school.

Running like the wind.

Charlie was convicted quickly in a trial that lasted two days. Thursday was the sentencing. Charlie was grateful for the support of his teachers, for showing up for him, for their testimony. We had no expert witnesses to explain Charlie's story to the judge and jury, so I took the stand to tell what I had learned over four days. He could have been their son, a nephew, a grandson – he was a human being whose life was worth saving. He had been raised in dire circumstances with limited options in the poorest area of Alabama, if not the southern United States. The jurors listened to all the testimony attentively, compassionately, and spared him from death, with a vote of 10-2 for life without parole. It was a procedure about as melancholy as any I have witnessed.

I don't know how Charlie felt about the sentence. He was whisked away from the courtroom. His lawyers and I were relieved, but for different reasons. Jimmy, the lawyer, knew there wouldn't be 20 years of appeals. None of us could be called ineffective.

This was the end of the line for Charlie. The prison doors would slam shut, never to open for him again.

Naively, in 2006, I thought we had somehow won by avoiding a death sentence. That was the objective of mitigation, and clearly, we had proven to the jurors his life should be spared. In those early days of my criminal defense investigations, I believed a death sentence was worse than a life sentence. Over time, I realized that a person could remain optimistic even when condemned.

But a sentence of life spent in confinement with hundreds of prisoners, without a chance of parole, extinguishes hope.

A brutal reality.

Murders in the Black Belt

I would choose a death sentence. That much I know.

That afternoon, I finished my invoice and emailed it to Jimmy. I'd had to reduce my hourly rate and shave off time to not exceed the $3,000 of approved funding. In those days, the first chair attorney gathered the invoices for those who worked on the team, submitted the billing to the state office of indigent defense, and one check was cut. Within weeks, Jimmy received payment for our work: his, the other attorney's, and mine. He cashed the check but failed to pay us. He disappeared. We learned he had stolen not just from us, but from the legal trust account that held client money, retainers for work he hadn't completed. He was stripped of his law license. He didn't even attend the administrative hearing.

I appealed to the state indigent defense office. I wrote to the Judge. The other attorney filed a petition for extraordinary expenses for both of us, but it was denied. Some suggested I try to find Jimmy, but I knew I would never receive a dime, so I managed my loss. Perhaps Martina had been right: maybe I should not have taken the case. Losing money stung, but the lessons I learned from Charlie's case were invaluable.

In the world of indigent defense, justice is an arrogant notion.

The Tornado

Overture

Just north of Dothan, the rain fell so hard I feared the road would wash away under a savage river current. The wipers whipped across the windshield at maximum speed, unable to maintain a sightline. I'd have to pull over, to wait for the rain to taper off, but where? The highway was too crowded, big trucks blew by at full speed, drivers undaunted by the storm; my economy rental car was buffeted by their slipstreams, then engulfed by water. The weather service issued a tornado watch that morning. In previous years, I would have stayed home and made this trip another day, but I could not reschedule this meeting. I no longer lived in Alabama. My flight home was early the next morning.

Act One

Nine days earlier, I had flown into Montgomery from Salt Lake City. When Peter's job relocated to Utah four months earlier, in January 2012, I had a dozen active capital murder cases in various stages of development in Alabama, and I dedicated this trip to five of my clients. I'd spent the first three days working in blighted and deeply impoverished areas of Birmingham, *ganglands*, where my last interview took place in a Medicaid-funded physical rehabilitation hospital. I met a young man, a rapper, not yet 30 years old, who had been shot 14 times while he performed at a nightclub. His assailant was a rival rapper, gunned down by retaliatory fire before police arrived on scene. This man I visited, a client's brother, was paralyzed from the waist down, and lost both legs due to infections that didn't heal. He expertly piloted a wheelchair to a patio garden. A blanket covered his residual legs, just enough bone to sit upright, to form a lap, enough bone left to eventually be fitted with prosthetics. He had a beautiful face framed by thick dreadlocks; his eyes were large and bright. He spoke lyrically, a cadence in a rich tenor; he laughed, he smiled. He then sang, a caged bird, mourning the loss of freedom. He smiled again. He was happy to see me, to talk about his brother, his mother, his extended family. He didn't get many visitors.

"Hey, when you come back, can you bring me a carton of cigarettes? I'll give you some money." I declined the money, one of my personal occupational hazards. I have paid water bills, and purchased diapers, meals, and groceries for family members of my clients, expenses that weren't tallied on my invoices. An hour later, I returned to the hospital and handed his ward nurse a bag with a carton of cigarettes, a couple of disposable lighters, a variety of candy bars, and a 12-pack of Pepsi, along with a card thanking him for the interview. I never saw him again. His brother's case was eventually settled without the trouble of a trial.

The next meetings were in Gadsden, then Auburn, with attorneys and witnesses, developing testimony and gathering records. Another day found me in Selma, where I sat on a couch covered by a sheet of Visqueen plastic and attempted to persuade an 84-year-old woman to convince her condemned son to take a resentencing deal that would allow him to live out his days in prison without a death warrant swinging like a noose over his head. He'd been on death row for a quarter century. She became irate, she wanted no part in this conversation. Her son was innocent, she believed. If he couldn't walk out of prison a free man, he would be rewarded in heaven for his persecution on earth.

"Jesus will set him free," she insisted. "Yes, ma'am. It's in God's hands."

Act Two

Sadness and miles linked my cases, and they took years to resolve. Happiness on these trips came from spending evenings and Sundays with my daughter and, eventually, my first grandson. By late April 2012, I'd made the Montgomery-Atlanta-Salt Lake City flights so

The Tornado

frequently airline attendants recognized me, not by name, but by beverage. My seats were occasionally upgraded from economy to business or even first class. I was often handed a complimentary glass of red wine once we reached cruising altitude. At home, I spent days writing interview notes and case reports. Then I'd tackle the monthly billing. Before 2015 pretrial work in Alabama paid only when a case was completed, so it wasn't unusual for my invoices to accrue a year or two of billable hours and expenses before finally being settled.[32] I took on the post-conviction cases to maintain a steady flow of money from the huge pro-bono coffers of international corporate firms, to keep my business solvent, my credit card bills paid in full each month. Two or three weeks later, I'd be on a plane again.

One day, after a particularly arduous work trip, I came home and looked at the tomato-red walls in my formal dining room and the adjacent piano room. The previous owner had installed beautifully lined red and yellow draperies when she'd built the house, custom-made for the wide expanse of windows in both rooms. That day I realized the paint colors and the heavy silk and brocade draperies upset me. I wanted light to pour into the rooms, through the windows. I needed to see my favorite tree: a Weeping Norfolk Spruce, planted when the home was built in 1996; years later, it had grown large and beautiful.

I got a stepladder from the garage and took down the draperies and curtain rods and put them in the trash. I left the custom blinds in place, for shade and privacy when I wanted it. I drove to Lowes and bought some paint rollers and brushes, a drop cloth, painter's tape, a gallon of primer, and another gallon of the light-yellow paint that covered the walls throughout the three-story home. I spent a week painting those two rooms, finally turning that house into our home.

That was work I could control.

Act Three

The drive from my daughter's home in Wetumpka to Dothan was just over 140 miles. I'd made this trip along U.S. Highway 231 often over the past sixteen years, but I'd never encountered turbulent weather. On those trips, I'd worked cases, served court papers, and driven my children to meet their father in Florida for court-ordered visitations. The timetable was as familiar as the route: two and a half hours to Dothan, four hours to Tallahassee, six hours to Gainesville, nine hours to Orlando. This road was slow but direct. I'd woken to a light, misty rain that morning, but as I drove south, the sky darkened with bulging, pregnant clouds, a lightning stroke away from rupture.

Just south of Troy, the wind picked up. I white-knuckled the drive for the next hour, radio off, senses focused and alert to avoid unwanted incidents. Anxious and worried, I made a left turn off 231 just inside the Dothan city limits onto a secondary highway and pulled into a strip mall. The rain slowed to a light drizzle. As I exhaled, then deeply inhaled, it felt so good to breathe I wondered if I had held my breath for the past hour. I waited a few minutes inside the car and spotted a parking space in front of a Subway sandwich shop. I needed a restroom before I reached my destination. I knew better than to use a bathroom at a client's home. I also knew Louise and Wayne, the people I would see that day, believed these sandwiches were healthy. A recent heart attack had prompted Wayne to eat foods that weren't fried, so I decided to pick up a sandwich for him to enjoy while we talked. Louise would take a nibble or two of her lunch, then set the food aside for later. She didn't have much appetite, especially when we discussed the last day of her granddaughter Shae's life, a little girl who had been beaten to death one night nearly a decade earlier.

Patricia Blackmon, Louise's daughter-in-law, was my client. She lived on Alabama's death row, one of five women in the state sentenced to death for committing a murder deemed heinous, atrocious, and cruel.

Several weeks earlier, I received a letter from Patricia, which could have been written by a southern matron, busy with her spring planting, rather than a woman who had been convicted of killing her adopted daughter, a two-year-old child, a murder she denied.

"I got my little garden up and going, and it's doing well so far. I've got tomatoes, lettuce, cucumbers, and jalapenos, as well as an orange tree. I don't know how big or if it will even produce any oranges. It's being grown in a bucket and I'm excited to see that it came up! I don't know if I'll grow any watermelons this year."

I pictured Patricia as she sat across from me during our visits, a wrist shackled to a heavy metal ring anchored on the scarred wooden visitation table. Her eyebrows plucked, her makeup carefully applied, her nails expertly manicured, her hair coiffed, her white uniform pristine and ironed. She was composed, relaxed, like she lived in the lap of luxury, rather than a death row cell. She was soft-spoken and gentle in our conversations, but I suspected she'd once had a deep well of anger that roiled just below her serene surface. I'd read the crime scene and autopsy reports. The evidence was some of the worst I'd seen.

Just after I pulled out of the Subway parking lot, a car on the opposite side of the highway lost traction and hydroplaned into the back bumper of the rental, bounced off, and quickly disappeared. I was alarmed but relieved I hadn't automatically braked hard when I was hit. I could have gone into a tailspin as well. I considered the situation, unsure if I should stop, call 911 to report an accident, or keep driving. I chose the latter. Wayne and I would check out the damage when I got to the Johnson's house. Just another mile or so.

Suddenly, the rain stopped altogether. Grateful for the break, I hoped this was the end of the severe weather, but my optimism faded when I saw the sky was a shade of light green.

A very bad sign.

The hairs on my arms and neck began to prickle, and the low-level headache I'd had all morning rocketed into throbbing pain. My neck ached; my teeth hurt. The barometric pressure had noticeably dropped, and my body reacted instantly to the shift. I shook three more aspirins into my mouth where they slowly dissolved. Hailstones pelted the rental; first the size of gravel, then the ice grew to the size of golf balls, which bounced merrily off the hood. I hoped the car would be drivable after the storm passed. I needed to get back to Wetumpka that night. My daughter planned a nice meal. My first flight left early the next morning for a connection in Atlanta. I couldn't miss it. I wanted to go home.

The rain poured down in sheets.

Coda

Just as I pulled into the Johnson's yard, there was a blinding lightning strike on the next block. *If I'd driven any further down this road...* The thunderclap was simultaneous; we were in the bullseye of the storm. I pulled as close as I could to the front door and briefly wondered about the wisdom of parking under the limb of a massive oak tree. Wayne opened the door to their sparsely furnished rental home and waved me in, "Hurry," he yelled.

The wind picked up. There was no sense in using the umbrella, so I grabbed the sandwiches and my purse. Once inside, soaked, Louise brought me a towel, and I attempted to dry my arms and face. I pulled my wet hair into a soggy ponytail. At once, the tornado sirens screamed from a nearby fire station, a terrifying, otherworldly sound, and Louise grabbed my wrist and pulled me down the hallway, where she had created a narrow enclosure by closing the bedroom and bathroom doors, away from windows. She had pulled a mattress from the bed to protect us from debris if the roof was torn off. Wayne sat calmly at the kitchen table and ate his sandwich. I pulled my phone from my purse and quickly exchanged some text messages with my husband, to give him the Johnson's address, so he would know where I was, to tell him I love him, just in case...

I said a silent prayer, although I'm rarely silent and not a pray-er.

I hoped I wouldn't die that day, not in that house, where dried cat shit sat in a pile on the living room carpet and had been there at least since my first visit a year earlier.

Lightning and thunder collided over the house, momentarily drowning the screams of the tornado sirens. Then the power went out. Louise reached over and held my hand. I closed my eyes. We waited for the roar of a freight train, the sound of a tornado.

The Murder House

Anyone who has driven from Dothan to Enterprise, Alabama, on Highway 84 has seen the house. It sits, deserted, just outside Wicksburg, on the way to Fort Rucker US Army base. It's a small cabin abandoned to the elements; left as it was when an elderly woman was brutally slain in January 2000. It's due west of Teaser's Gentleman's Club—a strip joint. Locals call it The Murder House.

Shortly before Rex Allen Beckworth was released from the Easterling Correctional Facility in Clio, Alabama, a cellmate named Mark Peacock mentioned his elderly grandmother, who lived alone, kept jewelry and money in her home. Beckworth, incarcerated for robbery, burglary, and theft, paid attention. Peacock described his grandmother's home, conveniently located on a highway but isolated from neighbors.

Once freed from prison, it didn't take long for Beckworth to reunite with his half-brother, James Earl Walker, and propose they rob the woman. Walker, himself recently out of jail, was living in a trailer in Etowah County. James was 20 years old, with a wife and a baby girl he was crazy about named Cherish. James tried to support his little family, but he had few skills as he'd spent a significant portion of his teens and young adult life incarcerated. He had dropped out of school in the seventh grade, after attending seven different schools. His mother moved him throughout Alabama each time she found a new man she hoped would support her and her drug habit. James was often homeless during his teenage years. He earned a GED while in juvenile detention.

Sometime near the end of 1999, James and Rex allegedly took a drive on Highway 84 out of Dothan toward Enterprise to scout the location. They found the house, and a car was parked out front with a for sale sign on the windshield. Rex went to the door and spoke with 87-year-old Bessie Lee Thweatt about the vehicle she was selling.

Several weeks later, on a night presumed to be January 5, 2000, Mrs. Thweatt's house was vandalized when someone smashed a window with a cinder block. The light bulb in the carport was shattered, and, according to a detective's statement, her telephone line had been cut. James claimed he had run off into the surrounding woods when Rex destroyed the window. He said he wanted no part of the crime.

The elderly woman was hit in the face, multiple times, with a blunt object. She was then shot in the head with a .22 caliber rifle. She lay dead on her living room floor while her assailant(s) ransacked her little house, searching for the money and jewelry her grandson had promised.

James' sister Angela worked the night shift as a housekeeper at Motel 6 in nearby Dothan. When James and Rex unexpectedly showed up in the early morning, she put them into an empty room. Days later, James and Beckworth were arrested. Angela told police investigators she had seen a rifle in the trunk of Beckworth's car. A .22 caliber rifle was found by a hunter in Power Dam Creek and retrieved by law enforcement officers. The bullets were badly damaged, and a positive match to the shell casing found inside Mrs. Thweatt's home could not be made. The rifle had been stolen in late 1999 from a house not far from the Thweatt home.

Since his arrest, James has adamantly denied being in the house the night of the murder. Although it was never conclusively determined who shot Mrs. Thweatt, both men were charged with capital murder, with burglary as the aggravating crime. The half-brothers remain on death row at Holman Prison in Atmore, Alabama.

♦ ❖ ♦

The Murder House

Attorneys with the New York law offices of Goodwin Procter, an international corporate firm, retained me in March 2008. The firm took on the appeals for James as a *pro bono* case. My job was to help them prepare the mitigation case for the March 2010 state habeas corpus appeal, which carried an Ineffective Assistance of Trial Counsel claim lodged against James' original trial lawyers. James and Rex had been charged in Houston County, and the habeas appeal was heard in the same Dothan courtroom where James had been found guilty in 2003. The case took me all over the state as the two men had lived primarily in the central area of Alabama, vacillating between Calhoun, Clay, Etowah, and Talladega counties. Their father had been institutionalized at Bryce Hospital with severe mental illness until his death. In between periods of incarceration, he spread his seed prolifically throughout the state, and his sons often lived with a variety of relatives, half-siblings, and tangentially related cousins.

Unlike many of my clients, I didn't spend much time with James. His lawyers visited him frequently on trips from New York, so they didn't rely on me to convey information to and from the client. James and I met only twice during the two years I actively worked on his behalf. But I logged long hours tracking down family members and acquaintances for interviews and records. The family tree of this crowd grew like Alabama kudzu—weedy ground cover rather than a forest.

When I conducted the interviews for this case, I was usually accompanied by a lawyer, typically a second or third-year associate, and each came prepared with a slate of questions. They would tell me what they needed to accomplish, whether it was to speak with specific family members or locate and interview the jurors who had sentenced James to death.

We never could persuade his mother to talk with us, but I had several meetings with his sister Angela, who used every opportunity to shake me down for money. Her living situation was precarious, and we met in diners and fast-food restaurants, where I would buy her meals. At times, Angela would bring her non-custodial daughter, and I'd feed her, too. I did find several people, including an employer who eventually testified on behalf of James, and a former stepfather, Tim, who had tried to teach James how to work a job, and care for his little daughter.

Tim verified the story that during his marriage to James' mother, she had carried on a long-term romance with Rex, James' half-brother, and co-defendant. I located and interviewed an incestuous clan of paternal family members in central Alabama who were mean, belligerent, suspicious, mentally ill, and dirt poor with extensive rap sheets, which included sexual crimes perpetrated against family members. Incest was a common occurrence in the White families I worked with—child prostitution seemed more likely found in Black families. Both of James' grandmothers had criminal histories. One of these women, living alone in a derelict single-wide mobile home without running water and no neighbors in sight, seemed so anxious I thought she'd pull out a gun or a knife and attack. Luckily, I was accompanied by clinical and forensic psychologist and mitigation expert Catherine Boyer for that interview. Grandma, in a very matter-of-fact manner, told us about being raped by both her father and grandfather. She had been molested frequently by a brother. Both of us, seasoned by years of capital murder work, were shaken from the encounter. We agreed to try to never do the Walker family interviews alone.

There was a cousin who allowed me and another attorney into his trailer. He poured out his heart to us. He talked about how James' father, his uncle, raped him repeatedly as a young boy. He cried. He was so emotionally damaged he was unable to work and lived on food stamps and a meager SSI check. He would not sign release forms for me to get his psychiatric records, nor would he agree to testify about the abuse he suffered, even though it would help his cousin, James. To get him to change his mind, I returned to his trailer twice more before the hearing, he never opened his door to me again.

I spent one odd morning with James' aunt Bonnie. I worked all day with Josephine, a third-year attorney who spoke fluent Mandarin Chinese and held doctorates in both chemistry and law. Josephine and I perched on broken white plastic chairs outside Bonnie's two weather-beaten side-by-side single-wide trailers, linked together by a rotting wooden bridge. We were surrounded by goats. The woman said she counted the goats three times a day, morning, noon, and evening, but never came up with the same number twice.

Bonnie had somewhere between eighty and too many goats. The place reeked of manure in 100-degree heat. Flies buzzed. We used our notepads to fan the air. I'm not fond of farm animals. I avoid eating goat cheese because, if it happens, my mouth senses hair, my throat constricts, and I gag. For a time, doing yoga with baby goats was a fad I didn't understand. I would never willingly allow goats to crawl on me.

We obtained little usable information from Bonnie aside from a jumbled-up story about how our client's father, who was her half-brother, may have fathered her son, whom we also met that morning. Josephine and I checked the bottoms of our shoes before we got back into the rental car. I blasted the air conditioning with all four windows open, and we aired ourselves for at least five miles. Goat stench was trapped in my nostrils for hours.

"Why didn't she invite us inside?" Josephine asked as we drove away. "It smelled terrible out there." I let the question hang while I tried to figure out how to get us back to town. She fidgeted in the passenger seat.

"I thought people in the south were supposed to be so friendly, offering iced tea and cookies."

"Josephine, did you seriously want to go inside those trailers?" I shuddered. "Can you imagine what it smells like in there? Did you really want to drink anything she would offer you?"

She laughed. "Yeah, you're right." Josephine flew back to Manhattan that evening. After this gamey exposure to Alabama, she never returned to work on this case.

Several months later, in 2009, I drove three hours to meet three young women lawyers for a 9:30 breakfast at the Dothan IHOP. One associate ordered hot chocolate rather than coffee and Rooty-Tooty

Fresh 'N Fruity© pancakes smothered in whipped cream. Honestly, I thought she was someone's little sister who tagged along because she was too old for a babysitter and too young to stay by herself. I hoped I wouldn't have to work with her.

But it was a first-year associate attorney, Shelby, who was to be my partner that week. We were to track down jurors from James' original trial. We planned to gently question them about their participation in the murder trial—which had occurred in August 2003—six years earlier. We sought to unearth any hint of juror or judicial misconduct they may have witnessed or experienced. We told them about the upcoming evidentiary hearing, and we were trying to get James out from under a death sentence. A new trial or a sentence of life without parole were our goals.

There are three questions an experienced investigator saves for the end of these conversations, which I call the golden questions.

The jurors are asked:

1. What made you decide to impose a death sentence?
2. The second question pertains to the sentencing phase of the trial, and we ask who testified on behalf of the defendant, and what does the juror recall about the testimony.

We want to understand the thinking of each individual juror.

Prosecutors portray defendants as monsters to frighten jurors, to goad them into guilty verdicts, especially in cases that carry a death sentence. It was the responsibility of the defense team to show the jurors why sparing James' life mattered, to explain how he ended up in this situation. A mitigation specialist is a required member of all defense teams handling death penalty-eligible cases, and her role is to gather information and prepare witnesses to tell the story of the defendant during the sentencing phase of a capital trial.

3. The third golden question was this: Was the juror coerced to vote for death during sentencing deliberations? Sometimes, there are jurors who, for religious or other reasons, want to vote for life without parole. When deliberations run long,

and patience runs thin, a juror may bow to peer pressure and vote with the majority.

These small communities, like Dothan, Alabama, are populated by people whose lives are deeply intertwined, for generations, through school, work, church, and daily activities like football games and potluck suppers. The jurors must resume their usual interactions once the trial is over, and we explore the go-along-to-get-along aspect of sentencing.

In Alabama, a minimum of 10 out of 12 jurors must vote for a death sentence for it to be imposed. But prior to April 2017, this rule was irrelevant, because a judge could impose the death penalty regardless of the will of the jury. This quirk in Alabama's judiciary rules did not affect James' case: all 12 jurors voted to give him a death sentence.

We wanted to know why.

If a juror is willing, these conversations can go on for well over an hour, and I've had several go on for much longer, particularly when a juror has struggled emotionally by imposing a death sentence. I've also had the door slammed in my face. Jurors tend to have a very good memory of their service on a murder trial, particularly when they've sentenced someone to death.

Shelby, the young associate, was in her mid-twenties and lovely enough to have been a beauty pageant winner. And, sure enough, she casually chatted about her pageant experiences during the drive from our hotel to the Dothan suburbs, to locate our first juror, a schoolteacher. As we neared a stately brick home in a manicured subdivision, I suggested she let me manage much of the interview and she could ask follow-up questions near the end. She agreed to this strategy.

"I'll take notes," she said, which was fine by me. Whoever took the notes had to write up the case report, which often took as long, if not longer, than the interview itself.

In this business, I rarely schedule an appointment unless it's with a professional: a doctor, a teacher, a mortician, a minister, or an attorney. I prefer to call on lay witnesses—regular folks—unannounced, and this ambush tactic generally works well for getting my foot in the door, catching a witness unprepared, and hoping for a scintilla of the famed southern hospitality that dictates politeness to strangers.

I pulled onto a curved driveway that led to the garage. The door was closed. We got out of the car and approached the entry. As I was about to ring the bell, a white Suburban came up the drive. We turned and walked toward the vehicle.

The juror, a petite blonde woman, exited the SUV with her two daughters, the eldest a teenager. The woman had used her remote control to open the garage door. They stood around us as I briefly introduced the attorney and myself and asked for about ten minutes of her time. We needed an hour, but no one would ever agree to this amount of time, so I always asked for ten minutes. She invited us into her house. A Golden Retriever bounded out of the door to greet all of us. The woman sent her daughters to the kitchen for snacks and homework. She led us into the living room.

I began by asking her what she remembered about the case, and James. She stated the facts of the case succinctly. We moved through her recollection of the prosecution witnesses, including the jailhouse snitch, Tim Byrd, who had testified James had confessed to shooting the woman while they were cellmates in the Houston County Jail. We slowly and methodically worked our way through the guilt-innocence phase of the trial, and I was about to ask the juror what the most significant aspect of the case had been when Shelby impatiently interrupted the woman:

"Did you find James guilty because of Byrd's testimony? Didn't you realize there was no concrete evidence against James?"

The juror was surprised by this question. I was, too. Shelby had just accused the juror of convicting a man of capital murder with no evidence. I gave Shelby the evil eye and shook my head. I spoke before the juror could take a breath.

"There was evidence, but nothing that definitively tied James to the shooting except for the testimony of the jailhouse snitch, right?" The juror nodded. I moved the conversation on to the penalty phase. I had noticed relics of a religious household around us—a painting of Jesus and his disciples at The Last Supper hung above the fireplace, a King James Bible on the coffee table with a bookmark holding the place of a passage, and the juror wore a small cross on a thin gold chain at her neck.

"I'm curious," I said. "Did you have difficulty dealing with the issue of imposing a death sentence because of your Christian beliefs?"

She sighed and fingered the cross. "I did. I had to pray on this all through the trial, to ask God to give me the strength and the wisdom to make the right decision."

The jurors, while not sequestered, had been repeatedly admonished by the Judge to not read newspapers, watch news accounts, or discuss the case with anyone, including their spouses.

"And did you seek counsel from your minister?" I asked.

She hesitated to speak. "I did. I spoke with my pastor because I was so troubled about the sentence."

And, *voilà*, she admitted she had committed an error during the trial. It was flimsy, but it gave us something to work with. I was about to ask her if, to her knowledge, any of the other jurors had consulted with their ministers, when Shelby, our raging bull in a china shop, knocked over a second display case.

"So, you violated the gag rule by speaking with your minister?"

The juror froze. It dawned on her she had confessed to discussing the case with her minister during the trial. Silence descended. Realizing she'd said too much, the juror stood up and asked us to leave.

The interview was over. The woman ushered us out of her house and would not speak with us again.

Shelby began to cry.

"I guess I blew it, didn't I?"

There was no need to respond. She knew she had messed up. We couldn't salvage what happened, we couldn't use what she'd said, but we had to soldier on. We had eleven other jurors to find, as well as the two alternates. But we needed to put a little time between this mess and the next interview, so instead of heading back into Dothan, I found Highway 84 and began driving west.

"Do you want to see the murder house?" I asked. People love crime scenes, and lawyers especially like a tour. It's a treat for them to visit the sites after spending hours studying case evidence and trial transcripts.

She brightened. "I'd love to."

Through experience, I developed crime scene rules, and I relayed these to Shelby. "I'm going to park on the side street, off the property, and away from the highway. We can walk around the house, you can look in the windows, and take photos, but don't touch anything. Okay?"

"All right," she said. "Is the house unlocked?"

"Yes, and the door from the carport is standing open; at least, it was the last time I went by."

"Have you gone inside?"

"No, but I've brought other lawyers here, to see the house."

"Why can't we go inside?"

I couldn't believe she'd asked that question. "Trespassing. It's still privately owned."

She thought about this for a moment, then promised to stay out of the house. We passed the sign for Teaser's strip club, and I slowed for a left turn. "There it is," I pointed to a derelict wooden structure barely larger than a cabin. The yard was overgrown with unpruned fruit trees and weeds.

I parked on a side street about a hundred yards away from the house. There were no neighbors close by, although a manufacturing business had opened across the side street in the years since the woman's murder. Kudzu continued to overtake the structure, and I knew one day the house would vanish altogether, leaving only a brick chimney as a reminder. As we walked down the road, I pointed out a large hole in the roof, at the back end of the small house.

"It's slowly falling in on itself, which is why we won't go in. That and the probability of a family of raccoons living inside." I stopped and took photos with the Olympus camera I grabbed from the trunk of my car. "Watch where you walk. This grass is lousy with burrs and thistles. Snakes, too," I warned as we cut through the overgrown yard to the one-car driveway. We walked up the fragmented concrete. I pointed out the broken glass from the lightbulb that had been smashed the night of the murder a decade earlier.

The door to the house had been pushed halfway open. I stuck my head inside and saw the house was just as it had been since my last visit, and the time before that. A letter from the Social Security Administration, along with discolored and yellowing bank statements addressed to Mrs. Thweatt, lay strewn across the floor, slowly mildewing, dissolving in the ever-present humidity.

To the left, in the crude kitchen area, dirty pots and pans sat on the stovetop. Mrs. Thweatt was murdered before she could clean up after her last supper. An unwashed plate and fork sat on the crude wooden counter. Someone had overturned a couch and coffee table. A file cabinet lay on its side, drawers pulled open, files ransacked. A television had been smashed, and glass shards sparkled on the floor. Dead leaves had blown in and lay scattered. The scent of musty decay hung in the entranceway.

"Let me show you something. Look inside," I said. Shelby stepped into the doorway.

"I think the house has been left exactly as it was the night of the murder," I said. "No one, not her daughters or their husbands, no one came and took care of her things."

"Oh, wow," Shelby said as she pushed the door wide open and walked right into the house.

Entitled brat. She must have been a joy as a teenager.

I considered saying something but shut my mouth. Shelby had no intention of listening to me anyway. She was the attorney, and I was the hired help.

Curiosity usually gets the best of me, and I knew I could have followed her inside, but there was something so sad about this house I couldn't enter it. I wasn't afraid, the violence had passed long ago, but what had been done to the old woman was monstrous. I was deeply troubled that no one from her family had cleaned up her belongings or secured the house from the elements.

Shelby described what she had seen as we drove back to Dothan. There was a large stain on the unfinished wood plank floor where Mrs. Thweatt had bled out from the gunshot wound. The ceiling had fallen onto the woman's unmade bed at the back of the house. Her few pieces of clothing had been pulled out of the drawers and lay on the floor.

That night, Shelby and I ate a quiet dinner. Neither of us felt much like talking. I nursed a glass of wine, and she drank something with an umbrella. We did more interviews over the next few days, but they yielded little in the way of useful information—she took notes and was reluctant to ask questions. I dropped her off at the Dothan airport on a Friday afternoon.

I made the drive home, and I never saw Shelby again.

Shortly before the March 2010 hearing, I accompanied a more senior attorney as we spoke with Mrs. Thweatt's family members, to see if they would agree to a sentence of life without parole for James. They wept. They spoke about how much they had loved the old woman and missed her and how her murder called out for the Christian retribution of an "eye for an eye."

That day, something about their demeanor, their crocodile tears, struck me as wrong. Their mother had lived in a shack for 67 years, and not one of them thought to either put it to rights or burn it down when she was killed. No one publicly blamed the grandson, who told Rex Beckworth she kept money and jewelry at her house. Her family abandoned the woman's personal effects and left the house of horror intact for all to witness.

I've been to the Murder House. It stands as neglected and forgotten as the woman who once lived there. And James remains on death row.

III

The Execution of Robert Butts

2005 to 2018

Robert Butts, Jr.

On May 4, 2018, the State of Georgia executed Robert Butts, Jr. Sentenced nearly 20 years earlier for a murder he might not have committed, Robert was executed because of the collapse of the support systems most of us take for granted: family, friends, teachers, community leaders, and ultimately, the American justice system. Robert was doomed from the moment he was born. Every significant person in his life failed him, from his mother to his court-appointed defense attorneys. But it is, perhaps, the district attorney, the representative of the state, who should shoulder the burden of Robert's death, because he lied about who fired the fatal gunshot in the separate trials for Robert and his co-defendant.

Meeting "Team Butts"

I was hired in October 2005 by William Clineburg, a senior partner at the Atlanta-based law firm King and Spalding, to work as a mitigation specialist on Robert's case.

Founded in Georgia during post-Civil War Reconstruction, King and Spalding is the oldest law firm in the South. Clineburg received a hand-written letter from Robert begging for help to appeal his death sentence, and the letter piqued Clineburg's interest. International corporate firms like K&S have the resources to tackle good conscience cases, and Clineburg assembled a team of associates to research Robert's trial and subsequent conviction. The financial commitment was steep: King and Spalding's efforts to gain Robert either a new trial or new sentencing through the State of Georgia's Rule 32 procedure cost millions of dollars.

Once the attorneys were satisfied they could find the information to support an ineffective assistance of counsel claim against Robert's original trial lawyers, the team hired a social worker as a mitigation expert. In turn, she asked me to develop the mitigation case that would form the basis of her testimony, and the testimony of other experts, for the evidentiary hearing.

The lawyers had scant information during our initial meeting. They knew Robert had a brother, a sister, and a mother who missed his trial in 1998. His grandmother and a great aunt attended the trial, but didn't testify during the sentencing phase, although they should have. There was mention of his mentally ill father, but no one knew how to find him. I left Atlanta after the meeting and drove three hours back to Alabama. I began to strategize my work out of Robert's hometown of Milledgeville, Georgia, a small town outside of Macon located five hours and a time zone away from my home.

Amy, a young mitigation investigator employed by the Georgia Resource Center (GRC) had been visiting Robert as a courtesy to the K&S team, acting as a placeholder until I could be contracted to join Team Butts. Attorneys from the non-profit center represented Robert's co-defendant, Marion Wilson, posing a tricky conflict of interest. Each had pointed the finger at the other as the shooter. A wall was needed between the two. Amy sent me what she had on Robert, which amounted to little more than addresses and telephone numbers for his mother Laura, a sister, and a brother.

I met Amy at the Georgia Diagnostic and Classification Prison in Jackson one morning in early November. We entered the facility together and went to see Robert.

Our first meeting was brief. Introductions are best made by someone the client trusts, and Robert was clearly smitten with Amy. His eyes lit up, his smile widened, and his demeanor became happy and upbeat the moment he saw her. Tall, model thin, and in her early 30s, Amy was adorable. She and Robert maintained a friendly, flirtatious banter during our visit. After initial pleasantries, I remained on the sidelines while Amy and Robert talked football. I spent the conversation observing Robert. He was 28 years old and had been jailed since he was 18. He was a tall, good-looking man with an easy, friendly smile. He enjoyed Amy's company. From the conversation, I intuited Amy spent much of her weekends watching the games, as did Robert, and they closely followed several teams in addition to the Atlanta Falcons. Near the end of the meeting, Amy explained I would be working on his case. She promised to see him when she could. Robert's shoulders sagged, and his smile faded as they hugged and said their goodbyes. I mentioned I would return for the afternoon session.

"A'right," he said. "Catch you then."

Procedures and Connections

Visits with a death row inmate are laden with security precautions—even for legal visits. Each time I went to this prison, I waited outside a small, run-down wooden building until the door opened and visitors were allowed in. I've stood in the blistering Georgia heat, freezing cold, and pelting rain, waiting to be allowed inside. There were two scheduled visitation times for legal business during the weekdays—from 9 to 11 a.m. and 2 to 4 p.m.

The door never opened before a quarter past the hour, and sometimes, it was much later before we were allowed entry. One visit lasted only 19 minutes because it took so long to be processed. Once inside, I identified myself and passed through a metal detector while my jacket, shoes, legal pad, and pen were sent through a scanner like the ones the TSA uses at airports. Then I was patted down, and my pants pockets turned inside out. I shook my shoulder-length hair to show I didn't have any bobby pins or barrettes that could be used as a weapon in the hands of a convict. Then I stood at a concession-style window to hand over a letter from a King and Spalding lawyer, a formal visitation request.

The warden's office would have received this letter via fax several days in advance, and a quick background check had been conducted on me. The letters contained a copy of my driver's license, my Social Security number, and birth date. The warden's secretary checked for felony convictions and outstanding warrants. Anyone with a felony, whether from a drug-related or violent crime, isn't allowed to enter a prison as a visitor, even in a professional capacity.

Next was the daily visitation log, where guests signed their names, occupations, and the names of the inmates they were scheduled to see. I lied every time I signed the log. Corrections officials throughout the country fear class action lawsuits, and many wardens don't allow private investigators into their facilities. To circumvent this issue, I had the attorneys list me as a paralegal on the paperwork.

"But you're an investigator, a mitigation specialist, building our case through your skills," lawyers said when I explained this protocol.

"You're so much more than an assistant," my husband exclaimed. Peter knew how invested I was in being an investigator. It was as much a part of my identity as woman, wife, and mother.

"I don't care what they call me," I said. "I just need to get into the prison."

After the sign-in, I approached a second window and handed my car key and driver's license to yet another officer. In exchange, I received a round metal disk with a number that corresponded to the hook on which my key and license hung. Surrendering these personal items was required at all jails and prisons, so in the event of a riot, fire or something bad, prison authorities knew who was inside. I left my wallet locked in the trunk of my car. I carried no money or credit cards into this facility. I wasn't allowed to buy treats or cigarettes for this client. I wore glasses with clear lenses—my prescription sunglasses remained in the car. My eyes had to remain visible in every jail and prison. The fact I used sunglasses to reduce brightness and ward off migraine headaches carried no weight with prison officials. It was futile to even begin the conversation. Dark glasses aren't allowed inside. Sunglasses—like cigarettes, postage stamps, and sex—have value. They're currency to inmates.

Having cleared these hurdles, I stepped into a sally port with other lawyers and paralegals and descended into darkness. Klaxons blared, signaling the opening and closing of barred gates. Upon exiting the gurney we were inside the prison.

In silence, our thoughts remained private as we hiked down a long hallway. The prison came alive through a rising din of voices as we drew closer to the inmates. Cheaply framed motivational posters—Hang in There! Soar High! Reach for the Stars!—were mounted on the dingy cinder block walls. Another poster warned I would get my own cell if I brought contraband to an inmate. *No need to worry about that.* I reached a third security area. The guard, a Black man in his late 50s, reliably greeted me each visit with a friendly smile and a wave.

"How are you today?" I asked in my most cheerful voice.

"You here to see Butts?"

"Robert. Yes, I am."

The guard unlocked an enclosed, chain-link walkway. Its gate clanged and locked behind me. A second gate was unlocked by a different, but equally friendly, guard who also greeted me with a smile. The gate slammed shut behind me as I was led into the visitation area for maximum security and death row inmates. There were two small, barred enclosures, cells bolted into the concrete floor, reserved for legal purposes, as well as a long, narrow room in which multiple legal conversations could be held simultaneously. The guards and I greeted each other with recognition from visit to visit, but I never knew their names. We didn't see one another often enough to be anything but cordial.

On this afternoon, my first solo visit, the guard opened the door to a cell opposite the enclosure we occupied earlier. There was a small, scuffed plastic table and two wooden chairs inside. The guard assured me Robert would join me shortly. I looked at my watch—2:50 p.m. I'd already used nearly an hour of my appointed time simply getting into the prison.

I waited for Robert to be brought up from his death row cell block.

The noise inside the Georgia Diagnostic prison was raucous and unsettling. A constant drone surged through the area and reverberated through the floor and walls. I could feel the sound. Doors crashed open and slammed closed. Men whooped when they saw a woman, any woman. Sounds were punctuated by an occasional scream of warning, of fear. Trays dropped. Metal chairs scraped floors. Clangs and bangs and rattles. Every sound, every word, bounced off concrete and steel, echoing throughout the prison. I often had a challenging time understanding what people said to me over the cacophony.

Ready for business, I had a questionnaire to work through with Robert to document his personal history, to identify his family members, school, and medical history. All of it would help me begin the process of mitigation, to better understand how Robert came to live on Georgia's death row.

Completing this questionnaire is an arduous process. Over the years, I edited the questions, trying to reduce the time it took to work through the form. It was a crucial tool and served to open communications between us. Many of my clients didn't understand the circumstances that led them to where they were: either in jail awaiting trial or convicted by jury and sentenced to death row. Lawyers were typically poor sources of personal information about their clients. They focus on the crime, the witnesses, the alibi, working through discovery and picking a jury. The lawyers depended upon me and I, in turn, relied on the clients to give me details to begin the mitigation process: parent's names, occupations, sibling names and ages, schools attended and contact information for family members. My investigations grew organically from there. But sometimes, the client couldn't give me even the most basic data, and I had to find it another way. Because of the time it took to process into the prison, it was unlikely we'd get through the mitigation form that afternoon.

My anxiety grew. Robert was a convicted murderer, and I'd be locked in this cage with him. My palms were sweaty. I worked to slow my breathing. No matter how many times I visited a jail or prison, an insistent internal voice always reminded me something bad could happen. Logically, I know harm can happen anywhere. But locked inside a prison, even as a visitor, I was straitjacketed, stripped of all control. Apprehension bedeviled me every time I waited for an inmate.

This is my prison mantra:

> *Don't let the lights dim, a fire start, or a riot break out.*

Robert Butts, Jr.

A guard appeared with Robert. He held Robert's forearm in one hand and a large ring of keys in the other. The guard motioned me inside the cell. Robert's ankles were chained together, so he shuffled his feet as he made his way inside the meeting area. His hands shackled behind his back. I wondered how Robert would be able to sign release forms with his hands cuffed. I was about to say something when the guard unlocked the metal cuffs. Robert placed his hands in front of his body, and they were re-cuffed. Robert entered the cage, we both chose a chair and sat. The guard locked us in and walked away. I looked at my watch. It was 3:06. There was less than an hour left. I knew better than to ask for more time.

Seated across from Robert, I took a moment to really notice him. He was a good-looking Black man. At nearly six feet, he was well built; muscular, but not bulky. To appear relaxed, he leaned back in the wood chair, the front chair legs off the ground and his head propped against the metal bars of the cell. A toothpick dangled from his mouth.

While we chatted about the lunch I'd shared with Amy at a strip mall in McDonough, halfway to Atlanta, I placed a yellow legal pad and three different sets of release forms on the table. All of them were free from staples, paper clips, or metal binders. Like bobby pins or hair barrettes, they could be used as weapons and were forbidden.

"Robert, in the little time we have, I'm going to ask you questions so I can get started in Milledgeville, where I'm headed when I leave here."

His chair's legs slapped loudly against the floor as he sat upright and leaned toward me. He took the toothpick out of his mouth, a flicker of interest crossing his face. "You going to Milledgeville?"

"I am when I leave here. I'm going for a few days. I want to meet your mom and your family. I'll start gathering records. Let's talk about your family."

"What do you want to see them about?" he asked guardedly.

"I need to meet everyone I can so we can begin preparing for your appeals."

"Why?"

I flipped idly through the information form, then looked him in the eye. "I need to understand how you ended up here."

"There's not much to know," he said. "My life was pretty normal."

I nodded as I picked up the first release. "Let's get these releases signed, okay?"

He extended his left hand for the pen.

I smiled and handed him the pen with my left hand. "I'm a lefty, too."

"This is a general release," I said. "I'll use this to get your school records and others, like any criminal ones, if you have them." I looked at Robert, and he nodded.

"Okay, sign here, put in your Social Security number and birth date." I pointed to the areas. He squinted at the words, held them away from his face, then pulled them closer to his eyes. The wrist shackles hampered his attempts to get a clear view of the documents.

"Shall I walk you through this, to make sure you understand what you're signing?" I had worked with people who couldn't read and tried not to embarrass them.

Robert sighed. "I can read. But I need glasses, and the prison won't get them for me." He rocked back in the chair again.

"So, you can't see to read, or you can't see at a distance?"

"I think a little of both," he said. "I have trouble seeing the words on a page, and I can't really make out faces or anything at a distance. I get bad headaches."

"Do you have a prescription? Is it just the prison won't provide glasses for you?"

"I've got a prescription. I saw the doctor, but I can't get any glasses."

ROBERT BUTTS, JR.

I shook my head. I picked up the general release form and walked him through it. I pointed out where he should print his name, his birth date, and his Social Security number. I noticed his birthday was in May, a few days after mine.

"Ah, you're a Taurus," I smiled. "Me too."

"Oh, yeah?" He looked up with interest. "When's your birthday?"

I told him, handed him a release form for his medical records, and pointed out where he should write his vital statistics. I asked if he had gone to a pediatrician as a kid or had a family doctor.

"Dr. Banks, or Banker, I think. At the health department." I made a note. I picked up the third form. "Were you in the military?"

"Nah." Robert stuck the toothpick back in his mouth.

"Was anybody in the military? Your mom? Your dad?"

"Not my mom. I don't know about my dad. My sister's in the military." I tucked the form back in with the others. "How about Social Security? Did you receive SSI benefits?"

"I don't know. You have to ask my mom."

Robert listed the schools he'd attended. He dropped out in 11th grade. He named his siblings, two sisters and two brothers. He was the second-born child. He gave me his mother's telephone number and address. He named two uncles, Tony and Johnny Waller, whom everyone called Pete. Both men lived in Milledgeville.

"Waller?" I asked and checked the spelling.

"Yes," Robert said.

"My maiden name is Waller," I said. "That's quite a coincidence, isn't it?"

"Where's your family from? Alabama?" he asked.

"No, I live there now, but I grew up in Miami. But both of my parents were from Iowa," I said.

"That so? Maybe we're related." We laughed at this twist. "You should ask my mom."

Robert surprised me by asking me about my family, my husband, and children. Most of my clients expressed little interest in my life. I briefly mentioned my son and daughter in college and my middle child in the Army infantry. This caught his attention. The Iraq war was escalating, despite hopes it would be over quickly before the country was devastated and countless lives were upended, damaged, and lost. I explained Danny was stationed in Germany but scheduled to be deployed to the Anbar Province in Iraq before Christmas.

"I'll bet you're worried."

"I am." I sat forward and placed my left hand over my mouth. A profound sadness engulfed me. I struggled not to cry. My husband, children, and I had gone to Germany for two weeks in early October to spend time with Danny before his year-long deployment to the Middle East. Since then, I'd been gripped with persistent feelings of dread, panic, sorrow, and abject fear.

I was grateful for my work. It distracted me from dwelling on personal horrors—which, compared to Robert's, seemed smaller and more manageable.

"Hey." He reached over and lightly tapped my right hand with the pen. "He'll be all right."

"Man, I sure hope so." I smiled. I felt relieved. Robert and I had begun to make a connection. I placed the signed releases between the pages in my legal pad and changed the subject. "Can someone in your family help you get a pair of glasses?"

He shook his head.

"Have you asked your attorneys?"

"Nah. They're doing so much for me already. I can't ask them for glasses."

"Do you have your prescription?"

"It's in my, uh, room." Death row prisoners live in small, solitary cells. They can't see their neighbors when inside their cells, but they can hear them. They're housed separately from other inmates. DR prisoners live on cellblocks, and each has a communal television room where inmates were allowed to gather to watch special shows, notably sports events. Robert lived on a different cellblock from his co-defendant to avoid any potential hostilities.

"Will you give me a copy of the prescription the next time I see you? Maybe I can get you a pair of glasses."

"You'd do that?"

"I can try." I pulled the questionnaire toward me. "Okay, let's talk about you. How would you describe your life growing up?"

He leaned back again in the chair. He fiddled with the toothpick.

"Well, I guess I had a normal childhood."

Milledgeville, Georgia

Over the next two years, I learned a normal childhood, if there is one, was not what Robert had. It took me several months to coerce his mother into a face-to-face conversation. It took me two years to piece together Robert's life from his birth to the time of his arrest right before his 19th birthday. This word, *normal*, would haunt him for years to come. I spent a lot of time with his siblings, his uncles, cousins and teachers to build Robert's biography, to understand the series of events that placed him, at 21 years old, on death row.

His maternal great-aunt Doris Cooper was initially reluctant to work with me. "I don't like White women," she said. "Especially ones with yellow hair." It turned out her husband David had a thing for blonde, White women. But Doris was the matriarch of Robert's maternal family, and I needed her to tell me their history. Robert's mother, Laura, was often unreliable. Mary Cooper, Laura's mother and Robert's grandmother, was comatose from a stroke she'd suffered years before. In a typical Milledgeville twist, Mary Cooper became a patient in the hospital where she'd been employed as a caregiver.

During my first interview with Doris, she sat in a chair across the living room from me. The late afternoon twilight caught her face, bathing it in an amber glow. At that moment, I saw my father's sisters in her face: my aunt Evelyn, my aunt Ginger, and then, my father.

"Doris, I think we may be related," I said.

"No, ma'am. We most certainly are not."

But our fathers were contemporaries and came from the same part of the country. Her father, Earnest Waller, was a White man born in 1918 in Iowa. As a young man he came to Milledgeville and became acquainted with Mary Lee, a young Black teenager. They had daughters Mary, born in 1938, and Doris, born in 1940. He had a wife and children in Chicago, but he visited Milledgeville often when the girls were young.

"When he was old and sick, someone brought him to our home on Jefferson Street for my mama to take care of him," Doris said. "They just drove up and dropped him off at the curb." Earnest Waller died in Milledgeville in 1993.

Her daughter said Courvoisier was the drink of choice for Doris. I brought her a bottle each time I needed to work with her. She'd sit in her chair, drinking Courvoisier and Coca-Cola, and we'd talk. She spoke about their family history, Laura's troubles with addiction, Robert's arrest, and the trial that she'd attended. Eventually, she welcomed me with home-cooked meals of fried chicken, cornbread, okra, and chitlins.

She came to agree with my theory that our fathers were cousins. All it took was a little cognac.

Milledgeville is a small town in the middle of Georgia. The population was estimated at 19,397 in 2005 and then registered 871 fewer residents

Robert Butts, Jr.

in 2020. The town is evenly split between Blacks and Whites. Milledgeville is situated on the Oconee River, 45 minutes northeast of Macon and two hours south of Atlanta. It was the capital of Georgia from 1804 through the Civil War and into Reconstruction.

A prominent feature of Milledgeville is the Central State Hospital, once the world's largest mental hospital with more than 200 buildings on 2,000 acres. Two underground tunnel systems linked the buildings, so patients could be moved between facilities during hurricanes, tornadoes, and the Civil War. When Union General William Tecumseh Sherman launched his famous "March to the Sea," a campaign marked by the burning of Atlanta and other cities, he led his troops to Milledgeville. He ordered the soldiers to burn the government buildings and penitentiary on the Central State grounds. But Doctor Greene—director of the Georgia State Lunatic, Idiot and Epileptic Asylum—convinced the general to spare the facility and give extra rations to the patients. At one time, the facilities were home to an estimated 13,000 patients. Today, only three operational buildings house up to 300 patients. Most buildings are closed and left to decay. Rumors of hauntings and ghosts persist, and people sneak onto the grounds for seances.

According to *Atlanta Magazine*, the first patient, Tillman B. of Bibb County, arrived in December 1842 chained to a stagecoach, but not allowed to ride inside the vehicle. He died six months later of "maniacal exhaustion." Many of Robert's relatives, including both his maternal and paternal grandmothers as well as his father, worked at the hospital and then became patients themselves.

Milledgeville is home to the Georgia Military College, an elite prep school, as well as the lifelong residence of esteemed Southern writer Flannery O'Connor. I love her stories of misfits and criminals. Her farm is now a museum I toured during one work trip.

My client, Robert Butts, known to his family as Junior, was born in 1977 to Robert Earl Butts Sr. and Laura Waller Butts. Laura was 18 years old, and Robert Sr. was 23. Laura gave birth to her first child, a daughter, when she was 16.

In 1978, when Robert was an infant, his father began to exhibit signs of mental illness. Laura's brother, Johnny Waller, stated in his 2007 affidavit and testimony for his nephew Robert Jr.:

"I got out of the Army at about the time Laura and Robert Senior were married. We lived together for a bit, and I knew Senior before mental illness took over. He was a nice guy, and he was very smart. He was in college and working at Central State Hospital. He and Laura were happy. They both were working, and things were good. But Senior began acting oddly around the time Robert Jr. was born. He would take buckets outside to collect rainwater. He built wooden crosses and put them up on the hill near our house. He started reciting verses of something, I don't know what, and he took to wandering all over Milledgeville. It wasn't long before Laura took Junior and left him. She was scared that he would hurt them."

His mental illness rendered him unable to work. In December 1978, when Junior was seven months old, Senior was committed to Central State Hospital with the diagnosis of schizophrenia, paranoid type. So began a cycle of arrests, commitments, hospitalizations, and releases to outpatient services and halfway houses for Robert's father, which continues to this day.

Locating Senior was a challenge. He was a big bear of a man. The first time I found him, I was intimidated, scared even. I explained I was trying to help get his son, Junior, off death row. He was pleased. He smiled broadly at the mention of Junior. *I love my son*, he told me and signed the releases, which enabled me to obtain thousands of pages of Senior's psychiatric treatment records.

When I needed to find him for an attorney or expert witness interview, I'd check with his elderly aunt, the matriarch of his family, to see if she knew where he was living. If she didn't, I dropped by the Oconee Mental Health clinic to look for him at mealtimes. Someone would tell me to which house or apartment he was assigned. If no one had seen him lately, I'd check the local jail. If those avenues of chance failed, I'd drive around downtown Milledgeville looking for him. Sometimes, I found him at the carwash on Jefferson Street, where he'd hang out with the workers and polish chrome for a bit of coin.

ROBERT BUTTS, JR.

With her husband descending into madness, teenaged Laura went looking for fun. She frequently left her two children with her mother or her elderly, alcoholic grandmother, Mary Lee Waller, and hit the streets in search of drugs, booze, and sex. Laura moved into a federally subsidized apartment with baby Robert Jr. and his 2-year-old half-sister. In May 1980, when Robert was three years old, Laura gave birth to his half-brother Tamayo. In 1982, just after Robert entered kindergarten, his half-brother Dominique was born.

Laura was 23 years old with four small children.

By the time Robert was in second grade, there were indications of what was happening to him. His teacher, Henrietta Reeves, wrote in 2007 that Robert:

"... had a great deal of difficulty accepting nurturing, hugs, pats on the back, words of encouragement... children who are not receptive to nurturing or affection may be reflective of a failure of a parent bonding with, or nurturing, her child. Robert was a quiet child. He was not aggressive, but he was a lonely child, a loner, and I believe that life, in the second grade, was a struggle for him. He was a little boy, and by that young age life had already taken him too much up and down. He always seemed tired, weary even, and I believe that when a child is living in a stressful environment, at home... this depletes the child's spirit."

In 1986, shortly after her youngest child was born, Laura was arrested and charged with driving under the influence. By September, when Robert was beginning the fourth grade, his mother had begun using crack cocaine. During a 2006 interview, Laura said a niece had come to her house one day and asked to borrow a baking pan. When Laura asked why, her niece said she wanted to make crack cocaine. Laura tried crack with her niece, a decision that rapidly developed into a daily habit. She was 27 years old, a mother of five small children, and addicted to alcohol and drugs. Except for Harold Burton, father to the youngest daughter, none of her children's fathers provided any income or assistance for their children, nor did they provide any parenting help.

Laura frequently disappeared for days at a time.

On August 1, 1987, Laura's mother, Mary Cooper, with the assistance of a federal program, helped Laura purchase a double-wide trailer on a small plot of land on Pettigrew Road on the rural outskirts of Milledgeville. Tammy, the eldest daughter, went to live permanently with her grandmother. Complaining about "too many children, too much trouble," Grandmother Mary and great aunt Doris brought bags of groceries to the four children left in the trailer. Ten-year-old Robert was in charge. Tammy reflected on this memory in her clemency petition to the Georgia Board of Pardons and Parole in 2018:

"I did not realize, until just recently, that once I was removed from my mother that Robert had no one to look up to, or to protect him or guide him. Suddenly, Robert was the eldest in the home, with no one to help him. That must have been worrisome for him, especially as he, and my other siblings, grew older. Once I was gone, Robert took care of our brothers and sister, and I wasn't there to help him."

By July 1988, younger brother Dominique began receiving a federally mandated Individualized Education Program (IEP) for special education services because of his behavioral and learning difficulties. His school records described him as "aggressive toward others and very disruptive in the classroom." Years of testing commenced for Robert's half-brother, which eventually led to a diagnosis of attention-deficit/hyperactivity disorder and oppositional defiance disorder. The medical evaluation, conducted by the Medical College of Georgia concluded, "both [diagnoses] were organic in nature due to exposure to alcohol prenatally... frontal lobe not working well." Laura admitted in a 2007 interview she drank heavily throughout all five of her pregnancies.

The same month that Dominique began receiving special education services, Isaac, Laura's live-in boyfriend and drug supplier, was arrested on charges of aggravated assault with a deadly weapon when he shot a man during a drug purchase. His plea deal required him to pay a third of his victim's hospital bills.

Up through the sixth grade, Robert managed to earn As and Bs. He finished that school year with only ten absences. By this time, his father had been arrested ten times and hospitalized on 20 occasions at the

Central State Mental Hospital to receive treatment for paranoid schizophrenia.

While Robert was balancing his grades against his troubled home life, his brother Dominique continued to behave badly in school. As he aged, he became increasingly aggressive toward both students and teachers. By May 1990, he was eight years old, but still in the first grade. It was reported he began making sexual overtures. "He came up behind Mrs. A, felt both her breasts, felt her on the legs; touched Mrs. B on her bottom... Mrs. Butts stated that Dominique exhibits the same behaviors at home." Nevertheless, Dominique was promoted to the second grade. It had been noted in reports throughout the year that Laura repeatedly failed to provide Dominique's prescribed Ritalin. Teachers' notes and school records portrayed a child out of control.

By November 1990, Dominique's behavior had become dangerous both at school and home. His mother often neglected to fill Dominique's prescriptions, which by now included Haldol, an antipsychotic medication, to control his auditory and visual hallucinations. There were documented incidents of Dominique jumping off a moving school bus and running through traffic. Laura consistently missed parent-teacher conferences. Her boyfriend, Isaac, came to the school in her stead. After Isaac was jailed, Harold, the father of Robert's youngest sibling, attended the meetings.

On Nov. 19, Jones reported to the school Dominique shot his brother Tamayo in the head with a BB gun. While Isaac claimed both he and Laura were home at the time, Robert recalled he was alone with his younger siblings cooking dinner when the incident occurred. Both Tamayo and Dominique corroborated Robert's version of the story. Robert was 13 years old.

It was during this time Laura received inpatient treatment for alcohol and drug abuse. She was hospitalized for 28 days. Medical records were included in her petition for Social Security Disability. "She was in two detox programs... 1991 and 1994. These records indicate she is unable to control her drug intake. The longest period she was abstinent was six months in 1991. There is a history of prostitution to get drugs. She was living on the street for a time, using crack and drinking approximately one pint of alcohol daily and leaving her children alone at home." There was a documented report about boyfriend Isaac chaining Laura to a motel bathroom sink for two weeks during this period.

In August 1991, Dominique was sent to Augusta University's Medical College of Georgia for an outpatient psychiatric examination, referred by the Georgia Division of Family and Children Services (DFCS) in Milledgeville. He was nine years old. The doctors in Augusta wanted to hospitalize Dominique for long-term, inpatient treatment, but Laura refused, later admitting she didn't want to lose his SSI check.

The reports generated by DFCS made it clear that child protective services investigators were fully aware of the children's unstable and dangerous living situation, with Laura often gone, and 14-year-old Robert trying to manage a mentally disturbed brother. DFCS reported Laura told them her boyfriend Isaac "physically abused her, and the police contacted DFCS about removing the children."

By this time, there was such an extensive record built around Dominique's behavioral problems that Robert's struggles to balance school and the home situation became widely known to the community at large. DFCS had an open child protective services case for years, yet the boys and their little sister continued to live alone—sometimes, as Robert reported, without electricity, running water, or a working telephone when their mother failed to pay the bills. His youngest sister wrote in her 2018 clemency petition:

"I remember that he would fix us breakfast in the mornings and made sure I got on the bus to school. He'd make dinner for us at night. He would try to fix my hair. He helped me with my homework. He took care of me, pretty much on a daily basis. He made sure that Tamayo and Dominique didn't tease me or pick on me. When our mother was gone, Robert tried to make life normal for us. I was a little girl in a trailer of big boys. We would all worry about our mother when she was gone. I recall being very tired at school as I never seemed to get enough sleep, and my grades were affected."

Robert Butts, Jr.

In August 1992, Robert began ninth grade at Baldwin High School. He had five absences. He passed his classes, except for one semester of Algebra I. This was his last good school year.

During our frequent visits between 2005 and 2007, I often shared with Robert stories from the people I met in Milledgeville. I recall asking him about his shoes and clothing. He said they were usually "raggedy," and his mother would get them from charities. He also said his maternal grandmother, Mary Cooper, would buy a few articles of new clothing and a pair of shoes at the beginning of each school year for each of the children. Robert recognized these purchases were a hardship for his grandmother, who worked as a housekeeper at Central State Hospital. He said as he entered high school, he was self-conscious about his appearance and tried to keep his clothing and shoes clean and in good condition, but "Dominique would get into my stuff and wear my clothes and make a mess out of them." At one point, Robert put a lock on his bedroom door to keep Dominique out. Dominique circumvented the lock by breaking Robert's bedroom window to gain entry.

Holding onto personal items was difficult. Robert told me that one year Harold Burton gave him a portable stereo for Christmas. "I loved that boom box," Robert recalled. "I loved being able to listen to music." Music took him away from his problems. His enjoyment was short-lived. When he came home from the first day of school after Christmas break, his boom box was gone. His mother had pawned it.

"Anything I ever got would disappear," he said. Harold said when he got his paychecks he would try to buy back some of the items Laura pawned.

In August 1992, Robert entered 10th grade at Baldwin High School. His grades showed he was struggling. He had 12 absences for the year and earned only four credits. He was not promoted to the 11th grade.

On June 14, 1993, Sheila Brown, a Baldwin County DFCS investigator, began looking into allegations Dominique had been sexually molested. She contacted Dominique's school liaison. The liaison later wrote, "... reportedly there were a number of children in the neighborhood who were being molested. It was discussed with Ms.

Brown the possibility of investigating the family for neglect issues. Ms. Brown reported that a file has been accumulated from previous investigations. She will currently assess the family for possibilities of current abuse and neglect."

There were no additional records about this, or any other, investigation.

In August 1993, Robert repeated the 10th grade. He earned 2.5 credits. In the meantime, his sister Tammy graduated with honors and began college, eventually earning a bachelor's degree and joining the military as an officer.

Baldwin High School teacher Henrietta Taylor noted in a 2007 affidavit that Robert was a loner and often slept in class.

"While I did not know the circumstances of Robert's home life, and I did not know that Robert's mother had a substance abuse problem, I did know there was something wrong. This was a young man with a lot going for him. I felt that Robert was trying to figure out who he was, seeking an identity… like many young people, he wanted to fit in somewhere—he wanted to be accepted and to have friends. I knew that his mother was not a positive influence in his life… it seemed to me that Robert was powerless. He had no security and no structure… this was a young man who was hopeless."

Tired of being made fun of for his clothing and shoes, Robert resorted to stealing items to pawn for cash. In early 1994, Robert committed two burglaries at nearby homes with a friend. He was arrested and confessed to four counts of burglary and criminal attempt to commit burglary. Robert was one month shy of his 17th birthday.

In July, Robert got a job at Burger King in Milledgeville, earning $4.25 an hour. In August, Robert was sentenced to four counts of burglary from neighborhood thefts. He was court-ordered to pay $1,223 in restitution to the victims. He was also placed on probation. Since Robert was employed, his mother demanded he pay $25 a week in rent. In the fall, he began the 11th grade. He earned no credit during the first semester and was referred to the Baldwin County Alternative School for the second semester. He earned 1.5 credits for the entire year.

Robert Butts, Jr.

On January 4, 1995, Robert pumped $11.67 worth of gasoline into his car and drove away without paying. Contacted by the sheriff's deputies the next day, he admitted to stealing the gas. He agreed to reimburse the victim for the gas to avoid arrest.

On January 13, a co-worker at Burger King seized Robert by the throat and began to choke him. Robert grabbed a hammer and tried to strike his assailant. The responding police officer noticed visible marks on Robert's throat as well as a hammer in the kitchen. Both were terminated by the restaurant manager.

Several weeks later, on February 3, Robert began work at a Taco Bell restaurant. His starting wage was $4.25 an hour, which eventually rose to $4.35. On July 5, now 18, Robert was charged with violating probation. He failed to report to his probation officer and had fallen behind in the payment of court-ordered fines and restitution.

In August 1995, Robert repeated the 11th grade at the alternative school. On Sept. 29, he was placed on probation for the burglary incidents in 1994, ordered to report weekly to a probation officer, and pay $30 per visit for restitution. As part of his probation, he was also ordered to present copies of his paychecks to his probation officer, attend school daily, make passing grades, and obey a curfew.

On October 16, 1995, Robert dropped out of school. Everything fell apart.

Robert confided to me, and the records supported his story, that by Fall 1995 his mother was deep into addiction and prostitution. Her long-time boyfriend, Isaac, was in prison and could no longer supply her with drugs. She pressured Robert to buy crack for her. He relented and did so to keep her at home and off the streets. He used the little money he earned from Taco Bell, money he needed to meet his restitution and court fine obligations, to buy crack cocaine for his mother. It was while purchasing drugs at the Milledgeville Manor, a grandiose name for the federally subsidized housing project, he met his future co-defendant, Marion Wilson.

"Man, look at your nasty shoes," Robert recalled Wilson saying to him. "Ain't you got no self-respect?" With this question, he pulled Robert into Wilson's orbit.

On October 20, Robert was arrested and charged with possession of one small piece of crack cocaine. He was also charged with possession of a firearm during the commission of a crime and with carrying a concealed weapon—a .380 Lorcin was found in his pants. Robert said the gun had belonged to Isaac, and he carried it when he went to buy crack to prevent being robbed.

The next month, Robert was arrested again and charged with theft by shoplifting. He and a friend were charged with stealing four music cassette tapes from a Blockbuster store in Milledgeville. The tapes were recovered. Robert entered a guilty plea and was sentenced to 12 months of probation with a $500 fine.

By this time, family members other than Robert's mother were aware of his legal problems. Robert's aunt worked as a court liaison for the Milledgeville Police Department. She admitted in our first interview in 2017 she was aware of Junior's troubles. "We all knew Junior was in trouble."

Yet, no one stepped up to help the troubled young man.

Robert got a job at the Concord Fabrics factory in December. He earned $6.25 an hour. A month later, his hourly wage was $6.75. On January 11, 1996, Robert was arrested yet again—this time for driving under the influence. He was sentenced to 12 months' probation and ordered to pay $530 in fines and $30 per month for probation services as well as complete 40 hours of community service.

On February 19, Robert entered a guilty plea to the charges of possessing a controlled substance, possession of a firearm during the commission of a crime and carrying a concealed weapon. He received a total of three years of probation for all three offenses. He was ordered to pay $1,235 in legal and court fees and $20 each month for probation supervision, as well as complete 100 hours of community service.

Robert Butts, Jr.

On February 27, 1996, Laura was hospitalized "... due to mental illness; and her condition has not improved significantly thereafter." Records provided by the Georgia Baptist Medical Center described "a diagnosis of major depression, cocaine abuse, alcohol dependence, alcohol withdrawal syndrome... unable to control her drug intake... the claimant has uncontrolled use of cocaine and alcohol." She remained in the hospital until March 11.

An 18-year-old Robert Butts Jr. was terminated by Concord Fabrics on March 1, 1996. He owed a total of $4,088 in court fines, restitution, and probation services. He had little education and no skills. Paying these fines must have seemed as unattainable as winning the lottery or flying to Mars. He knew he'd go to prison if he couldn't pay the money.

"I was overwhelmed," Robert told me in December 2006 after I had built his chronology through extensive interviews and records. As a teen, he had no one to help him navigate the legal system. There was no one who would extend a helping hand. He was on his own. He'd always been on his own.

He went to see Marion Wilson at the Milledgeville Manor housing project. Ironically, selling crack offered the only escape from his legal mess.

The Murder

Marion Wilson had a problem. He confided to Robert he'd lost all his money gambling, and someone stole the stash of drugs he sold out of the Milledgeville Manor apartments. Slightly older than Robert, Wilson had spent most of his life incarcerated for violent juvenile crimes, including shooting a migrant worker when he was 15, and multiple shootings when he was 17. Wilson had a sad upbringing as well: sexual molestation began when he was a young boy. He was thought to have made his first kill, a neighborhood dog, when he was six years old. Wilson hatched a plan to come up with some way to get the money he'd lost and owed to his dealer. Wilson's plan was to steal a car and take it to a chop shop for cash. He needed Robert to give him a ride.

This ride would forever alter three lives.

Southern Lies and Homicides

On the evening of March 28, 1996, Robert Earl Butts Jr., 18, and Marion Wilson, 20, drove to the Walmart in Milledgeville in Robert's car. Robert and Wilson entered the store. Video footage showed them standing in line behind Donovan Corey Parks, a corrections officer and part-time grocery clerk, as he bought food for his recently deceased mother's cat. Robert and Donovan knew one another. The Parks family lived next door to Robert's uncle Tony and his family. Robert purchased a pack of chewing gum, and the duo followed Parks to his car, which he'd left in the fire lane in front of the store.

A witness overheard either Robert or Wilson—depending on the trial—asking Parks for a ride. Parks agreed and moved items around in his Acura to make room for both young men. Robert said Wilson directed Parks to drive to Felton Street in an older, residential neighborhood. Once on Felton, Wilson told him to stop the car. When Parks stopped, Wilson exited the car, opened the driver's side door, "snatched [Parks] out [of] the car by his tie," and dragged him behind the car. Donovan Parks was forced to lie face down on the pavement. While Robert remained in Parks' car, he overheard Wilson say, "Give us all your money," followed by a single gunshot, which was fired, execution-style, into the back of Parks' head. Robert insisted to law enforcement he never got out of the car. After hearing the gunshot, Robert claimed he was "scared," "upset," "sick to his stomach," and "afraid of Wilson."

In a surreal sequence of events, the young men drove the Acura to Atlanta to find a chop shop. Unsuccessful, they drove back toward Milledgeville. Fearful police had discovered Parks' body, Wilson knew they needed to dump the stolen car before they returned to town.

They stopped at a gas station near Macon and bought gas. Wilson drove to a wooded area, doused the car with gasoline, and set it on fire. From a Macon phone booth near the burning car, Robert called his uncle, Earnest "Bobby" Waller, and said he needed a ride to Milledgeville. Although it was the middle of the night, Waller drove out and picked up Robert and Wilson.

Waller passed away in 2003. His daughter, Valeria Hightower, gave the following statement in a 2018 affidavit:

Robert Butts, Jr.

My father told us that when he got there, he saw that he had someone else with him. He said that Junior was 'looking scared and worried in the face,' and he described my cousin's demeanor as 'withdrawn and frightened.' But my dad described Wilson, the person with Junior that night, as 'calm, cool and collected.' My father asked Junior, several times during the ride, if he was all right. But Junior didn't say anything to my dad while they rode together. They never got another opportunity to talk about what had happened that night. Junior was arrested, and then my father was treated by the police like he'd been an accomplice to the murder. His van was impounded. He was interrogated. Which really bothered my dad because he did not know what was going on. He knew that something bad had happened and that Robert was too afraid to talk. He thought Junior was afraid that Wilson, or one of his associates, would hurt someone in our family if Junior cooperated with the investigators.

Robert was arrested outside his grandmother's home on April 2, 1996. Wilson was apprehended in the bedroom of his girlfriend's apartment. The murder weapon, a sawed-off shotgun, was found under her bed.

With these arrests, the wheels of the justice system began to turn. The State of Georgia announced its intention to seek the death penalty and try each young man separately. During the sentencing phase of Marion Wilson's 1997 trial, the prosecutor, Fredric D. Bright, told the jurors, "Beyond a doubt, Wilson was the shooter." Wilson was sentenced to die.

One Victim, One Fatal Gunshot, Two Death Sentences

In November 1998, Robert stood trial for capital murder for the death of Donovan Parks. His court-appointed attorneys could have given a mere presence instruction to the jury, signaling that while Robert was present at the time of the murder, he was not the shooter, and the weapon wasn't found on him. They also could have presented evidence Robert wasn't a gang member, although the prosecutors deliberately made the jurors fearful by warning of likely gang retribution.

On November 20, 1998, a jury found Robert guilty of malice, or intentional murder, and the necessary aggravating crimes of armed robbery, hijacking a motor vehicle, possession of a firearm during the commission of a crime, and possession of a sawed-off shotgun. When Robert was convicted of murder along with these aggravating charges, he became eligible for a death sentence. To be sentenced to death, a defendant must be convicted of committing a murder during the commission of another crime.

During the sentencing phase, his court-appointed lawyers made little effort to present a mitigation case, during which family, friends, and community members should have been called to speak on behalf of Robert and explain to the jury what had gone wrong in his life. Despite having a large family, only two women were present—Robert's grandmother, Mary Cooper, and his great aunt, Doris Cooper. Neither was prepared to tell the jurors why Robert's life mattered. His mother, Laura Butts, wasn't present. Her absence wasn't explained to the jurors. I later learned through court records Laura was jailed in Eatonton, a nearby town, during the trial, strung out from drug and alcohol withdrawal and unable to post bond.

At that trial in 1998, no one was prepared to humanize Robert. The jurors viewed him as a monster, a scary gang member, especially as Bright told the jurors Robert was so evil that not even his mother would come to court to defend him. Despite having paid a Georgia mitigation specialist and investigator $8,000 in state funds, the defense failed to present a mitigation case, an American Bar Association requirement for death penalty trials. The specialist said she had gathered many of the records I later spent months retrieving again, at great expense to Robert's appellate lawyers. She failed to prepare Robert's family members to speak for him at the sentencing portion of the trial. She later told Team Butts lawyers she lost the records during a recent house fire and couldn't remember much about the case.

No one told jurors, or the judge, that Robert's life mattered.

No one told his story.

Contradicting the words he'd spoken a year earlier at Wilson's trial, Prosecutor Bright told jurors Robert was unquestionably the shooter of Donovan Parks. Bright engaged in what was to be called during the appellate process an "inherently inconsistent one-murder, two-shooters theory of the crime." Sequestered for the duration of the trial because of the unsubstantiated gang retaliation rumors fostered by the prosecution, jurors heard nothing sympathetic about Robert. Terrified jurors listened intently as the prosecutor stated conclusively Robert Butts was the shooter. They sentenced him to death.

How was it possible both young men, Robert Butts, and Marion Wilson, were the triggermen when only one shot, one fatal shot, was fired from the shotgun found under Wilson's bed?

Despite years of unsuccessful attempts by Robert's lawyers to convince appellate courts he deserved a new trial—or, at the very least, new sentencing based on the prosecutor's erroneous statements and miscalculations and blunders committed by his court-appointed attorneys—Robert remained on death row at the GDCC. Throughout the state and federal appeals, judges said Robert wrote on his initial intake form he considered his childhood normal. The judges failed to understand Robert's crimes stemmed from desperation to pay his legal expenses and his inability, at the age of 18, to make reasoned decisions.

Dropping out of school, buying crack for his mother, selling drugs to pay his mounting legal bills, helping his dealer find a car to take to a chop shop—those were Robert's choices. But what choices are those for an 18-year-old to make?

What I learned from his case was this:

Every person in his life had failed Robert from the moment he was born until the day he went to live on death row.

Free Will, Preordination, and the Hearing

I met with Robert one day shortly before the September 2007 evidentiary hearing to explain some of the grim testimony family members, teachers and expert witnesses were going to present. He was visibly upset as we discussed how he'd been neglected, and when he realized the cards had been stacked against him from birth.

Southern Lies and Homicides

To calm him, I relayed a story I heard as I traveled through the Middle East in 1980. I interviewed a Jewish woman who survived the horrors of a Nazi concentration camp and then, in the 1970s, had been forced off her Rhodesian farm by the followers of despot Robert Mugabe. She'd been stripped of family members and homes twice in her lifetime. I asked her how she coped with those traumas. In response, she told me a Jewish folk tale.

The story was of Lailah, the angel of light, who takes babies on a journey through their lives before they're born. According to the tale, we are shown the highs and lows we will experience throughout our lifetimes. When we're returned to the womb, Lailah asks if we want to live this life or wait for another. If the child chooses the life he's shown, Lailah taps him below his nose, forming the indentation called the philtrum. The tap is to make us forget what we've seen. This story accounts for déjà vu, miscarriages, and stillbirths. I told Robert if we were to believe this Lailah tale, he must have chosen his life for a reason.

Robert cried as we spoke. But this myth, a story that presents predestination to explain situations that occur outside of our control, brought him comfort. Had Robert seen the particulars of his story and then actively chosen to live this life? For what purpose? We spent the remainder of our visit discussing free will, choice, and predetermination.

If we know we've chosen to live the trauma, does it, in some way, empower us?

During the three-day evidentiary hearing, held in a crowded prison hearing room, witnesses told the appellate judge the story of Robert's life. Their statements gave the judge, and Robert, a better sense of the circumstances of his birth, childhood, and adolescence. It allowed all the members of Team Butts to see the fruits of our labors. Robert cried throughout his mother's testimony as she told the court how she'd chosen drugs over her children and brought violent men into their home. She admitted she never told her children she loved them. She said she was sober but drank 12 cans of beer each day. "Beer isn't alcohol," she told us. That statement raised a few eyebrows in the hearing room.

Robert was also moved by the testimony of his uncle Johnny Waller, who acknowledged he'd known Robert was trying hard to manage, alone in the trailer with his siblings, but provided little help to his nephew aside from taking him fishing a few times. To punctuate the impact he could have had on Robert's life, Johnny mentioned his own son was attending law school at the time of the hearing, inspired by Robert's troubles to become a defense attorney.

Robert's two sisters and brother Tamayo also testified. Dominique was incarcerated, but his sworn statement was presented to the judge for her consideration and read into the record. Teachers and other lay witnesses traveled the distance to the prison to speak on Robert's behalf—to tell the court why his life mattered and to place on the record the fact they hadn't been contacted to speak at his trial. They apologized for not helping him when they'd seen him struggle, for leaving the children alone in the trailer for years, for ignoring a dire situation. Their heartfelt words meant the world to him. One teacher, a former coach and physical education instructor, lay dying at Emory Teaching Hospital in Atlanta when I interviewed him. He so strongly wanted to help Robert, I drafted a statement overnight based on our interview, and I arranged to have a hospital notary validate the sworn statement when the teacher signed it the next day. The hospital room was lined with witnesses who listened while I read the statement to the dying man. He slipped into a coma and died two days later. Sadly, Robert's uncle Tony Waller, an assistant fire chief for the City of Milledgeville, and his wife, a court liaison, declined to testify on Robert's behalf.

The victim's family were their friends and next-door neighbors.

Given the success of their own children and their excellent reputation in the community, we were struck by how Robert could have benefitted from his uncle's guidance, and his wife could perhaps have helped him navigate the juvenile justice system—and keep him out of trouble. They are good people, but they were in a difficult position. We understood.

Robert had no advocates growing up. Not one person gave him encouragement or a helping hand.

Opportunities were lost.

That week, I wrangled the witnesses. They were kept in a separate area of the prison before they testified so what other people said wouldn't influence their statements. The gathering of Robert's relatives, teachers, and community members lent a friendly, convivial vibe to the waiting room. People showed up to help Robert, and some likely would have shown up to help Robert at his trial in 1998, had they been asked. I went back and forth from the witness room to the hearing room, escorting them one at a time to testify. Most remained in the hearing room after they testified, curious, attentive, and supportive of this young man.

Donovan Parks, the victim of the fatal 1996 shooting, was not forgotten that week. His father attended the hearing, accompanied by his wife. Victims' family members react differently to these evidentiary hearings, and most are civil to members of the defense team. But not that week.

As I was about to step into the elevator with a witness, after a recess, I realized Mr. and Mrs. Parks were in the same elevator car. I hesitated, wanting to wait for the car to return, but the witness stepped inside. I followed. Believing I had to say something in the awkward space, I expressed my condolences to Mr. Parks, who didn't look at me.

His wife stepped forward, inches from me.

"We know who you are," she said, her voice angry.

She spat in my face.

I recoiled in horror. Then I reached into my pocket and pulled out a tissue.

During a recess on the final day of the hearing, Robert and I stood together outside the prison courtroom and spoke quietly. He wore the wire-rimmed glasses my optician made for him in 2005. I told him he looked smart in those glasses. He reminded me of our first visit and thanked me for working to help him, for stitching together his life story. He was overwhelmed by the number of family members, friends, and former teachers who had shown up that week to tell the judge why his life mattered.

Robert Butts, Jr.

"I know I told you my family was normal, way back when," he said. "But now I know how damaged we were. I thought everyone lived the way we did, until I came here, to death row. This is where I realized how different my life was from most other people. Now I know how bad things were."

Robert on Death Row

Robert and I maintained our friendship through letters for over a decade. Even though Robert was not allowed to pursue a GED in prison—"they won't educate me if they're going to kill me"—he taught himself to draw and write beautifully. With the help of friends, Robert published in 2009 a collection of his art and writings in a book titled *A Portrait of My Journey: Memories from Death Row*.

During those years, from 2006 through 2017, Robert was a faithful correspondent. I received an annual birthday card, usually hand-drawn by him. He sent me Christmas cards. His letters were often full of family news. His grandmother died in 2011 after lingering in a coma for a decade. His great aunt, Doris Waller Cooper, perished in 2014 when her home burned to the ground. Robert's brother Dominique died on Father's Day 2016 of a massive heart attack while serving a life sentence at Valdosta State Prison. Robert Butts Sr., his father, was incarcerated at the Georgia Diagnostic Prison, and Robert had tried to find a way to see him. His mother found sobriety, then lost it again; her cycle continues to this day. I keep his correspondence, as I keep the cards and letters my children send to me. Robert was my family.

Robert went to live on death row at the Georgia Diagnostic and Classification Prison on November 23, 1998, the day after his sentencing. I visited him frequently from October 2005 through September 2007. When he received a death warrant in late 2017, I was brought back onto Team Butts by King and Spalding attorneys and attorneys with the U.S. Federal Defender office in Atlanta.

I last saw Robert on December 14, 2017. He was still wearing the same glasses I bought for him all those years ago. He was older, wiser, and enthusiastic to see us. He cracked jokes and laughed. He hugged us all, strongly and with heartfelt emotion.

On Friday, April 27, 2018, Robert was given an execution date. He was scheduled to die on Wednesday, May 2. He was moved to a glass observation cell overlooking the death chamber. Robert was under 24-hour surveillance to ensure he didn't commit suicide and upstage the executioner and the State of Georgia. He was given unlimited phone access and called me often, multiple times a day, mostly to obtain the updated telephone numbers of women he'd "dated" over the years so he could call them to say goodbye. He knew a lot of women.

"Staring at the room where you'll die. There's nothing cruel or unusual about this, is there? No violation of the Eighth Amendment, right?" I asked.

"Nah," he said. "It's all about making sure we know these folks are in control, I guess."

I fumed. Robert remained calm.

The Parole Board reviewed his clemency case on Tuesday, May 1, and issued a 60-day stay of execution—much to the relief of Robert and Team Butts.

Robert was pleased with this development but also guarded when he called. "Don't get too excited. The stay means nothing. They're going to kill me anyway," he told me matter-of-factly. His reaction revealed a pragmatism forged by a lifetime of disappointment.

Twelve hours later, and with no official comment, the Parole Board rescinded the stay of execution order and rescheduled Robert's death. Federal Defender Victoria Calvert, who had been one of Robert's King and Spalding lawyers for the 2007 hearing, and remained on his legal team through the years, kept me updated with texts. There were no more phone conversations with Robert. I silently whispered my goodbyes.

On May 4, 2018, Robert Butts Jr. was executed by the State of Georgia, 10 days before his 41st birthday. "He's gone," Victoria texted after she left the execution chamber.

Robert Butts, Jr.

Robert was buried beside his brother Dominique in Milledgeville. His accomplice, Marion Wilson, was executed on June 20, 2019.

One victim. One gunshot wound. Two executions.

A month or so after his death, I received a letter from Robert. I was startled when I pulled it from the mailbox. There it was, lying atop catalogs and junk mail, his handwriting a cheerful sight. A letter that immediately brightened my day, until I remembered he was dead.

It must have been among his belongings retrieved from the prison, likely given to his lawyers after the execution. This letter was remarkable for what it didn't say. In the face of his impending death, he remained optimistic, inquiring about my family members, mentioning how much our last visit meant to him, Robert asked if I would arrange to get him a new pair of glasses. The envelope held his new prescription. There was no mention of worry or anxiety.

That final letter was written in March, but he never mailed it. Maybe he didn't have any stamps, or felt self-conscious about asking for help, or worse, knew he wouldn't live to wear the glasses. I wished he'd asked me. I would have bought him those glasses. I put that final letter in with all the others, along with a silent prayer:

Vaya con Dios, mi amigo, until we meet again.

A Note from the Author

Some names have been changed in the telling of these stories. I have retained the integrity of the details based on my memories and the extensive documentation included in official records, interview notes, and case chronologies.

Acknowledgements

Many thanks to those who have shared their heartbreak and tragedies and allowed me to navigate them through uncertain waters. I'm humbled by your trust.

While this work is often solitary, I would not have been successful without the support of the many attorneys who contracted, referred, and championed my services throughout the years. Much appreciation to the lawyers, particularly Jacqueline E. Austin, who gave me my start in the business.

Kindest regards to each of my fellow Writers on the Brink members for your wisdom, support and friendship as I presented these stories on our Monday night Zoom calls. You inspire me to keep telling my tales.

I could not have done either the work or written this collection of stories without the unwavering love and support of my husband Peter.

About the Author

Susan Lehmann is a licensed private investigator, a criminal defense and capital mitigation specialist, a journalist, and award-winning author. She lives in the western U.S. with her husband, two Golden Retrievers and a black cat.

Social Media Handles:

- Substack: susanlehmann@substack.com (The Weight of Words)

Also by Susan Lehmann

Visions of Ted Bundy: The Psychic and the Chi Omega Murders (White Rhino Press, 2017)

Echoes from the Mind: The Psychic and the Gainesville Student Murders (White Rhino Press, 2016)

25 Ways to Drive Your Mom Crazy, children's book with Joann C. Hall (White Rhino Press, 2016)

Notes

―――――――――――

¹ Krokow, Eva M., Ph.D. Sep. 27, 2018. *How Many Decisions Do We Make Each Day?* Psychology Today.

² The image of Ouroboros-Zanaq is licensed under the Creative Commons Attribution-Share Alike 2.5 Generic license.

³ In a strange twist of fate, the grandfather of my death row client Robert Butts, Jr. was the grandson of this uncle. Robert's story is the final chapter of this book.

⁴ Allegato, Rose. (1960, March 6) Here's Gold Coast Murder Timetable. *Miami Herald Archives*. https://miamiherald.newspapers.com

⁵ Allegato, Rose. (1960, March 6) Here's Gold Coast Murder Timetable. *Miami Herald Archives*. https://miamiherald.newspapers.com/

⁶ Allegato, Rose. (1960, March 6) Here's Gold Coast Murder Timetable. *Miami Herald Archives*. https://miamiherald.newspapers.com

⁷ Allegato, Rose. (1960, March 6) Joy, Anger, Sadness Greet Killer's Capture. *Miami Herald Archives*. https://miamiherald.newspapers.com

⁸ Allegato, Rose. (March 8, 1960) What Drives a Youth to Kill… and Kill? *Miami Herald Archives*. https://miamiherald.newspapers.com

⁹ Shaw, Joy Reese (March 13, 1960) Rough Childhood Too, But-. *Miami Herald Archives*. https://miamiherald.newspapers.com

¹⁰ Domonoske, Camila. *NPR.org*, "Alabama Sheriff Legally Took $750,000 Meant to Feed Inmates, Bought Beach House." Mar. 14, 2018. Accessed Mar. 8, 2024. https://www.npr.org/593204274

In the perfect definition of "double-edged sword," this same sheriff was also required to borrow $150,000 to keep his inmates fed, after the previous sheriff died in office and, per state law, the remaining funds earmarked to feed Etowah County inmates went to the late sheriff's estate. It took years to pay off the unexpected debt, but not as many years as it might have taken had it not been for the bonus that was automatically included in an Alabama sheriff's income.

[11] Blinder, Alan. nytimes.com, "Alabama Moves to Limit Sheriffs from Pocketing Jail Food Money." Jul. 11, 2018. Accessed Feb. 12, 2019. https://www.nytimes.com/2018/07/11/us/alabama-jail-food-money.html.

[12] Joe Hasell (2022) - "From $1.90 to $2.15 a day: the updated International Poverty Line" Published online at OurWorldInData.org. Accessed Mar. 8, 2024. https://ourworldindata.org/from-1-90-to-2-15-a-day-the-updated-international-poverty-line

[13] Edin, Kathryn J., Shaefer, Luke H. $2.00 A Day: Living on Almost Nothing in America. (New York-First Mariner Books, 2016.)

[14] Michelle. Frugalityandfreedom.com. "Lessons from Eating on $2 a Day: Live Below the Poverty Line Challenge." May 31, 2019. Accessed Jun. 19, 2020. https://www.frugalityandfreedom.com/eating-on-2-dollars-a-day.

[15] The operative word here is *accused*, as the fate of most inmates in county jails has not been decided.

[16] Connell, Lindsay. WTVM News. "Suspects Identified in Murder of Camp Hill Man." Jun. 3, 2008. Accessed Apr. 7, 2018. https://www.wtvm.com/story/8420030/suspects-identified-in-murder-of-camp-hill-man.

[17] Askew told prosecutors Frankie Bradford had been the ringleader of this group, and that Bradford had intended to kill Timothy Heard. In exchange for his testimony against Bradford, Askew received a twenty-year sentence for his participation in the murder. It was structured so he would serve five years, with five years' probation to follow. He was sentenced on March 25, 2010, and paroled on May 1, 2013. His probation was revoked later that year when he tested positive for cocaine.

[18] This group of four young men identified as "The Crips." Sociologist and Expert Witness Dr. John Hagedorn met with Frankie, his brother, and others in Chambers County to assess the gang-related charges levied against Frankie in the Capital Murder charge. He summarized his findings in a report prepared for the court: "The "Crips" gang Mr. Bradford belonged to appears to be like other such

NOTES

informal peer groups in small towns in the south and across the nation. Research finds young people respond to media images and gossip, imitating what they imagine to be big city gangs. All such small-town gangs are explained by peer group interaction and never by hierarchical ties to a big city gang. Bradford's 'Crips' gang apparently consisted of four young men: Jonathan Askew, Dexter Martin, Michael Morris and Frankie Bradford."

[19] Court records support this claim.

[20] According to the 2020 U.S. Census, the median national household income was $67,521, and 11.4% of all households lived below the poverty line. U.S. Department of Census. Accessed Jul 31, 2021. https://www.census.gov/library/publications/2021/demo/p60-273.html

[21] One of Frankie's attorneys also received a thank you note from Frankie, who said he'd written the letters with help from a guard.

[22] Domineque Ray and his co-defendant Marcus Owden were charged with the 1995 abduction, rape, and murder of Tiffany Harville, a 15-year-old girl from Selma, Alabama. Domineque received a death sentence for the Harville murder and was also serving consecutive life sentences for the murders of two teenage brothers, who were killed while playing video games in their home.

Despite numerous petitions for a new trial in the Harville case or a sentencing commutation from death to life without parole, Domineque was executed on February 7, 2019.

Gladys J. Ray, his mother, died in 2012 at age 55.

[23] Health Information Portability and Accountability Act.

[24] All of the names and locations of this story have been changed at the client's request.

[25] Amanda was immediately suspected of harming her child. First responders assume the caregiver at the time of injury or death was either negligent or caused harm to the child.

[26] The hospital is now called Children's of Alabama.

[27] Capital murder is a non-bondable offense.

[28] My funding was capped at $7,500 and there were no provisions for travel expenses.

[29] A pseudonym.

[30] Tennyson v. State of Alabama, https://law.justia.com/cases/alabama/court-of-appeals-criminal/2012/cr-10-1128.html.

[31] This was ironic as his mother worked for a bail bond company.

[32] And sometimes it took much longer to be paid. In 2023 I received a check from the Alabama Office of Indigent Defense for work I had conducted in 2011.

www.ingramcontent.com/pod-product-compliance
Lightning Source LLC
Chambersburg PA
CBHW030335010526
44119CB00047B/505